friendly competitors

FIERCE COMPANIONS

friendly competitors
FIERCE COMPANIONS

Men's Ways of Relating

Frank B. Leib

The Pilgrim Press
Cleveland, Ohio

The Pilgrim Press, Cleveland, Ohio 44115
© 1997 by Frank B. Leib

Biblical quotations are from the New Revised Standard Version of the Bible,
© 1989 by the Division of Christian Education of the National Council of the
Churches of Christ in the U.S.A., and are used by permission

Published 1997. All rights reserved

Printed in the United States of America on acid-free paper

02 01 00 99 98 97   5 4 3 2 1

Library of Congress Cataloging-in-Publication Data

Leib, Frank B. (Frank Bartine), 1944–
    Friendly competitors, fierce companions : men's ways of relating /
Frank B. Leib.
        p. cm.
    Includes bibliographical references (p.).
    ISBN 0-8298-1211-3 (pbk. : alk. paper)
    1. Homosexuality, Male. 2. Male friendship. 3. Men—Psychology.
4. Masculinity. 5. Carpenter, Edward, 1844–1929—Views on male
homosexuality.
    I. Title.
        HQ76.L44 1997
        305.3—dc21   97-35247
                                                                           CIP

For my friend and teacher
John C. Raines
and
In loving memory of
Basil O'Brien

I don't see the divine spirit—whatever it is—wanting us to experience guilt. I see the divine as a very positive, very loving, very gentle, very sensuous, sacred force in our lives. I think all this guilt is a very patriarchal thing, and the sad part of it is that women have cooperated with it. Sexual recovery is the process of healing our psycho-sexual woundedness, letting go of the old blueprints of shame, guilt, and fear. People want to know how to reinvent sexuality. These are unprecedented times. If we are going to avoid destroying ourselves, it is important that we build a sexually healing community of people who are totally committed to speaking and living their truth. I think we get too isolated as individuals when we over-identify with the nuclear family. I see us coming back to a sense of community that supports people, helping them to midwife their sacred sexual selves.

—Marina Raye

CONTENTS

PREFACE

In the idyllic 1950s, when we thought of Marilyn Monroe and Joe DiMaggio as the perfect couple, the forbidden subject of love between men remained very much what D. H. Lawrence had called it: one of the dirty secrets of Western civilization. Many people, perhaps even most people, would have denied that such a love was possible. Men were natural competitors, even predators. Men fight each other; they don't love each other. Men can work together as teammates, business partners, comrades-in-arms, buddies. But no real man ever wants or needs anything more from a friend.

Even in high school, however, I knew from reading Homer and Socrates—not to mention the historical books of the Bible—that in the remote past men had loved one another passionately and that they had consummated that love in celebrated acts of heroism and self-sacrifice. Damon and Pythias, Achilles and Patroklos, Hercules and Iolaus—these names had a magic for me when I was sixteen. I thought I saw a capacity for such companionship in some of my classmates. In fact, I knew I did. But they didn't talk about it, and I learned not to.

Perhaps passionate friendships had no place in the modern world, I thought. Perhaps they were no longer natural. Perhaps they precluded normal love for women and the healthy pleasures of family life. As an adolescent, I pondered these issues endlessly, and like Saint Paul, I began to think of myself as "one born out of due time," as though my enthusiasm for my training partner in the weight room were an atavism from some lost civilization.

In college, I discovered the novels of D. H. Lawrence and found them profoundly disturbing. Given the essential innocence of that time, I never considered the possibility that Lawrence wrote about homosexuality; as my professor of modern literature assured me, he

wrote about relationships, all kinds of relationships—even those between men. Nevertheless, the closing scene of *Women in Love* haunted
me for years.

Birkin, the poet, tries to explain to his wife, Ursula, that he needs
the love of another man. "Aren't I enough for you?" she asks, under-
standably upset. "No," he answers. "You are enough for me as far as
a woman is concerned. You are all women to me. But I wanted a man
friend, as eternal as you and I are eternal." Ursula answers with the
voice of common sense: "You can't have two kinds of love. You can't
have it, because it's false, impossible. . . . It's an obstinacy, a theory, a
perversity." Birkin's reply is the closing line of the novel: "I don't believe that." I realized that, like Birkin, I didn't believe it either. At the
very least, I wanted an explanation. Just what was it about the conditions of modern life that made this one form of love—that between
men—seem so impossible, so out of the question?

And then came the sexual revolution of the 1960s. In 1969, when
the gay riots in Greenwich Village occurred, I lived only a few blocks
from Sheridan Square, the focus of the violence. I remember how astonished I was to hear gay people shouting the slogans of Malcolm X
and Martin Luther King and imitating the tactics of H. Rap Brown
and Stokely Carmichael. I had never thought of myself as a member
of a minority group; at the time, most gay people didn't. It had never
occurred to me that I had the civil right (as one manifesto of the period told me) "to make love with anyone, anyhow, any time, independent of any external control whatsoever." I enjoyed my new sense of
belonging to a community of like-minded individuals, but I questioned the ways in which that community had begun to define itself.

For one thing, I seriously doubted that men capable of sharing
love were actually in the minority. It ran counter to my own experience, and I didn't think that the facts of history and anthropology
supported it. I had become convinced that there is an element of homosexuality in every close friendship between men, just as there is
an element of heterosexuality in every close friendship between a man
and a woman. In most cases, that sexuality is not and can not be expressed. But still, because human nature is sexual, sexual feeling enters into every intimacy—even between men. Kinsey had found that
most people—though not quite all—were capable of a homosexual
response. Masters and Johnson would later confirm this. Anyone who

knows anything about gay bars and hangouts knows just how many happily married men frequent them. My own experience suggested that it was really very normal for one man to want the love of another. And if I couldn't bring myself to believe that gay people were really all that different from other people, I objected still more to the idea that they necessarily lived outside all rational standards of human decency or even good sense. I winced when pioneer gay activist John Rechy announced, "Promiscuity is our noble revolt. When gay people f— and suck in the streets, that too is a revolutionary act." Even before the advent of AIDS, I could hardly believe my ears when a thoughtful, educated person like Edmund White announced publicly that "gay men should wear their sexually transmitted diseases like red badges of courage in a war against a sex-negative society." Michael Callen (afterwards the founder of People With AIDS) has admitted to once sincerely believing, "Every time I get the clap, I'm striking a blow for the sexual revolution." Long before AIDS, I couldn't help but wonder where this sort of sexual revolution would lead.

Two years before the Stonewall riot, I had joined the Mattachine Society, the first gay organization in American history. It had been founded in the unlikely year of 1950 by an old-style New Deal radical named Harry Hay. For decades, Hay had preached the moral value and the spiritual beauty of love between men, and I knew he hated the ghetto mentality cultivated by so many gay people. I asked Hay how he felt about the new developments in the movement he had started. He smiled patiently and told me that if I wanted to know what gay liberation really meant, I should read the works of Edward Carpenter, a late-nineteenth-century Anglican priest, poet, and mystic. Carpenter, Hay said, had given D. H. Lawrence his greatest inspiration, and he was the true father of gay liberation. No one to date, Hay thought, had understood better the peculiar dynamic of relationships between men under the special conditions of modern life. Given the exciting atmosphere of that time, I was in no mood to spend my time in a library, but I did remember Hay's advice.

Within months after the Stonewall riots of 1969, Hay's Mattachine Society dissolved. No one considered it radical enough. Like everybody else, I joined the Gay Liberation Front, the most militant of the new gay organizations. It borrowed its name from Ho Chi Minh's Vietnamese National Liberation Front, and it was closely allied with quasi-military groups such as the Black Panthers and the Young Lords. For several years, GLF's Maoist philosophy and confrontational tactics attracted a wide following. But then, the Vietnam War ended, and the "big chill" of the Reagan years began. GLF also disappeared, and no one organization would ever again claim to speak for all gay people.

During the long drought of "Reaganomics" and in the midst of the tragedy of the AIDS (and perhaps because of it), I made it my business to master the philosophy of Edward Carpenter. Since then, his ideas have become for me the meditation of a lifetime. This book is the product of that meditation, but it is also something more.

Over the years, I have lectured on Carpenter's ideas at universities all over the country and to a wide variety of audiences, from veterans' organizations and police clubs to women's groups. I am always surprised at how eagerly many people respond to Carpenter's philosophy. There is a real hunger for Carpenter's insights. This book is aimed at people like the ex-convict who told me that Carpenter understood prison life better than any counselor he had ever talked to, or the middle-aged mother of seven who learned from Carpenter how to love and help her oldest son. It is aimed at anyone, in fact, who is interested in rethinking the phenomenon of love between men and its relationship to a moral, humanistic, or religious way of life. Andrew Holleran once described love between men as an attempt to swim up Niagara Falls: "Eventually you have to admit: the water is flowing the other way." A century earlier, Edward Carpenter had seen himself as one called, Moses-like, to part a Red Sea of hate so that we might all pass through dry-shod.

Several individuals have helped me put this book together. First, I am indebted to the memory and the inspiration of a special friend, Basil O'Brien, who both loved the ideals of Edward Carpenter and lived them. I want to thank Sam and Evelyn Laeuchli for their generous emotional support, and Zalman Schachter for his invaluable insights into Cabala—both Christian and Jewish. I also want to mention my editor at Pilgrim Press, Timothy Staveteig, who helped me move from rough to final draft, along with Ed Huddleston, associate managing editor. Finally, this book is dedicated to John C. Raines, my teacher and advisor; he encouraged me to pursue this project when everyone else was telling me that it was impossible.

chapter one

THE LINE BETWEEN FRIENDSHIP AND LOVE

Friendship

When we were idlers with the loitering rills,
>The need for human love we little noted;
>Our love was nature; and the peace that floated
On the white mist and dwelt upon the hills,
To the sweet accord subdued our wayward wills:
>One soul was ours, one mind, one heart devoted,
>That, wisely doting, ask'd not why it doted
And ours the unknown joy that knowing kills.
But now I find how dear thou wert to me;
>That man is more than half of nature's treasure
Of that fair beauty which no eye can see,
>Of that sweet music which no ear can measure;
>And now the streams may sing for other's pleasure,
The hills sleep on in their eternity.

—Hartley Coleridge (1796-1849)

Men in American culture, no matter how friendly they try to be, often seem to relate to each other as competitors—striving to outdo their peers in sports, business, and many other facets of life. At the core of this behavior is an almost obsessive fear of sensitive male friendships. The concept of masculinity that results from this cultural construct defines manhood in ways hostile to the formation of loving friendships between men.

Many have suggested that the myth of the rugged individualist—the man who glories in his self-sufficiency and spiritual isolation—is the cause. The myth is deep-seated and enduring, with

1

exemplars ranging from pioneers taming the wilderness and cow-boys riding the range, to modern-day extremists dropping out of the mainstream to live in the woods and prepare for war against the government. For such men, competition is the only natural way to relate to other men because any closer relationship—especially one that involves emotional or physical connection—is the quint-essential unnatural act. Even the gay rights movement has, per-haps unwittingly, adopted this perspective when it declares anony-mous promiscuity as a civil right; in this view, the so-called sexual outlaw is little more than a homosexual version of the American rugged individualist.

This book reclaims another side of American culture. From Walt Whitman and Herman Melville to Ernest Hemingway and Jack Kerouac, many of America's most popular novelists and poets have celebrated love between men. American and cultural history contains surprising examples of such love. Our religious heritage, from young David and Jonathan (1 Sam. 18:1–4, 19–20; 23:16–18) to David Brainard and Jonathan Edwards, has taught a reverence for this love. Even when such relationships became fierce, these men maintained a companionship that did not negate their mas-culinity. Perhaps most surprising are the many cultural sources for exploring this shift from friendly competitors to (sometimes fierce) companions.

This book argues that love between men is psychologically healthy and biologically normal. It is based on the premise that men must learn to love each other without fear. The fear of male companionship, homophobia, is not primarily a fear of sex but a fear of love and intimacy of every kind. The task of this book is to show how the so-called sexual outlaw is not the natural enemy of family values but a means for all men to achieve more-loving, inti-mate relations with others. Men who learn not to fear love and not to glorify the violence that destroys love should make better—not worse—husbands, fathers, and brothers.

RUGGED INDIVIDUALISTS AND BOSOM BUDDIES

The primary source for this book is the work of Edward Car-penter, a turn-of-the-century Anglican cleric who sought to redefine our ordinary understanding of homosexuality in order to shift the emphasis from sexual behavior to emotional needs, from the genitals to the heart. He sought to revive the classical Greek notion that romantic attachments between men promote the common good of society by building up a spirit of communal love. Such love supplements and completes the biological family by extending brotherly feeling outside of the family circle until it embraces the whole of the human community.

Friendly Competitors, Fierce Companions is my way of getting at this fundamental shift in thinking, not only to introduce Carpenter's thought but also to extend it to gay studies and men's studies, in short, to apply to our contemporary situation Carpenter's sense of the moral insensibility of love as the greatest expression of friendship between men. Carpenter is not the only source of my thinking: North American culture today is replete with inadvertent calls for this very approach. Therefore, to engage more-current sources, we first explore four paradoxes.

Male Friendship and the Need for a Sacrament

The first paradox comes from a surprising venue, Christian fundamentalist men's devotional literature. *The Men's Devotional Bible*, published in 1993, is typical of a genre of religious literature that has become popular in recent years: it is designed to make the Bible readily accessible to today's fundamentalist Christians. Thus, it combines easy-to-read study aids with a rather loose translation of the ancient texts—so contemporary and even colloquial in its idiom that it frequently amounts to little more than a rough paraphrase of the original. The editors also provide a daily reading plan that enables the average busy Christian to go through the whole Bible every year. Each of the daily readings includes a page or two of contemporary devotional commentary specifically designed to relate the spiritual meaning of the so-called inspired author to the needs of those modern men who are sincerely interested in learning how to be real men as well as real Christians.

"Becoming a real man in a fast-paced, demanding world is hard work," the introduction informs us. "Where can a man find answers to tough questions about being a man?" it continues and then answers its own question reassuringly: "*The Men's Devotional*

Bible is designed just for you—one of today's men tired of trying to measure up to society's standards of manhood and eager to discover the Biblical model of masculinity and maturity."[1]

If this response sounds like an endorsement for what Jerry Falwell and his Moral Majority are pleased to call "family values," then the devotions that follow certainly live up to their billing. The authors show little sympathy for what they would consider liberal ideas of any kind: these Christians consider *Murphy Brown* subversive and regard AIDS as God's punishment for sin. Yet even against such a background, *The Men's Devotional Bible* (perhaps only because its editors do sincerely mean to be faithful to the spirit of Christ) does in fact contain some observations strangely at odds with the professed values of organizations like the Moral Majority.

Take, for example, the story in which Jesus grieves passionately for the death of Lazarus (John 11:35). The daily meditation specifically calls attention to the tears of Jesus: "The text states simply and profoundly, 'Jesus wept.' Seeing his tears, friends of the family remarked, 'See how he loved him!'" These tears are, it seems, a silent commentary on modern notions of manhood: "In that incident, once and for all, Jesus refuted by his tears the notion that 'big boys don't cry.' He who remains history's perfect and complete man stood by a graveside and wept."[2]

In any other context, such an endorsement of emotional sensitivity might seem commonplace, but coming from staunch fundamentalists, it seems somehow surprising. In commenting on the story in 1 Samuel where David and Jonathan pledge their undying affection for each other, *The Men's Devotional Bible* offers this interesting suggestion: "Virtually every important relationship or event in our society is acknowledged with ritual and ceremony in the presence of others. Marriage is the best illustration of this." In the modern church, they note, only one relationship is exempted from this rule: the important relationship of friendship is devoid of any type of ceremony and covenant formation, in that "when we decide to commit to a friendship, rarely is there a public testimony or occasion for acknowledgment by family and other friends." This is not a truly Christian situation, however: the Bible encourages the establishment of a covenant when men become friends.[3]

One can hardly help but wonder about the innocence of the authors. Do they really imagine any fundamentalist or even mainstream Christian denomination creating a sacrament of friendship, a public rite comparable in seriousness to the marriage ceremony, in which two adult men stand up before a congregation and declare or symbolically enact their unconditional love for each another? How many modern churchgoers could view such a ceremony without discomfort or embarrassment, without some sense (in the words of one biographer of John Henry Newman) that "this unusual capacity for emotional friendship . . . seems unhealthy and even indecent, except in the very young"?[4]

The editors of *The Men's Devotional Bible* could respond that this modern embarrassment over emotional male friendship is without biblical precedent, that it bespeaks a guilty conscience, that the tears of love appropriate between Jesus and Lazarus or David and Jonathan are certainly appropriate between any two modern Christian men. And were they to assert this, I could hardly agree more.

The fact is, however, that the sense of indecency remains, that such a sacrament of friendship has not been established, that the mainstream denominations still militantly promote the fears and suspicions that make such a sacrament unthinkable in the context of modern Christian life. If such attitudes contradict the spirit of Christ, that makes them no less deeply felt or widely held in today's churches.

Heroic Friendships and Sports Icons

The second paradox calling for a fundamental shift from male competition to companionship comes from the heroic friendships in American literature (even in our popular cartoons and comic books) as well as from the sports celebrities who embody such heroic relations. If the worship of competition is equally an American cult, then the previously mentioned capacity of men to love each other and overcome enormous obstacles side by side has also been celebrated by America's favorite writers and has become a fixture of our popular culture. Every Lone Ranger has his Tonto and every Batman his Robin. Many literary critics have identified heroic friendship as the single most prominent theme in American literature: men alone, escaping from their womenfolk as they take to the open road together, heading for new frontiers.

The real test of manhood in this literature is a man's ability to love another man—to work with him, fight at his side, listen to his troubles, bolster his courage, even die with him should the need arise. High-school football coaches and Independence Day orators love to wax eloquent about what Walt Whitman called "the beautiful and sane affection of man for man welded together into a living union."[5] This is the essence of team spirit, the soul of patriotism, the cement that holds the nation together. And this cult of male friendship still apparently thrives in spite of all our homophobia. The popular success of a "tearjerker" such as *Brian's Song* (a tragic love story about two football players) demonstrates this.

Most Americans, when asked whether two real men can love each other sincerely, are apt to offer a distinction: Isn't it obvious that different kinds of love exist? Why confuse the issue by comparing the genuine love between two real men with the deviant fixations of perverts? As Americans, we have nothing but respect for genuinely masculine friendships. After all, it is common knowledge that Washington loved Lafayette, that Sam Houston loved Andrew Jackson, that Lewis loved Clark. Most of us have no difficulty at all distinguishing between such manly attachments as these and sexual perversion.

But if we are so sure that we know the difference between a strong, loving man and a homosexual, what makes us so uncomfortable with overt expressions of affection between men—even if they are only verbal? (Perhaps this is the reason that such historic icons as George Washington and Sam Houston have not entirely escaped the charge of homosexuality by the occasional iconoclast, although mainstream historians still loudly defend their honor.) This apparent contradiction warrants the attempt to search further for a resolution.

An illustration of our ambivalence on this issue can be seen in the flamboyant displays of affection between athletes on the playing field. Sports fans will applaud an affectionate hug between football players, even a loving pat on the butt or an energetic smooch on the cheek. The crowd went wild when Yogi Berra leaped on Don Larsen and wrapped his legs around Larsen's waist after he had pitched a "no-hitter" in the 1956 World Series. Here was the exact kind of "beautiful and sane affection of man for man" that we most prize.

In contrast, when Magic Johnson locked the dignified Kareem Abdul-Jabbar in a tight, prolonged embrace and kissed him repeatedly on the face—congratulating Abdul-Jabbar after he had sunk a winning basket—David Halberstam described his behavior as "dangerously close to an unnatural act." Apparently Magic had already aroused suspicion in some minds by his emotional courtside smooching with Isiah Thomas, his partner in what one journalist described as a "weird marriage."[6] (God only knows what the gender-bending antics of Dennis Rodman might mean to the average sports fan; in his case, for no obvious reason, boasting about bisexual adventures seems to reinforce rather than undercut a bad-boy image.)

In short, expressions of affection between men—even the most obviously competitive and aggressive of men—are never entirely above suspicion. The line that separates heroic friendship from perversion, the sublime from the disgusting, is always dangerously thin in the American mind—however reluctant we may be to admit it. This deep division in the American psyche between the true nature of masculinity and the proper relationship of man to man shows up time and again as a signal for further exploration.

The Beauty of Men and Bodybuilding

A third paradox arises from contemporary observations regarding the beauty of men. Does the male body have a beauty comparable, in its own way, to the beauty of the female? Many men (and even more women) will readily agree that it does. When Arnold Schwarzenegger points out that in the animal kingdom the male of the species is usually the more beautiful, he does not arouse much opposition. People think they know the difference between aesthetic appreciation and sexual desire. But even a champion bodybuilder can invite ridicule when he says, as did Steve Michalik, Mr. America of 1979, that "like the male lion and the peacock, I feel that a man has as much to offer as a woman."[7]

In ordinary usage, we almost never describe a man as beautiful, and when we do, it is not always a compliment. A woman, of course, can be beautiful; she can even be referred to as "a beauty," as though she actually embodies that abstraction. By extension, a car can be a beauty, as can a curveball. A man, however, is never a beauty, and a beauty contest in the United States never involves the male of the species.

Yet popular journalist Charles Gaines notes that the United States has "the art and sport of bodybuilding." Sportswriters never refer to a bodybuilding competition as a male beauty contest, although this would not be an unfair description. Contests like "Mr. America" and "Mr. Universe," the best-known championships in the sport, clearly derive from much more popular beauty pageants for women. Perhaps for this reason some modern bodybuilders seem to go to great lengths to look grotesquely bulky and even freakish so as to avoid being thought of as "beautiful." However, Gaines argues, "to enjoy or understand [bodybuilding] you need to suppose, first, that the male body is a potentially beautiful thing, capable of being worked and perfected like a piece of sculpture, and second, that the product of that work can be a serious subject for contemplation and visual enjoyment."[8] Unintentionally, of course, Gaines may be articulating the reason most people still do not take bodybuilding seriously, as either a sport or an art form.

Gaines insists that no one should feel embarrassed about admiring the beauty of men. He draws on the obvious argument that, from Polyclitus and Myron through Michelangelo and Rodin, the whole of the Western tradition in art has glorified the athletic male nude. Greek sculpture in fourth and fifth centuries B.C.E. as well as "the painting and sculpture of the Renaissance, were based on and inspired by a vision of the perfected male body as the most articulate and satisfying form in nature." Yet, Gaines asserts, however much we may admire an ancient statue or a Renaissance painting, we still tend to see bodybuilders "as narcissistic, coordinatively helpless muscleheads with suspect sexual preferences."[9]

So much for bodybuilding as an art form. What about bodybuilding as a sport? Gaines writes: "It seems effete to a lot of [people] for a sport to require nothing more of the body than just to be presented for viewing. What are all those muscles good for? I mean what can those guys do with them?"[10] Simply posing for spectators strikes many people as somehow passive and feminine, not manly. But interestingly, male ballet and stage dancers get even more abuse than bodybuilders, and these dancers can do amazing things with their bodies. Rigorous training, obvious strength and coordination—these cannot overcome the problem that by exhibiting their physical beauty for public admiration, these men appear effete, even vaguely ridiculous, to most Americans. (Perhaps only Chippendale-type male striptease dancers, whose sexually provocative beefcake gyrations are intended for the amusement of women—as a balance to female striptease artists for men—evade this judgment. Oddly, people think of them as more macho than classical dancers but also as rather sleazy. But the chorus boy remains a vaguely ridiculous figure in the popular mind, unlike the cover girl or the beauty queen, who are taken seriously.) But the reason again has to do with our cultural definitions of masculinity and femininity.

Most people seem still to assume that, because this is, after all, a man's world, only a woman should exhibit her body. Such exhibitions showcase her physical desirability, which is itself a silent affirmation of the culture that makes women into objects of men's sexual desire and ownership. A woman will readily comment on the beauty of another, perhaps because both are judged similarly in the sexist context. But when a man admires the beauty of another man, the admiration is insulting because it reduces him to the status of a woman. As everyone knows, the worst thing you can call any young man in this culture is a "girl." And the worst thing you can call any young woman is a "slut." Because this indicates the true value we place on sexually active women in this society, any man who exhibits his body for public admiration risks being categorized as nothing more than a sex object. Few men will risk demeaning themselves in this way. Thus, as feminists often remind us, women are still the sex that is looked at rather than the sex that looks.

In short, male beauty embodies the same paradox as male love: the sublime once again verges on the debased. What we admire so closely resembles what we despise that it is hard to tell them apart. Millions of people trek through the Sistine chapel to admire the male nudes of Michelangelo, but no man can comment on the beauty or grace of another without appearing perverse. We can listen with pious attention to the words of Jesus when he says, "Greater love hath no man than this, that he lay down his life for his friends" (John 15:13). Yet no man is permitted to tell another man that he loves him without feeling embarrassment and arousing suspicion.

Popular thinking on bodybuilding and male beauty as well as on male domination of women must involve some profound misunderstandings, but what do we not understand? Do we misunderstand the nature of homosexuality or the meaning of love between men? Should we rethink our concept of beauty or find a new definition of masculinity? Why have the most creative eras in Western civilization found the beauty of men so full of spiritual meaning, so profoundly suggestive of all that is most moving and dignified in human aspirations? Why in certain times and places, have men have found it so easy to love each other and form enduring, nurturing partnerships? Where do we even begin to think about such questions?

Feminism, Profeminism, and Gay Liberation—and Plato

The fourth paradox calling for a fundamental shift from male competition to companionship comes from the postmodern movements: feminist, profeminist men, and gay liberation. For decades now, feminists have worked at the deconstruction of conventional notions of masculinity; they could hardly have done otherwise. How can one evolve new ideas about what it means to be a woman without asking significant questions about men as well as about notions such as friendship, romance, and power?

Men have not always responded with sympathy to feminist ideas, but they have at times shown a willingness to entertain searching questions. As one popular journalist put it, "No longer can we [men] rely on old breast-beating certainties, that men are the bread-winners, or the warriors, or the protectors, or the hunters. We have come to the realization that women can do all this stuff too, and have been doing it for centuries but without making a big fuss."[11] Some men even proudly describe themselves as profeminists and welcome the project of redefining masculinity as a liberating process. But such an affirmation by this wing of the men's movement does not necessarily involve a renewed interest in love between men or the aesthetics of male beauty. Of course, both wings of this movement—represented by sweat-lodge drum-beating and by the Promise Keepers—seek to reestablish male self-esteem and male bonds, but with even less apparent interest in male friendship and desire.

Some in the profeminist men's movement tackle head-on the overriding masculine fear of intimacy, and to that extent they have challenged the pervasive homophobia of American men. Even though this element of the men's movement has produced creative new ideas about what it means to be a man today, it has not really focused its attention on the moral dilemmas or spiritual significance of passionate attachments between men. These issues can even appear as secondary to men who see their main challenge in life as developing "the emotional insight . . . which will enable a man to win the love of a modern woman with whom he can form a true and lasting bond."[12]

Gay liberation as a movement has always moved in tandem with feminism. In fact, there has been some overlap of membership—for example, the lesbian feminists—although the two movements have rarely pursued the same goals or addressed the same problems. Even so, one might expect that gay liberation would at least be sharply focused on the moral and emotional challenges of love between men. This turns out not to be the case, however. The contemporary gay movement is focused instead on guaranteeing the civil rights of homosexuals—employment protection, access to spousal benefits, legal recognition of committed relationships. As important as such civil rights may be, their pursuit may serve only to endorse the dominant culture's assumptions.

The history of the gay liberation movement has been a complex one. Viewed as a whole, it resists generalizations. Although the term "gay" in this context is new, the movement itself is quite old. Some use the term narrowly to refer to the movement in the United States initiated by several days of rioting in New York's Greenwich Village, outside a popular bar called the Stonewall, during the spring of 1969. This radical fringe of the gay movement continues to receive a great deal of publicity in the mass media, often highly sensational. However, the extent of its real impact on the cultural values of ordinary people remains debatable.

In a much broader sense, gay liberation really began with Plato (c. 428–348 B.C.E.), or even earlier. If gay liberation means recognizing the right of men to love each other freely, then few thinkers have written more powerfully on this subject. Time and again in his dialogues, Plato defended love between men against its moral critics—both within Athens and among foreign visitors, most notably the hostile and aggressive Persians.

The Persians not only thought ill of love—including love between men—but also disdained both philosophy and sport, according to Plato, because of the despotism under which the Persians lived. They tended to lump together Grecian indulgence in public nudity with their fanaticism about sports and their love for philosophical debate. The Greek cult of love between men somehow exemplified the worst elements of all three. In Plato's mind, this said more about the Persians than it did about the Athenians: "I suppose it does not suit tyrants for their subjects to indulge in high thinking, or in staunch fellowship, which love more than anything else is likely to beget."[13]

The love of one man for another—more than any other form of love, Plato thought—fills individuals with the spirit of freedom and defiance. For this reason, tyrannical governments inevitably persecute it: "I know there are some people who call [male lovers] shameless," Plato admitted, "but they are wrong. It is not immodesty that leads them to such pleasures, but daring, fortitude, and masculinity—the very virtues which [men] recognize and welcome in their [male] lovers." Men who can deeply love other men—men who will devote their whole lives to such a love and even die for it—always make the best citizens, Plato believed, "which is proved by the fact that . . . they are the only men who show any real manliness in public life." Any attempt to legally prohibit or morally restrain such love, he asserted, is itself a proof of despotism: "Wherever the law enacts that it is wrong to yield to the [male] lover, you may be sure that the fault lies with the legislators—that is to say, it is due to the oppression of the rulers and the servility of their subjects."[14]

Western civilization has never forgotten Plato, of course, but his understanding of love between men—whatever its merits or defects—was severed from the remainder of his philosophy long ago. Indeed, most students, when they first encounter Plato's reverence for male love, react with blank disbelief. Classical civilization itself has inspired generation after generation of philosophers, but the Greek cult of love between men, although sometimes admired, has resisted translation into other cultural settings. Plato's point seems well taken: that cultural oppression leads to the suppression of male (and also female) companionship—indeed, to the suppression of free thought and republican forms of government. This fourth paradox, like the three discussed earlier, calls for examination of the ways in which the culture of male competition needs to be transformed into a culture that promotes male companionship.

EDWARD CARPENTER AND MALE COMPANIONSHIP

If a historical moment is needed from which to date origins of the modern gay liberation movement, then the 1969 Stonewall riots make a poor choice; these riots stand more as a climax to a larger drama than as a starting point in history. The year 1894 works much better, and the place is Manchester, England, in a church hall often used by workingmen's groups and labor organizers. A young Anglican clergyman—whose lean build, luminous eyes, and wistful smile struck his listeners as Christlike—delivered and later published a lecture entitled "Homogenic Love, Its Place in a Free Society." It was an event unthinkable before it actually happened.

"Homogenic" and "Homosexual"

The term "homogenic" was Carpenter's own invention to refer to affection (not necessarily physical) between two persons of a tribe. He explained that he would not use the term "homosexual," calling it a bastard word, improperly formed from mixed Latin and Greek roots (*homo* is Greek for "same," whereas *sexualis* is from the Latin and can be understood as distinction by genitalia or by characteristics such as the usage of genitalia). Moreover, the whole idea of "homosexuality," Carpenter argued, could be misleading, hardly more than a rationalization of popular prejudices and prerational fears. (The term was coined by an obscure German physician name Benkert in 1870 to describe what he called a condition of moral insanity: a woman's soul trapped in a man's body.) Because in 1894 people still thought of the word "homosexual" as rather technical, a medical term rather than a part of everyday language, Carpenter's neologism "homogenic" had a real chance of replacing it.[15]

By taking the "sex" out of "homosexual," Carpenter thought he had given the word a much less sensational ring. It is wrong, Carpenter said, to define a human being by sexual behavior alone, a definition that "of course, turns the whole subject upside down, and gives rise to violent and no doubt very natural disapprobation; and to endless recriminations and confusion."[16] Not that Carpenter shared the Victorian distaste for sexuality—even between men—but he wanted to start at the other end of the human equation. In healthy people, sex is an expression of love. If one needs to classify people, then why not start with the heart instead of the genitals? Thus, Carpenter defined homogenic love not primarily as a form of sexual activity, but more fundamentally as a kind of feeling—the feeling of camaraderie for those of the same social group as well as for a person of the same sex.

The *genic* in "homogenic" comes from the Greek word for "kind" (as in "humankind"), but it can also refer to a tribe—or more exactly, to a confederation of related tribes, as in a city state such as Athens. Homogenic love, then, is also community love or even communal love. Echoing Plato, Carpenter suggested that love between men has a broadly social value rather than a strictly biological one. Love between a man and a woman reproduces the tribe; love between men helps hold it together. Reproductive love turns inward toward the restricted world of the family circle. Homogenic love turns outward toward the marketplace and the workplace. It helps subdue male competitiveness, replacing it with a sense of solidarity and shared endeavor as the motive force of community life.

At the same time, Carpenter believed, homogenic love means love for the same kind of person as oneself. In loving a woman, a man loves difference; it might even be said that he loves a mystery. In loving what makes her different from him, he may be loving that about her which he never can fully comprehend. This mystery often gives to heterosexual love its special magic and glamor.

Not all desire, however, focuses on difference—or mystery. When one man loves another, he loves what resembles himself. Such homogenic love has the potential for complete mutual understanding and sharing. Carpenter borrows a poignant phrase from Aristotle when he says that, at its best, love between men means "one soul in two bodies." More literally, it offers to a man the possibility of finding himself in another who also inhabits a male body. It has the potential for a complete mutual understanding and sharing.

Carpenter insisted that one form of love (say, the love of what resembles the self) should never preclude the other (say, the love of what is different from the self); both forms complement rather than rival each other. If mystery has its fascination, then so does the possibility of sharing what is most secret, most private. In this respect, homogenic love gives a new meaning to masculinity. Such brotherhood can become the motive force that drives society toward its common goals.

The scientific literature of Carpenter's time often argued that the true homosexual was incapable of love. Carpenter countered that one who knows even a little literature or history recognizes that real men can love each other as profoundly as they love women: "If the confronting of danger and the endurance of pain and distress for the sake of the loved one, if unswerving devotion and life-long union constitute proofs of the reality and intensity of an attachment, then proofs have been given in numberless cases of such attachment as existing between men."[17]

Some might object that such historical examples of love between real men have little in common with what science defines as genuine homosexuality. Perhaps this is true, but love between men (even at its most heroic) has not always remained totally pure—especially if pure love means totally spiritual or even disembodied love, as though men somehow stepped outside their flesh when they loved or closed their eyes to the physical presence of their friend.

On the contrary, when one man loves another, he loves a whole human being, not a pure spirit: "We may say that to all love and indeed to all human feeling there must be a physical side."[18] Despite the enforced reserve of the masculine persona, especially in

Anglo-Saxon cultures, men do not really need less physical affection than women do. Men also need affection, even if only the rowdy public displays between athletes. And one does not have to spend much time in a gymnasium to realize how intensely aware men can be of one another's bodies. Most men will as readily admire as envy the strength or symmetry or grace of another man. "Sport allows men to dissect other men's bodies in fetishistic (yet sporting) detail," writes Tody Miller, "It proffers a legitimate space within which men can gaze on and devour the male form. The fetish of admiring individual bodily components ('look at those triceps') gives a scientific pleasure."[19] Carpenter believed, on the one hand, that "this love of man to man, in its primitive purity, proclaims itself as the noblest and least selfish utterance of a man's sense of beauty." On the other hand, Carpenter also liked the old maxim of the Platonic Academy which taught, "Love attempts to win friendship by a show of beauty."[20]

Even to a modern audience, Carpenter's observations have the ring of truth, and yet they also have the effect of arousing suspicion. Where is all of this leading? A century ago, audiences responded in exactly the same way: "In the common mind any intimacy of a bodily nature between two persons of the same sex is so often (in the case of males) set down as a sexual act of the crudest and grossest kind," Carpenter acknowledged.[21] Then as now, the degree of physical affection permitted, even between athletes, stopped dead at what Carpenter called, for lack of a better term, "genital contact." Cross that line, and a man ceases to be a man; he becomes a pervert, a freak with a woman's soul trapped in a man's body, a person incapable of real love, and a pariah to all decent society.

Passionate Friendship, Romantic Love, and Caring. Carpenter made light of the terrible distinction between physical affection and genital contact in a way that shocked his contemporaries and may still shock us. "Love between men probably demands some amount of physical intimacy," he said offhandedly, "but the degree of intimacy is a matter which can only be left to the good sense and feeling of those concerned."[22] Society assumes that only a queer sort of person, a kind of moral monster, confuses affection with love or aesthetic admiration with sexual desire. Carpenter thought otherwise. In real people, emotions do not come in watertight compartments; they flow into each other. Affection and desire are not opposed—at least not in healthy people. The sexually attractive and the aesthetically pleasing can resemble each other closely, so that ordinary people can mistake one for the other, or allow one to color the other.

Again, emotional men can easily blur the thin line that separates passionate friendship from romantic love. Many men (and women) expect their best friend and their spouse to be the same person. Similarly, some men treat their best friend with a devotion that verges on romance—especially when they happen to feel keenly aware of his personal beauty or glamour.

Popular feeling covertly recognizes the fragility of all such distinctions and responds with suspicion to any displays of affection between men, even on the battlefield or the basketball court. Carpenter simply points out that, at the conscious level, popular prejudice attaches excessive importance to essentially unreal categorizations. "No hard and fast line can at any point be drawn effectively separating the different kinds of attachment," he explains. "We know, in fact, of Friendships so romantic in sentiment that they verge into love; we know of Loves so intellectual and spiritual that they hardly dwell in the sphere of passion."[23]

This is true even of married heterosexual couples. Some consider sexual satisfaction absolutely pivotal to the success of their relationship. Others place much more emphasis on shared understanding and shared commitment. Some marriages, by turns, fit both patterns. Which heterosexual marriage is qualitatively better, the one based primarily on sexual passion or the one based primarily on emotional intimacy? Surely only the partners involved can decide that. Carpenter believed that we should judge love between men no differently.

Some sexually motivated men can hardly imagine a deep attachment of any kind that does not include a sexual element; others separate their sexuality from their emotions so completely that they never bring them together—even in marriage. In every case, however, what really matters is the quality of the caring involved. To attach such enormous importance to the simple fact of genital contact is to give it a significance that it may not merit.

Certainly sexual activity does not pollute an intimate friendship, but then neither does a lack of sexual contact negate friendship's value. In those cases where sexual expression might enhance the love—by adding a new dimension to the sharing of experience and human intimacy—it might be cruel, on the basis of irrational phobias, to frustrate the natural desire for such contact. In the final analysis, the extent and degree of sexual intimacy should matter only to the men involved.

Carpenter had all of the standard objections to casual sex prevalent in his time, as in ours; promiscuous sexual behavior between men could be as unlovely, he thought, as promiscuous sex between a man and a woman. Yet even when promiscuity is condemned, its importance is exaggerated. Promiscuity is not the real problem; love—and our fear of it—is the real problem.

Masculinity and the Fear of Love. Carpenter thought that what we really feel about love between men is exactly the reverse of what we think we feel. We think we condemn emotional attachments between men because they might turn out to be sexual in origin. In fact, we condemn sex between men because we fear that they might love each other too much. If they love each other, then they have replaced the culturally sanctioned definition of masculinity— that is, competitiveness and its will to dominate—with companionship and cooperation. Tampering with such a sacred convention means threatening to collapse the whole social and economic structure which has been built on top of it. Unconventional sex acts, by comparison, are trivial.

This threat to conventional ideas of manhood, and conventional ideas of society, is the reason that love between men has always been identified as contrary sexual feeling, sexual inversion, and even moral insanity—popular prejudice cross-dressed in pseudoscientific terminology. In reality, no man becomes a woman by the simple act of loving another man. Anyone familiar with the so-called gay scene in the United States knows that no real correlation exists between a romantic interest in other men and so-called feminine personality traits. Often, the reverse is true.

History is replete with many homosexual men who flaunted their masculine interests and manner, men such as Richard the Lion-Hearted, Alexander the Great, Lawrence of Arabia, and Ernst

Roehm—not to mention Julius Caesar, said by Suetonius to have performed as husband to every woman in Rome and as wife to every man. And even popular homosexual or bisexual entertainers such as Rock Hudson and Marlon Brando have been paid astronomical salaries for their ability to project masculinity on film. By contrast, the traditional ladies' man can often impress other men as effeminate: Rudolph Valentino is a famous example, as was his once equally famous friend Ramon Navarro, the first of America's many "Latin lovers." Great lovers in history, such as Lord Byron and Count Casanova, illustrate the same point. Concepts of feminine and masculine behavior usually remain subjective and are always culturally conditioned. The British consider French manners effeminate, and the Germans think the same thing about the Italians. In France, homosexuality is the German vice; in Germany, it is the British vice; and so on.

Carpenter, however, simply cut the Gordian knot of all this confusion by rejecting the traditional equation of masculinity with competition. He fervently preached the essential evil of the whole cult of machismo, especially the identification of manhood with a penchant for violence. This, he thought, is not a problem in our time: it is *the* problem of our time. For him, teaching men to love each other means the healing of the nations, and without such love, the modern world will drift inexorably, through widening circles of escalating violence, toward its own eventual destruction. When men have learned how to care for each other, they will in the process discover a new definition of manhood, based not on conflict but on love, not on competition but on companionship.

Carpenter did not mean that men should love each other instead of loving women, or instead of loving their children or their parents or their families or God. Although controversy still dogs all recent attempts to gather reliable statistics on this subject, most studies agree that, while a comparatively small minority of men are exclusively homosexual, most men (though not all) do have a potential for bisexual behavior, a fact that pre-Christian history amply demonstrates. Until recently no one ever thought it strange that one man might fall in love with another, although some moralists considered this reprehensible. In Carpenter's view, however, gay liberation need not be the enemy of family values; rather, it is the natural ally and complement of such values. Families never can be safe in a world that praises and even requires masculine aggression and conflict. A world in which men feel free to love each other would be a much safer world for women and children than a world where men must continually fight to prove their manhood.

Homogenic love entailed, for Carpenter, "a new conception of life—yet ancient as creation, the life of the heart, the life of friendship: society forming freely everywhere around . . . the larger dedication to humanity, the wider embrace that passes all barriers of class and race."[24] Such love teaches men a whole new ideal of manliness, of what it means to inhabit a male body with its own special sort of spiritual beauty and creative power. It even makes men more understanding of women and more sensitive to their needs. In short, it is genuinely a redeeming love.

Carpenter felt that the call of masculine beauty and masculine love was "the word which is on the lips of God today." Echoing the famous "I am" statements of Christ in the Gospel of John, he dramatizes this call: "I am the ground of thy soul; I am that which draws thee unbeknown—veiled Eros, Visitor of thy long night-time; and I that give thee form from ancient ages, thine own—yet in due time to return to Me, standing beyond Time."[25] The concept of spiritual eroticism offends many Christians, but for Carpenter, the calls of love are always the calls of God, the only final proofs of God's existence, the only real clues to God's nature.

LOVE AS A BLISSFUL SACRAMENT

Saint Teresa of Avila used to joke about those sour-faced saints who had turned religion into an ordeal and love into a painful duty. They had forgotten the basic principle of Classical theology that the inmost nature of the Godhead is pure bliss. In writing of God's delight in God's own divine perfection, Aquinas pointed out that "joy and delight are a certain resting of the will in its object." But God's own nature is the principle object of God's own contemplation. Thus, "God rests supremely in the contemplation of His own perfection."[26]

The concept of divine eros reminds us of what was, for Aquinas, a basic truth of theology: that bliss is the natural comple-

ment of divine perfection, just as "beauty is the natural complement of youth." Sour-faced saints never associate religion with joy
or beauty with holiness, but, in fact, the alliance of these concepts
goes back to the dawn of philosophical thought.

Centuries before Aquinas, Socrates had taught that the delight we take in human beauty should naturally remind us of the
deeper and more mysterious delights of contemplating the Divine
beauty. "The rainbow is I suppose a reflection caused by the sun's
rays falling on a moist cloud," Plutarch wrote, explaining the
Socratic concept, "and similarly erotic fancy in the case of noble
souls causes a reflection of the memory from things which here
appear and are called beautiful to what is really divine and lovely
and felicitous and wonderful."[27] Plato said that Socrates learned
from a priestess named Diotima that the only way to divine beauty
lay through the contemplation of human beauty, "He who has
learned to see the beautiful in due order and succession, when he
comes towards the end will suddenly perceive a nature of wondrous beauty . . . beauty absolute, separate, simple and everlasting."[28]

Does the Christian church need a "sacrament of friendship"?
Carpenter answered that love between men—like the beauty of
men—is already a sacrament, an outward and visible sign of an
inward and spiritual grace. This is the key to the mystery of the
beauty of men: not biology but spirituality explains the value of
love between men. Such beauty reflects God's pure delight in Divine perfection. This love teaches persons to rise above the mundane pursuit of the biological necessities of life here below toward
a Divine perfection which has no reason for existing outside of its
own nature.

Asceticism has condemned all sexual feeling that does not
result directly in the procreation of children. Puritanism (which is
often wrongly characterized as being prudish about sex) encouraged sex within the bonds of heterosexual marriage but too often
seemed to confine charity both to begin and to end at home. Jesus
taught otherwise, and it is far from clear that his teachings support what fundamentalists today call "family values."

Jesus had a much broader conception of family and could be
quite harsh toward those who placed the interests of their biological families above everything else. On one occasion, when his

mother and brothers called for him, Jesus said to the crowd that had come to hear him preach: "'Who are my mother and brothers?' And looking around on those who sat about him, he said: 'Here are my mother and my brothers! Whoever does the will of my God is my brother, and sister, and mother'" (Luke 5:34, 35).

Unlike Plato, Edward Carpenter was a modern man writing about a society that is much like our own; it could be said that he understood how to apply Plato's moral insights to the modern situation. But if the world has forgotten Plato's ideal of love between men, how much more completely has it forgotten Carpenter. In his own lifetime, Carpenter actually had considerable impact. D. H. Lawrence, E. M. Forster, and Mohandes Gandhi were among his disciples, as were such pioneer psychologists as Havelock Ellis and Magnus Hirschfeld. He wrote on the theme of the social import of love between men, and in the teeth of incredible opposition, he found publishers for almost all of his work. By the time of his death in 1926, societies to promote his vision had appeared in several countries, the most famous of which was the Institute of Sexology in Berlin.

Within five years of Carpenter's death, however, his world came to an end with the Great Depression and the rise of fascism in Europe. Christopher Isherwood, in his autobiography, describes how on one sunny May morning in 1933 he saw a gang of Hitler Youth loot and destroy Hirschfeld's Berlin Institute for Sexual Studies; they arrived in a column of trucks, carrying guns and axes, and were accompanied by a brass band.[29] All of the Carpenter-inspired organizations for the understanding and promotion of love between men disappeared during the fascist era. And after fascism's bloody demise, gay liberation started out in another, much more dangerous direction.

chapter two

A HISTORY OF LOVE BETWEEN MEN

For the Beautiful Youth Diocles

In holy night we made the vow;
  And the same lamp which long before
Had seen our youthful passion grow,
  Was witness to the faith we swore.

Did I not swear to love you ever;
  And have I ever dared to rove?
Did you not own a rival never
  Would shake your faith or steal your love?

Yet now you say those words were air,
  Those words were written all in water,
And by the lamp that saw you swear,
  You give yourself with joy to another.

—Meleager (150-94 B.C.E.)

In 1969, on a balmy evening at the end of June, the New York Police Department made a routine raid on a Greenwich Village gay bar called the Stonewall. Such harassment of gay watering holes occurred often in that era; in the preceding two weeks, the police had hit five bars in the Village area alone. Usually the humiliated and frightened patrons left quietly, desperate to preserve their anonymity; owners paid off the police, and in a month the bar reopened.

This time was different. An angry crowd gathered in the street, taunting the police and chanting slogans about gay power. When

23

one policeman tackled a demonstrator and began clubbing him, a hail of stones and bottles forced the police to barricade themselves inside the bar. In moments, the crowd had become a mob, spilling over into Sheridan Square, stopping cars, chasing traffic cops with bricks and Molotov cocktails, pulling straight couples out of their cars and shouting at them that the Village streets now belonged to the queers. In the end, the city had to call out its special tactical force, which massed at one end of the street in full riot gear—with clubs and shields—charging into the crowd and breaking heads. The next day, the rioting resumed.

THE CHARACTER OF MODERN GAY RIGHTS

Like Athena springing full grown from the head of Zeus, the modern gay rights movement suddenly burst into the full glare of national publicity on that evening. Overnight, it grew from a handful of secretive splinter groups, largely composed of village Bohemians, into an international mass movement. Overnight, what Oscar Wilde once called "the vice that dare not speak its name" had become the vice that will not shut up. The initial drama of that night in June, and its confrontational style, have characterized the movement ever since—often with the unintended results that sensationalism takes the place of serious debate and publicity takes the place of real change. The simple fact is that the American media—hitherto blind to the mere existence of homosexuality—had discovered that gay rights could make good press. Even though the union of the movement and the media was hardly a love match, it worked only too well as a marriage of convenience.

Today, when gay issues are a staple of daytime television talk shows, housewives find themselves listening to graphic accounts of the intimate sexual adventures of male prostitutes and transsexuals. Groups such as Queer Nation and Act Up stage carefully publicized experiments in street theater, as they shock middle-class housewives by shouting obscenities in shopping malls or as they offend even nonbelievers by interrupting church services and trampling on consecrated communion bread. On a daytime talk show, a lesbian in full leather drag sets the ratings soaring when she shouts that she would like to burn down every church in

America, while a concerned mother in the studio audience expresses her fear that "teaching that homosexuality is normal . . . you twist a child's mind."[1]

The Calvin Klein organization attempted to cash in on this hoopla when it publicly hired a well-known gay pornographer to design an advertising campaign using half-clad adolescent boys in sexually provocative poses. Although public outrage finally forced the company to cancel the ads, the sale of its products jumped. In the same spirit, punk-rock groups like the Red Hot Chili Peppers and Extra Fancy got themselves banned from popular radio stations as having lyrics that are "too gay for radio play," but their tapes and videos sell briskly among teenagers.

Significantly, however, these same teenagers, in one survey after another, have emphatically asserted their belief that homosexuals are legitimate targets who deserve to be openly attacked. In spite of all the sensational publicity in the popular culture—or perhaps because of it—adolescents and college-age young people apparently hold far more negative views of homosexuals than do their middle-aged parents.[2] Given the nature of much media coverage, this may not be so surprising. Sensationalism, after all, does little to break down stereotypes or to encourage human understanding; it may indeed have the reverse effect.

Has the Gay Rights Movement Failed?

A great deal of evidence suggests that in its attempt to change public attitudes, the gay rights movement has made little headway. Eighty percent of all Americans still consider it always morally wrong to engage in homosexual behavior, whatever the circumstances. Hate crimes against homosexuals increase every year, while those responsible for making and enforcing the law stubbornly refuse to protect gay people. The Supreme Court, for example, has consistently refused to strike down antiquated sodomy laws, even though these laws originally banned all oral or anal sex, even between married couples. Whereas the court ruled that laws against heterosexual sodomy violate the constitutional right of every citizen to privacy, the justices have decided that there can be no constitutional right to engage in homosexual sodomite behavior that for centuries has been considered morally deviant and "not in the best interest of humanity."[3]

"Homosexuals are a threat to every American," declares a representative of a well-financed organization called Christians for Family Values. Conservative Christian groups demonstrating against gay rights in New Orleans carry signs that read "AIDS is the Cure." And not only right-wing fundamentalists or bigots preach against the lavender menace. Even scholars and intellectuals, who consider themselves open-minded and who really do strive for objectivity, often find the paranoia contagious. Consider the case of the Ramsey Colloquium—a group of Jewish and Christian theologians from such prestigious institutions as Princeton University, Rutgers, and Amherst. As recently as the mid-1990s, they issued a position paper on what they called "The Homosexual Movement," contending that "permissive abortion, widespread adultery, easy divorce, radical feminism, and the gay and lesbian movement have not by accident appeared at the same historical moment." In their view, all homosexuals, along with all adulterers and all abortionists, "have in common a desire for liberation from constraint." As the declared enemies of spiritual values, "They also have in common the presuppositions that the body is little more than a instrument for the fulfillment of desire, and that desire is the essence of the self." In short, the current assessment—that the gay agenda mandates hedonism, moral anarchy, and the overthrow of every sane standard of human decency—has not changed much.[4]

Edward Carpenter on Love and Responsibility

The gay rights movement has failed to achieve a serious reevaluation of the place of love between any two persons in a free society because it ignores the basic warning of Edward Carpenter: gay rights is not really about sex, but about love. Decades of media hype have done much to obscure this distinction. But gay activists have not helped. Such well-known gay writers as Leo Bersani and Armistad Maupin, for example, have enthusiastically endorsed the impression given by Calvin Klein and John Rechy that gay rights means endorsing anonymous promiscuity and self-destructive self-indulgence as moral norms.[5]

This mistake is a natural one. On the subject of male sexual promiscuity, our society has profoundly ambivalent, even schizoid, double-standard attitudes. On one hand, our schools and churches hold up the family man as the ideal of masculine behavior; on the other hand, men privately express quite different values in bars and locker-rooms, in any place where they gather away from their wives and daughters. More than a few men like to boast about the number and variety of their sexual conquests. Indeed, middle-aged executives openly flaunt their so-called trophy wives—attractive and expensively dressed young women who have replaced the now middle-aged women on whom these men depended in building their careers. Many men do not seem to admire let alone demand sexual purity in their fellow-men. On the contrary, they tend to see discreet sexual adventures as evidence of masculinity. Whether Jerry Falwell or Larry Flynt speaks for the majority of American males is unclear. Perhaps they both do. The one voices a man's public conscience, the other his private one.

Homosexual men naturally carry over these values into the gay subculture. Given the fact that marriage does not exist in that culture, the family man can hardly be a gay icon. To young gay men, this freedom from responsibility can look like real freedom. Particularly in the emotional climate of the late 1960s, when Hugh Hefner's much-publicized "*Playboy* philosophy" became the manifesto for a sexual revolution of sorts, rebellious young gay men naturally saw promiscuity as a revolutionary gesture.

But nothing is revolutionary about male promiscuity. The gay rebels were only buying into the darker side of heterosexual male culture, as it had existed for centuries. For gays and lesbians, the institution of marriage does not exist, either as restraining force or as a safety net. On the contrary, many gay men feel condemned to anonymous promiscuity as the only way to protect their dirty secret. Promiscuity can seem like a prison. Thus Jean Genet speaks of the "extraordinary limitation of the pederastic universe," in which no romantic relationship ever survives the first sexual experience. The promiscuous experience must forever be started over.[6]

Edward Carpenter had argued a century ago that if one accepts the equation of gay liberation with promiscuity, the struggle will have been lost from the outset. It only places a powerful weapon in the hands of bigots and puritans. Moreover, heterosexual males may take pride in their own sexual conquests, but they will hardly extend that courtesy to gay men, whose adventures they will condemn with the full rigor of inquisitors. In addition, anonymous promiscuity—though it may protect gay men in a homophobic environment—virtually guarantees that they will never lead emotionally fulfilling lives, either as a individuals or as a community. What is truly revolutionary is not male promiscuity but male love.

For Carpenter, however, freedom from responsibility can only be freedom from human relationships, which is no freedom at all. People who refuse any responsibility for the welfare of others ultimately marginalize themselves. To say, as some gay activists have said, that homosexuality is fundamentally lawless or even amoral is to guarantee pariah status for gay people. Sexual outlaws, by definition, remain on the fringe of normal life. At best, society will regard them as tolerable because harmless; at worst, it will despise them as incapable of meeting the simplest obligations of common humanity.

But are romantic attachments between men fundamentally lawless? Is love between men identical with sexual license? The work of Edward Carpenter invites us to rethink such questions from a historical and cross-cultural perspective. If the whole web of lies and misconceptions can be untangled, then the Victorian condemnation of homosexuality as essentially hedonistic and amoral will be shown as a red herring. Moralists denounce the fact that men cannot really love each other; what they fear, however, is the possibility they really can.

Although often interpreted as a sign of weakness and effeminacy, this love threatens people because, at some level, they intuit what Carpenter wants to prove: that romantic attachments between men are not now and never have been peripheral to the human experience; they are central, even indispensable to the healthy functioning of society and to the flourishing of culture. They have the power to change the world. Thus, Plato could argue that love between men, even though it has no biologically reproductive function, is yet spiritually fertile with progeny of wisdom and beauty essential to the growth of the human spirit: "A [male] lover . . . by constant association with so much beauty and by thinking of his friend day and night . . . will attain a union more complete than that which comes of bringing up children, because [male lovers] will create something lovelier and less mortal than human seed."[7]

In our own time, Urvashi Vaid states a similar conclusion: "That gay people are so universally regarded as a threat to be harshly suppressed suggests that gay and lesbian culture contains ideas that are deeply transformational—and I believe redemptive— to the political, moral, and social order now in place." This redemptive potential is the import of Carpenter's work.[8]

HOMOPHOBIA AND THE TRADITION OF CHRISTIAN FRIENDSHIP

Two generations ago, psychologist Wainwright Churchill made an observation about the often paradoxical nature of what he terms "homoerotophobia" (fear of desiring the same sex): "It is a bizarre paradox that in the homoerotophobic atmosphere of our culture, many males seem more able to enter into sexual relationships with other males than into significant friendships." In his practice, Churchill observed "the willingness of a great many young men to enter into furtive sexual relationships with other men," even though they would suffer an enormous loss in their sense of personal worth if they were ridiculed for "some innocent gesture of affection between themselves and a friend.[9]

Men apparently can tolerate a maverick sexual streak in a man, especially if it is accompanied by a penchant for violence, but they cannot overlook or tolerate real intimacy between men. Indeed, the masculine fear of intimacy is an obvious fact of life to anyone who bothers to think about it. Churchill writes, "The great need of American males—especially in youth—to be tough and aggressive, to seem to go about with a perpetual chip on the shoulder is a function of homoerotophobia."[10]

The gay Christian movement has agitated for decades, within the churches and outside them, for legal and sacramental gay marriages. Poet and journalist Bruce Bawer says he has learned, in his own work, "that most heterosexuals have less trouble dealing with gay sex than with the idea of gay love." He cites polls confirming that straight people are more tolerant of homosexuals than they are accepting of gay unions. Bawer explains such attitudes by observing that people tolerate homosexuals for libertarian reasons (to each his own) and disapprove on moral grounds ("how dare they pair off as if they were legitimate married couples?").[11]

If such observations are accurate, then American homophobia represents a strange inversion of traditional Christian morality. The Christian religion has never condemned affection between men. As John Boswell has beautifully demonstrated in a recent study, the church actually has a proud tradition of Christian friendship, familiar in some of its manifestations to most Sunday-school students: David and Jonathan, Sir Philip Sidney and Hubert Languet, Paul and Timothy, Basil and Gregory, Luther and Melanchthon, Newman and Ambrose St. John, Jonathan Edwards and David Brainard, Don Bosco and Domenic Savio—the list goes on and on. Jesus himself wept without restraint for the death of Lazarus, occasioning comment, though not reproach, among his contemporaries. The church always boasted of the fact that its Savior, Jesus Christ—whose love fell, like the rain, on just and unjust alike—also had a special friend, a beloved disciple singled out for a private and privileged intimacy with him.

All of these friendships were pure, but that's the whole point. Christian tradition exactly reverses the judgment of most modern Americans. Kisses and embraces, even tears of love between men, have not offended Christians historically, any more than they offended Christ himself. Indeed, Boswell has shown that many branches of the church, at different times in history, have actually blessed friendships at formal ceremonies vaguely resembling the marriage service. On the other hand, impersonal sex and sexual brutality have always been considered a violation of Christian ethics in every age of church history.

Not everyone quite realizes how narrowly physiological the traditional Christian objection to homosexuality really was. It rests on one obvious and unarguable fact: homosexuality is not fertile. Even before the Christian era, Philo of Alexandria compared sodomy to the irrational sowing of seed in a foul-smelling swamp rather than in a fertile field. Anyone at all familiar with the paintings of Hieronymous Bosch realizes that the medieval condemnation of homosexuality played up a physical disgust with anal intercourse—and inadvertently fostered a corresponding fascination with it, as Aldous Huxley has documented. The so-called Satanic kiss (on the devil's anus) became, in the popular imagination, the central act of worship at a witch's Sabbath.[12]

It is interesting to speculate by what process of cultural evolution the medieval disgust with a specific sexual act, anal intercourse, became generalized into a pervasive horror, not only of any emotion between men but even of any emotion in men at all. Maralyn French has observed that anger has become the only emotion permissible to men in our culture—an idea that would certainly have startled Augustine. So great has this horror of male emotion grown that, for some, overt homosexual activity (or sodomy) now seems less intolerable if it is brutal and anonymous.[13]

The Modern Medical Explanation of Homosexuality

Little in the modern medical or psychological literature on homosexuality will help explain the reasons why anonymous sex has made homosexuality more tolerable. The possibilities of love between men and the reasons why they inspire such horror in modern Americans have hardly been the focus of the scientific attempt to understand homosexuality which began a century and a half ago. In the modern world, when people have asked for an explanation of homosexuality, what they usually have wanted to know is its cause and possibly also its cure. They have almost never wanted to know why so many people feel so threatened by it, even when they have no obvious reason to be.

Certainly there has been no dearth of answers to questions about the cause and cure of homosexuality. Scientific and pseudoscientific literature on the etiology of homosexuality actually makes entertaining if voluminous reading. Every imaginable physiological and psychological abnormality has been targeted for blame. Defective glands, brain malformations, nervous degeneration, air pollution, noise pollution, overcrowded housing, malnutrition, pregnant mothers suffering malnutrition, overfeeding, emotionally unstable mothers, dominating mothers, clinging mothers, cruel mothers, mothers with defective glands, cruel fathers, demanding fathers, weak fathers, indifferent fathers, effeminate fathers, incestuous fathers, cold fathers, bullying fathers, too little male hormone, too much male hormone—and so forth.[14]

When it comes to therapy for homosexuals, the medical imagination has been equally fertile. At the turn of the century, with the science of endocrinology still in its infancy, doctors began experimenting with injections of an extract derived from the testicles of dogs. This line of research ended in the 1920s with the notorious monkey-gland therapies of the colorful Russian charlatan Serge Voronoff. In the 1940s, a more sophisticated brand of American researchers, with generous government funding, treated homosexual subjects remanded to them by the court system with various steroids of the type now used by bodybuilders to cause muscular hypertrophy and general "virilization." The subjects had "accepted organotherapy by compulsion," the police said. In any case, the results were disappointing. Raising the testosterone levels of homosexual men does not affect their sexual orientation at all; it does, however, increase their sex drive.[15] Dr. Ruth Westheimer is still praying for a cure, she says, but evidently without much hope for the near future. When so much effort and so much ingenuity yield such meager answers, surely the time has come to wonder if we have been asking the right questions.

The Art of Loving

In *The Art of Loving*, Erich Fromm observes, "Any theory of love must begin with a theory of . . . human existence."[16] How surprising a claim from a practitioner of scientific psychology! Theories about the meaning of human existence are usually the domain of theologians and philosophers who operate outside the realm of scientific verification.

In the modern world, we have grown so used to a tightly restricted way of thinking about homosexuality—as a narrowly defined medical or psychiatric problem—that we experience great difficulty approaching it in the spirit of Eric Fromm. The great bulk of scientific literature on homosexuality certainly contains nothing so bold as a theory of human existence, and even theologians tend to discuss homosexual relationships quite independently of any theories they might entertain concerning the nature of love and the role of friendship in the Christian life. C. S. Lewis actually denies that what exists between homosexuals can be called love, and Fromm suggests this as well. "The homosexual," he says, "suffers from the pain of never-resolved separateness, a failure, however, which he shares with the average heterosexual who cannot love."[17] One wonders just what sort of scientific evidence he might have had for such a theory—especially in the light of the fact that he often quotes Plato, whose whole theory of love derives from homosexual experience.

Edward Carpenter saw clearly in the 1870s what Bruce Bawer and Wainwright Churchill have only recently discovered, and what C. S. Lewis and Erich Fromm never did understand: the problem of homosexuality is, in reality, the problem of love and our fear of it. Eschewing the jargon of pseudoscientific psychology, he wrote in a light, common-sense philosophical style that is as old as the humanist tradition. From the *Symposium* of Plato and Ovid's *Art of Love* to the *Philosophy of Love* by Leone Hebraio and Castiglione's *Book of the Courtier*, the humanistic discourse on love has been an enormously popular and profoundly moving literary genre. In fact, Fromm's *The Art of Loving* is a contribution to this genre (rather than to any putative discipline of scientific psychology), as is C. S. Lewis's *The Four Loves*. And it was in this tradition, rather than in the elaborately learned style of the medical sexologists of contemporary Germany, that Carpenter also chose to write.

In his autobiography, Carpenter recorded his efforts to keep up with the medical literature on homosexuality pouring out of Germany throughout his lifetime. "Their books—'more Teutonico'—are generally overladen with detail, huge jungles through which it is difficult to find one's way," he complained.[18] Carpenter was sympathetic in principle to this enterprise and even friendly with some of its more liberal practitioners (notably Dr. Magnus Hirschfeld). Some of it had some value, he suspected, but his own concerns lay elsewhere.

When, in 1894, Carpenter delivered his lecture entitled "Homogenic Love," Brian Reade described it as a thing unimaginable until it happened because Carpenter had attempted the first truly humanist discourse on love between men since the end of the classical period. His lecture, although comparatively brief announces all of the major themes that he would subsequently explore in a lifetime devoted to understanding masculine love. The lecture opens on a distinctive note: "Of all the many forms that Love delights to take, perhaps none is more interesting (for the very reason that it has been so inadequately considered) than that special attachment which is sometimes denoted by the word Comradeship."[19]

Carpenter wants to place his readers squarely within the humanist tradition of the discourse on love, where love is still a source of delight and its endless varieties a manifestation of the divine. He leads us to expect that he will use references to the classic poets where his contemporaries use case histories, and he complains that "the medical inquirer is bound on the whole to meet with those cases that are of a morbid character, rather than those that are healthy since indeed it is the former that he lays himself out for."

With purely moralistic studies of homosexuality, or sodomy, considered as a vice, Carpenter is equally brief. In the notion that love between men violates natural law, Carpenter sees the social conditions of another age, "dating, as it certainly does, from far back times when the multiplication of the tribe was one of the first duties of its members, and one of the first necessities of corporate life." Under the conditions of nineteenth century life, when overpopulation was already a specter on the horizon, such notions no longer have a place. For human beings, love certainly means more than reproduction: "No one would seriously maintain that the mutual stimulus, physical, mental and moral, which flow from embraces and endearments are nothing, and that because these things do not lead to actual race propagation, therefore they must be discountenanced."

Carpenter dismisses with equal common sense the disease-theory of homosexuality. The research of his day, he concluded, could not support such a conclusion. "By the tabulation and comparison of a great number of cases and 'confessions,' it has become pretty well established that the individuals affected with inversion in marked degree do not after all differ from the rest of mankind, or womankind, in any other physical or mental 'particular' which can be distinctly indicted."

In dealing with the question of the cause of homosexuality, Carpenter tended to turn the tables on the moralists and bigots. Perhaps what needed to be explained was our modern terror of love in men. Why was it, he wondered, that "the subject had never since classical times been once fairly faced in the arena of literature or public discussion, but has as a rule been simply dismissed with opprobrious epithets."

Homophobia and the Rise of Capitalism

Carpenter understood that one part of an adequate explanation was the ascetic bias of the medieval church. He also recognized, however, that modern homophobia—the kind that dreads even the thought of emotional intimacy between men—was of much more recent origin and not essentially related to Christianity at all. Carpenter judged that this sort arose with capitalism and its accompanying phenomena of militant secularism and radical individualism. It had begun in the seventeenth century, he suspected, roughly contemporaneous with the Puritan revolution: "Especially perhaps during the last century or two of European life—it has generally been treated as a thing to be passed over in silence, as associated with mere grossness and mental aberration."[20]

One might wonder just how much the great libertarian revolutions that marked the rise of industrial capitalism and the triumph of scientific thought had relaxed the religious taboos against homosexuality. Surprisingly, these revolutions exacerbated such taboos. To be sure, the church had long proscribed sodomy, along with all other forms of nonreproductive sexuality (including masturbation). Yet serious efforts to enforce such bans were rare before the advent of the Age of Reason. In the words of a recent study of sexual behavior, "It was not until the eighteenth century that a true campaign against it [homosexuality] began. The opening shot in this campaign was part of the early medicalization of sexuality."[21]

This campaign coincided with a widespread process of social change that Maralyn French has termed "the masculinization of Western culture." Gradually the aristocrat, who prided himself on his sensibility, had given way to the industrial magnate, the steel or railroad baron "who adopted an image, still popular today, of hardheaded hard-heartedness, toughness, realism."[22] To such leaders, anything even distantly resembling love affairs between men necessarily became the greatest sin. The change in men's dress, from the flamboyant silks and feathers of the aristocrat to the drab three-piece suits of the bourgeois, symbolized the new masculine identity.

The whole thrust of Carpenter's argument is to allow his listeners to understand the sheer oddness of this sort of social arrangement. Never in history, he said, had men so deadened themselves emotionally. Other historical cultures had been cruel and unjust, but never had they made affection between men into a sin. To some, this dread of emotional ties might seem trivial, a fact of little significance in the history of the modern world. Carpenter saw it as the single most important sin of our civilization: "It is difficult to believe that anything except this kind of comrade-union which satisfies and invigorates can supply the force and liberate the energies required for social and mental activities of the most necessary kind." He felt sure that the markedly materialistic and commercial character of the last age of European life explained the fact that "the only form of love and love-union that it has recognized has been on the necessary but comparatively materialistic basis of child-breeding."[23]

A Cross-cultural Study of Love between Men

In order to suggest just how truly odd the modern attitude toward male emotion is, Carpenter described some of the markedly homosexual friendship customs that have prevailed in many historical cultures. From Herman Melville's South Sea novels *Omoo* and *Typee*, for example, Carpenter had learned that "in the annals of [Tahiti] are examples of friendships, unsurpassed by the story of Damon and Pythias [yet] they were frequently entertained at first sight for some stranger from another island." Melville had observed (through personal experience) that Tahitian men scarcely minded sharing their women with male friends, but they would share a male friend with no one: "Though little inclined to jealousy in ordinary love-matters, the Tahitian will hear of no rivals in his friendship."[24]

In the memoirs of the Scottish missionary David Livingstone (who gained fame by means of his medical work in Africa), Carpenter discovered the friendship customs: "among the Balonda and other African tribes, . . . regular ceremonies of the betrothal of comrades take place, by the transfusion of a few drops of blood into each other's drinking bowls [and] the exchange of name."[25] Carpenter's initial research into the lives of the Africans disabused him permanently of the illusion that Europeans were necessarily more civilized than all other peoples on the planet. It gave him a definite bias in favor of peoples labeled by whites as primitive, and it made the study of the role of homosexuality in early cultures a major preoccupation of his.

From his classical education, Carpenter made a great deal of the cult of pederasty among the ancient Athenians and Spartans, stressing the enormously creative role it played in Greek culture as a whole. Plato's *Symposium* would always remain something of a sacred text for him because of its spiritual foundation in homogenic experience. This interpretation has become a commonplace of much modern scholarship, but it was still a novelty in Carpenter's time—seldom alluded to and always either explicitly or implicitly denied. Notable is Carpenter's conviction that wherever the Greek spirit reasserted itself in its authentic form—as at the Platonic academy in Florence, for example—idealized friendships in the Platonic pattern would be discovered as its motivating force.[26]

Carpenter quoted in full one of Michelangelo's sonnets to Tomasso Cavalieri, which seemed to express the eternal spirit of Greek companionship expressing itself in Renaissance Italy. He saw in the work of Michelangelo that sensuous mysticism, that discovery of the divine in the human (and vice versa) that was for him the essence of both religion and sexuality. He believed that Michelangelo's art perfectly expressed the peculiar tendency of love between men to induce the divine frenzy described by Plato.

At this point, in his discussion of Michelangelo, Carpenter finds himself face to face with an issue that had already become discussion topic. Michelangelo was a hero to the Victorians, and his unconventional private life was something of an embarrassment to them. Although Michelangelo called Tomasso his bridegroom and his Ganymede (after the Greek myth of a beautiful youth raped by Zeus), and although he wrote of his desire to kiss the young man's chest and neck, no evidence confirms that the two men consummated their shared love, which both described as essentially spiritual. Victorian critics made as much as they could of this. Evidence was available that Michelangelo was actually a devout Catholic, and Victorian biographers often made this an occasion for celebrating his so-called personal purity (largely a euphemism for his lack of sexual interest in women).[27]

Moreover, Carpenter knew that his allusions to homosexuality among primitive peoples were also vulnerable to criticism. The homosexual nature of friendship customs in various cultures had already occasioned much heated debate among the Victorians. Again, Carpenter has relevance for the contemporary discussion. For example, an angry conflict arose in the mid-1980s concerning the real nature of the *berdache* ("man-woman") customs of many American Indian peoples. One group of scholars has argued that even Greek pederasty was not homosexual in any meaningful sense. Deconstructionist historians have recently asserted that the psychological realities of classical Greek life differed so much from those of modern European or American homosexuals that the same word can hardly be used to describe both. Redescribing same-sex contact as homosexuality is not innocent because it obliterates the many different ways of organizing sexual roles in different societies. "Does the classical Greek adult, married man who enjoys sexually penetrating a male adolescent share the same sexuality with the 'berdache,' the adult male Indian who from childhood has taken on many aspects of a woman and is regularly penetrated by the adult male to whom he has been married in a public ceremony?" Does either share the same sexuality with the modern homosexual in New York or San Francisco?[28]

Because of old and new debates such as these about the correct application of the word "homosexual" in a cross-cultural context, Carpenter preferred his own neologism, "homogenic." Rather like the protagonist of Lillian Hellman's groundbreaking drama of lesbian love, *The Children's Hour*, Carpenter often felt that he could never find the words to discuss the homosexual predicament fairly. Hellman's heroine tells her friend, and reputed lover, that: "Every word will have a new meaning [for us]. Woman, child, love, lawyer—no words that we can use in safety anymore. We would have to invent a new language, as children."[29]

Homosexuality versus Love between Men

The problem, as Carpenter saw it, was the tendency to understand "homosexuality" in an excessively narrow sense that would make it appear a much more restricted phenomenon than it really is. For example, in Carpenter's time, ordinary people still used the word "sodomite" interchangeably with "homosexual," considering the two terms identical in meaning. In this sense, a homosexual is a man who acts as the passive partner to anal intercourse; no other form of sexual intimacy between men properly counts as homosexual, so that Oscar Wilde could honestly say at his trial that he had never engaged in unnatural vice.[30]

Again, even in the twentieth century, a homosexual is often understood to be a man who wants to be a woman, but alternatively, a homosexual can be thought of as a man who hates women. And when used interchangeably with the word "pervert," "homosexual" can also suggest a deliberate cultivation of the abnormal, the grotesque, the bizarre, or even the satanic. On the basis of just such confusions, C. S. Lewis made his well-known judgment that nothing is less like real friendship between men than a homosexual love affair. Those who see a similarity "betray the fact that they have never had a friend," and Lewis flatly refused to believe that anything resembling modern homosexuality had ever existed in classical civilization. "All those hairy old toughs of centurions in Tacitus, clinging to one another and begging for last kisses when the legion was broken up—all pansies? If you can believe that, you can believe anything."[31]

Carpenter rebelled against all such excessively narrow or willfully distorted uses of the word "homosexual." In particular, he took issue with the view so concisely articulated by C. S. Lewis when he wrote that "Nothing is less like friendship than a love-affair." Carpenter's view coincided more closely with that of Lord Byron when he wrote, "Friendship is love without wings." "We know, in fact, of friendships so romantic that they verge into love; we know of loves so intellectual and spiritual that they hardly dwell in the sphere of passion," Carpenter observed. Thus, men fear friendship because they know that at its deeper levels, it shades off into love. The only way effectively to guard against this is to limit oneself to that shallow form of amiability which Lewis called "clubbableness" and which he admitted most men mistake for friendship.[32]

Dismissing such male bonding, some feminists, such as Maralyn French, feel strongly that most men are incapable of any sort of true intimacy: although many men have buddies with whom they play or drink or compete in sport, the relationship between them is rarely permitted to dip below surface bantering, rivalry, and bravado. French thinks that the competition of the workplace carries over into private life; most all-male activities involve other forms of competition or ritualistic discussions of competition— conversations about sports or politics. Buddyship is a particular kind of relation, not to be confused with friendship. "Most men do not have friends and are not capable of friendship."[33]

If clubbableness and buddyship are not friendship, then what is? And how does friendship differ from love? Carpenter quoted Richard Wagner, who told King Ludwig of Bavaria that real friendship between men was "no egoistic yearning, but a thorough stepping out of self into unreserved sympathy with the comrade's joy in himself."[34] In this sense of friendship, it makes little difference whether Michelangelo ever shared a sexual climax with Tomasso Cavalieri; the total involvement expressed in his poems to the young man is homogenic. Similarly, Wagner and Ludwig of Bavaria were hardly buddies; they shared far more than mere interests. The question as to whether they had sexual relations together, or of what sort, hardly seems relevant.

C. S. Lewis felt that even at its deepest levels, male "Friendship, unlike Eros, is uninquisitive." "You can become a man's Friend without knowing or caring whether he is married or single or how he earns his living," because, according to Lewis, male friendship involves pure intellect only. "This love essentially ignores not only our physical bodies but that whole embodiment which consists of our family, job, past and connections." "Eros," Lewis says, "will have naked bodies." Among men, friendship demands "stripped minds."[35] He may be right about actual practice among modern males—especially in a university setting. To Carpenter, however, such bloodless intellectual exchanges made a mockery of any meaningful notion of friendship. He knew that all emotions affect the body: "The most delicate emotion which plays through the mind has, we cannot but perceive, its corresponding subtle changes in the body. But if this be true of love in general, it must be true of Homogenic Love."[36]

For Carpenter, then, homosexuality is primarily a human relationship, which might be emotional but not very passionate, as seems to have been the case between John Henry Newman and his friend Father Ambrose St. John. On the night Father Ambrose died, for example, Newman clung to the body of his lifelong companion for hours, weeping hysterically. Or it might be all sexual passion and essentially devoid of affection, as seems to have been the case between the novelist Jean Genet and Armand, who often shared violent sado-masochistic sex until they betrayed each other to the police.[37]

Carpenter would actually have agreed with C. S. Lewis's observation that "Lovers are normally face to face, absorbed in each other; Friends, side by side, absorbed in a common interest," except that Carpenter would have thought it a travesty to call any man a friend if one shares only a common interest, without knowing or caring whether he is married or single and how he earns his living. Homogenic love is the response of one whole person to another and should involve some degree of physical closeness. Exaggerated fears of sexual intimacy should never stand in the way of this closeness, but neither should a homogenic relationship be marked out by sexual activity as a necessity. "Summarizing, then, . . . we may say that the homogenic love, as a distinct variety of sex-passion is in the main subject to the same laws as the ordinary love."[38]

For Carpenter, the irony of the redesigned and strengthened British sodomy laws in 1870 is that whereas they were intended to check unrestrained sensuality, they further deformed and degraded homosexual life. They also weakened social bonds by increasing industrial-age homophobia: men dreading even superficial intimacy or warmth; men finding it easier to live like a Jean Genet and harder for them to live like a John Henry Newman.

What kind of a society is it, Carpenter asks his audience, that restricts itself to this sort of human interrelatedness? The cultural pathology involved runs deep, and Carpenter does not attempt to answer his own question within the limits of his lecture. Instead, he leaves it hanging and concludes his address by appealing to his audience for positive action. This problem is not trivial, he says; it goes to the heart of national life. He then quotes Plato, "In countries which are subject to the Barbarians, the loves of youths share the evil repute of philosophy and gymnastics because they are inimical to tyranny." Plato thought he knew the reason—"because the interests of rulers require that their subjects should be poor in spirit and that there should be no strong bond of friendship or society between them."[39]

THE SPIRIT OF FREEDOM AND
THE POWER OF MASCULINE LOVE

In the nineteenth century, with its many libertarian and egalitarian movements, Carpenter was sure that people would soon realize how freedom requires, even presupposes, close and voluntary bonds of affection and cooperation among men. Tyranny is always puritanical, as the careers of Stalin and Hitler both demonstrate. Genuinely free societies are described in the funeral oration of Pericles as allowing enormous private freedoms but encouraging community spirit and public cooperation.[40] In contrast, those societies that care least about the welfare of ordinary citizens are the ones that try hardest to police these citizens' private lives.

At the close of his address, Carpenter quoted Walt Whitman as the prophet of a new age: "I will make inseparable cities with their arms about each other's necks, by the love of comrades. I say Democracy infers such loving comradeship, as its most inevitable twin or counterpart." And again, "It is to the development of such fervid comradeship that I look for the counterbalance and offset of materialistic and vulgar American democracy, and for the spiritualization thereof."[41]

To a considerable extent, Carpenter's own experience in the British labor movement validated Whitman's language about comrade love. Carpenter had found true affection and communication among his radical friends, and among working men he had also found love. It did not seem fantastic to him, or even visionary, that an openness to homogenic love among the general population might really help to change the world. He asked his working-class audience to consider what it had done for Periclean Athens: "For if the slaughter of tyrants is not the chief social duty nowadays, we have with us hydra-headed monsters at least as numerous as the tyrants of old, and more difficult to deal with, and requiring no little courage to encounter."[42]

Carpenter wrote a lecture to explore the relationship between comradeship and general politics, and, more importantly, to answer his own question about the genesis of the growing homophobia of the modern world. In his own lifetime, this lecture, "Civilization: Its Cause and Cure," would be most often associated with his name. It was this essay that earned him the nickname "Noble Savage Carpenter."[43]

The word "civilization" in Carpenter's title has a somewhat ambiguous meaning, as he himself admits at the outset, confessing that he may use it, "with a good deal of imaginative 'elan'." He says clearly what he does not mean: civilization is not for him "an easy term denoting all that is ideal and delightful in social life." He gives it "an historical instead of ideal value, as applicable to a certain period only in the history of each people." On the vital subject of the definite marks and signs of "the civilization period in history," however, he admits he has perhaps been insufficiently precise.[44]

In practice, Carpenter sometimes uses the word broadly, rather as Freud did in his famous study, *Civilization and Its Discontents*: "What we call our civilization is largely responsible for our misery, and we should be much happier if we gave it up and returned to primitive conditions."[45] In this sense, "civilization" seems to mean almost any organized social structure that inhibits the free play of instinctual life. However, Carpenter sometimes uses the word "civilization" in a very narrow sense—rather as any typical nineteenth-century Englishman might use it: to denote Protestant, democratic, European industrial capitalism.

The most important sources of Carpenter's understanding of the concept of civilization, however, lie in German philosophy of a particular sort. Carpenter had turned to Friedrich Engels's *The Origin of the Family* for insight into the relationship of sexual morality to political economy. When Carpenter spoke of civilization, it was most frequently Engels's sense of the term that he had in mind. Engels writes: "Civilization is the stage of development in society at which the division of labor, and the commodity production which combines them both, come to their full growth and revolutionize the whole of society."[46] Engels stoutly maintained that at all earlier stages of society, production was essentially collective, just as consumption proceeded by direct distribution of the product within larger or smaller communistic communities.

For Engels, civilized alienation resulted from the dissolution of primitive tribal societies into complex nation-states, stratified by class and characterized by the struggle between individuals and groups for control of the means of production. Carpenter firmly believed that both this stratification and struggle explained the rise of modern homophobia: "Men sometimes speak of civilizing and ennobling influences as if the two terms were interchangeable but whether the actual tendencies of modern life taken as a whole are ennobling is, to say the least, a doubtful question," Carpenter observed. The human conquest of nature, whatever its benefits, had come at an enormous cost. Carpenter accepted Engels's notion that the simple tribal life of many early peoples had involved higher moral and spiritual values than those prevailing in modern urban civilization. Primitives had known how to share and cooperate with one another. The knowledge of how to control nature had created wealth, but it had led also to the desire of some men to control and manipulate others. More particularly, it had led to the desire of men as a class to control and even own women: It destroyed the ancient system of society based on the "gens," that is, a society of equals founded on blood relationship, and introduced a society of classes based on differences of material possession. In this system, the whole female sex became a special class of slave. As French has noted more recently, "Patriarchy destroyed the ancient system of mother-right and inheritance through the female line, and turned woman into the property of man."[47]

So far, Carpenter follows Engels rather closely, as has much of modern anthropology. Colin Turnbull, a twentieth-century anthropologist and noted researcher on primitive peoples, has written that throughout much of modern history, the average worker in industrial societies must work "under conditions that no self-respecting Bushman or Iroquois would have tolerated." Turnbull flatly contradicts the traditional Hobbesian view that before civilization, life had been "nasty, brutish, and short." "On the whole, anthropologists have found otherwise, and have accumulated an enormous mass of data to support their view." Such evidence confirms Carpenter's belief in the moral superiority of primitive life.

In the "conscious dedication to human relationships that are both affective and effective, the primitive is ahead of us all the way," Turnbull writes. The communal life of tribal cultures supports the belief that all people are of, "worth and value and importance to society from the day of birth to the day of death."[48]

In order to understand the modern terror of love between men, Carpenter said that one had to start with Engels's basic insight: "The first class opposition that appears in history coincides with the development of the antagonism between man and woman in monogamous marriage, and the first class oppression coincides with that of the female sex by the male."[49] To Carpenter, it seemed natural to assume that early tribal life had centered around the mother and had been roughly anarchical; people ruled themselves by consensus and without the need for designated rulers. Even today, many tribes live more or less this way. Of these, the Eskimos are an example well known to Carpenter.

Once men are defined as the natural rulers of women, it follows that some men will want to rule over others, so that the natural way for men to relate to one another will also be hierarchical. In short, some men will be defined as women. French writes: "Homosexuality is seen as tainted because in it, according to ancient lore, one partner must lower himself to become a woman."[50]

The division of the human race into two categories—the vanquished and the vanquishers—has a high cost, and not only for gay men. To date, archaeologists have found no evidence of violence throughout the whole of the Paleolithic (from about three million to ten thousand years ago), "no remains of weapons used by humans against humans, no signs of groups of humans being slaughtered."[51] Since the advent of civilization, weapons and human slaughter seemingly have increased.

Carpenter agreed with Engels that any class structuring of society—even that which defines men as the rulers of women—necessitates widespread violence. And usually this violence is defined as legal, as the defense of law and order. "The old community of life passes away, and each man tries to grab the utmost that he can," Carpenter argues, "and artificial barriers of Law have to be constructed in order to preserve the unequal levels." The final term of this hierarchical restructuring of the human community is the emergence of the military strongman: "When the central inspiration departs out of social life, so does it writhe with the mere maggots of individual greed, and at length fall under the dominion of the most monstrous egotist who has been bred from its corruption." Carpenter would have agreed that the primitive "actually lived more in harmony with himself and with nature than does his descendant."[52]

Primitive Cultures and Love between Men

What is original with Carpenter is his conviction that the primitive life of the gens was by its nature conducive to the uninhibited acceptance of homogenic love. Here his reasoning breaks dramatically with Engels. Today, feminists often object to Engels's frequent insistence that "women are naturally pure (that is, uninterested in sex)."[53] Even though Engels and Marx had an interest in classical civilization, they failed to acknowledge, for whatever reason, that love between men occurred in ancient times.

Carpenter suspected that in the replacement of the communal life of the gens by repressive patriarchal class structures lay the seeds of what would become homophobia. In a state of natural anarchy, before these structures developed, sexual feelings would be allowed free play. The patriarchal sense of sex as an act of possession, in which the male conquers and the female surrenders, would have been preceded by a sense of sexuality as an experience of communal sharing.

The casual acceptance of social nudity among most primitive peoples, Carpenter thought, indicates this different attitude toward human sexuality. Carpenter liked to repeat the story of the British missionary in Central America who asked an Indian why he felt no shame at exposing his naked body in public. In reply, the Indian asked the missionary why he felt no shame at showing his face naked. The missionary answered that the face expresses the emotions of the soul. "Ah," said the Indian, "we are all face."[54]

The civilized horror of nakedness symbolized for Carpenter the need for civilized persons to isolate themselves and to cut themselves off, not only from the life of the community but also from the life of nature. If individuals could realize their essential oneness with others, then they would lose this absurd sense of physi-

cal shame and break out of the cage of useless taboos and meaningless guilt. "During the civilization period, the body being sys-
tematically wrapped in clothes, the head alone represents the
man—the little finikin, intellectual self-conscious man." By comparison, Carpenter thought that the cosmical human being was
represented by the entirety of the bodily organs. The body has to
be delivered from its "swathings" in order that "the cosmical consciousness may once more reside in the human breast."[55]

Carpenter felt a real fascination for what he perceived as the
primitive sense of the sacredness of sex. What Christianity con-
demns as unholy and middle-class morality hides away as shame-
ful, the ancients celebrated in their temples as a mystic ritual. Hegel
had defined as primitive "those religions in which spirit has not
yet gained the mastery over nature, in which spirit is not yet recognized as supreme and absolute."[56] Carpenter questioned this
"triumph of the spirit," this glorification of the "finikin self-conscious intellect" at the expense of all that united an individual with
nature and even the natural processes of his or her own body.

"Man has sounded the depths of alienation from his own divinity," Carpenter wrote, "he has descended into Hell; henceforth
he turns, both in the individual and society, and mounts deliberately and consciously back again towards the unity which he has
lost." Carpenter felt that modern man could never be free without
"a resurrection of the body," without a rediscovery of primitive
"body-consciousness." "The bitter experience that mankind had
to pass through is completed," he told the Fabian Society. "The
meaning of the old religions will come back to us. On the high
tops once more gathering, man will celebrate with naked dances
the glory of the human form and the great procession of the stars,
or greet the bright horn of the young moon."[57]

Such highly dramatic passages in "Civilization: Its Cause and
Cure" aroused intense emotion in Carpenter's day—not all of it
negative. In his youth, D. H. Lawrence felt inspired by Carpenter
to write The Plumed Serpent, his particular attempt to create a
neopagan or phallic religion for the modern age. But Lawrence
spoke for a tiny, daring, and youthful minority. Fifty years later,
Anthony Burgess still speaks for most critics when he calls this
book "the least liked of all Lawrence's novels."[58]

In the 1880s when Carpenter first published this lecture, most readers—even educated readers—found the idea of sacred sexuality truly distasteful. Writing of his first delivery of the lecture, Carpenter said, "I shall not easily forget the furious attacks which were made upon me on that occasion." Even the feminists turned their backs on him. Christabel Pankhurst—the Susan B. Anthony of British feminism—felt that she spoke for the whole of the Women's Social and Political Union when she asked Carpenter "to concentrate on the vote and not to explore the sexual implications of feminism."[59]

In the twentieth century, an age that has known rock concerts and fascist monster rallies, Carpenter's talk of naked dancing and sun worship can take on odd connotations. It is important, in this respect, to keep clearly in mind just what he thought the sacred orgies of antiquity had meant. Such twentieth-century pagan rituals as today's slam dancing or the Lebensborn festivals of the Hitler Youth are essentially celebrations of male aggression. What Carpenter had in mind here might be aptly summarized in the words of Erich Fromm: "The human race in its infancy still feels one with nature. The soil, the animals, the plants are still man's world." Humans identify themselves, he points out, "with animals, and this is expressed by the wearing of animal masks, by the worship of a totem animal." Thus, for Fromm, "Rites of communal sexual orgies were a part of many primitive rituals. Inasmuch as these rituals are practiced in common, an experience of fusion with the group is added."[60]

For Fromm, as for Carpenter, the core meaning of the primitive sacred orgy is the absolute unity of the whole human family, with itself and with surrounding nature. He also would have emphatically seconded Fromm's opinion that the civilized sense of shame in the presence of nudity originates in the loss of the primitive consciousness of the gens.

On one crucial point, however, Fromm parts company with Carpenter, for whom the modern horror of love between men is also the result of social fragmentation and individual isolation. Fromm chose to follow the school of thought—as prevalent in this century as in the last—that homosexuality is, both literally and metaphorically, a social disease, a symptom of decadence and degeneration. To Fromm, as to most of his contemporaries in the psychiatric profession, it seems obvious that a healthy, wholesome, sane individual would have to be entirely heterosexual. Surely unnatural vice only occurs in the overrefined and overcivilized environment of modern life; surely the primitives, who lived so close to nature, could have known nothing of it.

In this view, the fundamental difference that separates people is not cultural but natural. It was God who separated the male and the female (Gen. 1:27). Granted, as Fromm allows, that the essential meaning of sexuality is the individual's "need to overcome his separateness, to leave the prison of his aloneness," it follows that the only true union between people must overcome the fundamental biological distinction of male and female. For Fromm, the idea of polarization is strikingly expressed in the myth that originally man and woman were one, that they were cut in half, and from then on each male has been seeking for the lost female part of himself. Fromm thought that the meaning of the myth is clear enough. "Sexual polarization leads man to seek union in a specific way, that of union with the other sex."[61]

Fromm assumed that among primitive peoples, because they were so close to nature, the biological distinction of male and female would have been more pronounced than among civilized people—for instance, in the familiar myth of the cave man dragging his woman off by her hair. He equated with modern decadence the notion that "the soul has no sex." The suffragettes receive sharp criticism in *The Art of Loving* for their unromantic notions about gender. "The polarity of the sexes is disappearing, and with it erotic love. Men and women become the same, not equals as opposite poles."[62] Fromm takes it for granted that widespread homosexuality will be one symptom of this homogenization of the sexes.

THE MYTH OF THE DIVINE ANDROGYNE

After the sensation of "Civilization: Its Cause and Cure," Carpenter wrote his two most important books on homogenic love in an effort to refute those who, like Fromm, fear that widespread homosexuality will result if the polarity of the sexes abates. Carpenter begins at the same place as Fromm—namely, with the myth of Aristophanes (in Plato's *Symposium*), the double-backed monster, the primeval Androgyne. His first major study of homosexuality, *Intermediate Types among Primitive Folk*, Carpenter reverses in the opening paragraph Fromm's judgment about androgynous personalities: "That they might possibly fulfill a positive and useful function of any kind in society is an idea that seems hardly if ever to have been seriously considered."[63]

Perhaps because he had known Carl Jung, Fromm himself grants that "the polarity between the male and female principles exists also within each man and each woman."[64] Fromm seems not to have realized the full implications of this concession, however. If one takes the myth of the primal androgyne seriously, then the truly whole human being would be one who evenly balances the feminine and masculine sides of his own nature. In Carpenter's terms, it would not be the so-called normal types, who embody the extremes of the masculine and feminine social personae, but the intermediate types who would represent the most balanced embodiments of human nature.

It might even be more correct to say that the androgyne is literally the most primitive human type, because masculine and feminine sex roles (being defined differently by various societies) are not truly natural at all. They are, in fact, cultural artifacts. People do not conform to them spontaneously or naturally. A young boy must be taught repeatedly to earn or prove his manhood. Ideas about what is manly or ladylike behavior vary from one age to another and from place to place. Behind them lies authentic human nature, divided naturally into biological male and biological female but not necessarily divided into masculine or feminine social roles as these are cultivated in various specific historical societies. If these assumptions are true, then one would expect that primitive cultures might actually be closer in their workings to natural human androgyny than civilized ones, in that the latter would tend to take their own artificial categorizations more seriously and to mistake them for absolutes.

Carpenter believed that the problem of love between men would remain insoluble so long as it was studied apart from its social context, as though it were an isolated phenomenon, some sort of medical or biological anomaly to be quarantined and cured.

For him, the solution lay in the recovery of the primitive gens. The fear of homogenic love originated in alienation; the acceptance of homogenic love could help restore the lost sense of community. When fully accepted, love between men never promoted moral chaos. What it promoted was human connectedness: "These earlier folk who lived so much more out in the great open of Nature than we do, and who also lived in the great open of the tribal life of their fellows, their outlook on the world was in many respects far saner than ours."[65]

Androgyne as Priest and Warrior

From his cross-cultural studies of homogenic personalities, Carpenter felt that he saw a pattern emerging. Within those societies that had encouraged love between men, individuals with a markedly homogenic temperament tended to make their chief contributions in two areas of life vital to the ancients (although apparently antithetical by modern Christian standards)—war and religion. As odd as it may seem, homosexuals in history seem to have performed most notably in the roles of warrior and priest. John Boswell correctly observes, "Modern military leaders tend to find this improbable or even unbelievable."[66] What these vocations have in common is their emphasis on community service over individual rights.

Carpenter suspected that among intermediate types, those men closer to the masculine pole in their personal attitudes would have gravitated toward the army; those closer to the feminine pole, to the priesthood. He admits that his case for this is a bit shaky, because the warrior heroes of antiquity seldom fit into modern notions of what constitutes truly masculine behavior. In mythology, Hercules, the most famous strong man of the ancient world, dressed as a woman for three years and served the Queen of Lydia, Omphale, as a handmaid. "The great hero Achilles passed his youth among women, and in female disguise."[67]

Nonetheless, Carpenter tended to believe that the military cult of male love—notable among the classical Greeks and the medieval Japanese—tended to promote what Westerners today would consider masculine values. He speculated that a certain type of homogenic man might be described as supervirile, standing in the same relation to other men as the normally sexual man stands to women. "Such a man is able to bewitch men, just as they, in the passive way, bewitch him," so that in a real sense, he feminizes them. Alexander the Great, with his inexhaustible energy and his boundless aggression, who cried at reaching the Atlantic Ocean in Northern Africa because he had no more worlds to conquer, would be a perfect example of this sort of gay man.[68]

Interestingly, D. H. Lawrence seems to have been fascinated by this concept in Carpenter's work. In fact, he liked to portray himself as a supervirile type, both in life and in literature. Apparently, he did not always succeed in this—at least not in the eyes of his wife, the strong-minded Frieda. Lawrence's interpretation, however, is a misreading of Carpenter, who never sets up the supervirile man as ideal, but quite the reverse. What interests Carpenter about such men is the way in which they bring out the androgyny of more ordinary types. In any case, they have a feminine streak themselves, insofar as they fall in love with other men. And they illustrate a principle dear to him: "As the varieties of human type are almost endless, so the varieties of sex-relation between these types are almost endless."[69]

The classical cult of military comrade-love has received so much discussion in the literature of gay rights during the last two decades that little in Carpenter's presentation of it would now come as a surprise. To summarize: most educated people today know that the armies of the ancient world—and especially those of classical Greece and Rome—encouraged love affairs between soldiers as a way of building up group morale. The Greeks reasoned that men fight with more spirit when they stand side by side with the friends they love and that such love renders the sacrifices of military life bearable and even sweet. In a way, General Colin Powell recognizes the same phenomenon when he says that a strong military force depends on male bonding to hold it together. Powell, at least publicly, denies that this bonding can ever have a sexual dimension. One can hardly imagine, however, that he is not aware of what most veterans certainly know. Men forced to live apart from their wives and girlfriends for long periods of time, while living together with other men in close proximity, often develop homogenic (if not homosexual) attachments among themselves. Powell argues that such attachments necessarily disrupt military discipline; Julius Caesar and Alexander the Great thought otherwise.[70]

Perhaps more interesting to many American readers would be Carpenter's discussion of the comrade-lovers of the Japanese Samurai, a cultural institution less well known in the West. Carpenter had a special love for Japanese civilization, and he had developed a following there by the turn of the century. His young disciple Ishikawa Sanshiro became more than a friend, and he shared with Carpenter his rich knowledge of *Bushido*, the code of chivalry practiced by the medieval Japanese knights and their male lovers.

What comes across as original in Carpenter's treatment of this subject is that these long-extinct social institutions have import for the modern world. What interested Carpenter, as a pacifist, about Greek pederasty and Japanese Bushido was their shared emphasis on self-discipline, fidelity, morality, courage, and civic pride. In the modern world, homosexuality has become so identified with dissipation and self-destructive self-indulgence that it still comes as a bit of shock to consider that it once was associated with heroic virtue and militant patriotism.

That these virtues were employed in defense of the realm interested Carpenter less than the fact that they were expressive of strong community spirit. In the ancient world, he noticed, aggression was directed outward at the enemies of the tribe. In a society based on competition, aggression is directed by each citizen against all. We might not want to imitate the military adventures of the classical Greeks, but we can learn from the communitarian spirit of their democracy—and that was based on their respect for homogenic relationships.

Love between Men as the School of Virtue

Carpenter stresses that homogenic unions were, in no sense, peripheral to the life of these societies. Among the Greeks, he says: "For the beautiful and high-born not to have a lover is disgraceful, since the neglect would be attributed to a bad disposition." The most famous statesmen, intellectuals, and generals of the ancient world proudly took homosexual lovers and were celebrated in song and story for doing so: "Solon of Athens' great and wise law-giver wrote poems in praise of [homogenic love], and in his laws placed the pursuit of it and of athletics on a par, as worthy of, and to be encouraged in free men but as forbidden to slaves."[71]

Like the Samurai, the Greeks delighted in stories of famous lovers, and the theme of these stories is always the same: the amazing loyalty of the lovers to each other and to the community. The lovers Harmodius and Aristogeiton were regarded as the founders of Athenian democracy because they slew the tyrant Hipparchus; Cratinus and Aristodemus offered their lives in order to propitiate the gods and end a plague in the city; "the love of Philolaus the law-giver of Thebes, and Diocles, the Olympic conqueror, lasted until death; and even their graves were turned toward each other in token of their affection." And then there was "the splendid heroism of the Theban band, composed solely of lovers—which perished to a man at Chaeronaea, B.C.[E.] 338, in the last battle of Greek Independence against the huge army of Philip of Macedon."[72] Of such relationships, John Boswell writes, "Most ancient writers—in striking opposition to their modern counterparts—generally entertained higher expectations of the fidelity and permanence of homosexual passions than of heterosexual feelings."[73]

Such unions, Carpenter emphasizes, "became a sort of foundational element in their life, a publicly recognized source of political and social activity and a bulwark of security to the state." As such, they were "not by any to be entered into unadvisedly or lightly, but reverently, discreetly, advisedly, soberly, and in the fear of God." Philosophers and moralists, like today's marriage counselors, gave good advice on what wise men should look for in a prospective lover. "They do not regard as an object of affection a youth exceedingly handsome, but him who is distinguished for courage and modesty," Plato warns, and in the *Symposium*, Pausanias suggests that no man should take as a lover a mere stripling who cannot appreciate philosophy, but rather a young man in the first blush of maturity who already displays a love of virtue and learning.[74]

All of these cultures recognized some sort of sacrament of friendship, with solemn rites and celebrations that could resemble a marriage but were seen as something quite different. The exchange of vows, the offering of sacrifices, a priestly benediction, family banquets, and dances usually marked the occasion, but some cities had very characteristic rites of their own. Aristotle records the Theban custom: "On the grave of the hero Iolaus lovers and their beloved youths still pledge their troth with one another because Iolaus was the favorite of Herakles." Carpenter took particular interest in his discovery that in rural Albania, the homeland of the Dorians, some branches of the Orthodox church still blessed brotherhood-unions of two men. The ceremony included an exchange of vows, and then, "the two made incisions in each other's fingers, and sucked drops of each other's blood the two partners sharing the Eucharist immediately after."[75]

Carpenter advised his English-speaking readers that they would find the love stories of the Samurai all but incredible for their high romantic lyricism. Along with many of his generation, Carpenter admired Japanese art, but, unlike most Anglo-Americans, he had developed close Japanese friends and his books had attracted a readership in Japan. Carpenter felt impressed by what he saw as "the remarkable combination of the masculine and the feminine in the Japanese character—of the sensitivity to beauty with heroic endurance and courage."[76] Some of Carpenter's Japanese friends began to organize and promote his ideas, but eventually his works were banned in nineteenth-century Japan and his followers threatened with imprisonment.

Eros and Divine Androgyne

Carpenter complains of the strange working of the British mind that made the idea of real intimacy and passion between men seem inconceivable. Unlike the Japanese, the modern Englishman requires proof that men can love each other at all. Carpenter particularly resented the notion that a capacity for tenderness in a man is a sign of weakness. Thus, C. S. Lewis refused to believe that "those hairy old toughs of centurions" could ever have fallen in love with each other. After all, they weren't pansies. Carpenter thought that love always makes a man stronger—if it is sincere. Thus, the Greek word for "lover" also means "inspirer." Carpenter thought that romantic love, in some form, was the motive force of all the great achievements of civilization: "Probably, where-ever there has been a great and inspiring ideal of this kind actually moving among a people, there has lain at or very near the root of it that wonderful thing, human love."[77]

It struck him as the most obvious mark of decadence in the industrial age that what has been called "love" among us has been so trivialized. Carpenter agreed with Engels's view that the middle class had essentially turned marriage into a business proposition: "The bourgeoisie remains dominated by the familiar economic influences and therefore only in exceptional cases does it provide instances of really freely contracted marriages," Engels wrote.[78] Carpenter tended to agree, but of one thing he was sure: "The love that had built the Parthenon or the Cathedral of Chartres" was not one of the real motive forces of capitalist civilization. "Strangely enough there is little sense in modern times of the sacredness of love, even in its most gracious forms, nor any inclination to connect it with religion." Because our understanding of sex has become so secular and even physiological, Carpenter felt that we had become almost blind to the "marvelous and mysterious process by which the soul, the very being, of one person passes over and transfuses that of another."[79]

On the subject of the connection between homosexuality and religion, Carpenter makes his most interesting, original contributions to modern thought. His research into primitive religion convinced him that shamanism around the world was connected to homosexuality—and frequently to some form of ritual transvestitism as well. For example, Christian exegesis had long recognized the presence in the Jerusalem Temple, previous to the reign of the reforming King Josiah (638–608 B.C.E.), of the *Kedeshim*, or sacred male prostitutes, who conducted the rituals of sacred sex in the service of Yahweh (2 Kings 23:7). In addition, classical scholars knew that men similar to the Kedeshim had been active as a regular feature of religious worship all over the ancient world. Carpenter had learned during his trip to India that Hinduism still had homosexual rituals, as did the Sufi monks of Turkey and North Africa.

This suggested to Carpenter that some sort of instinct for mysticism is innately associated with androgynous personalities. He felt he saw it even the modern West, among British poets of a mystical bent—such as Tennyson, for example. "The feminine traits in genius, as in a Shelley or a Byron, are well marked in the present day." On a more pedestrian level, Carpenter felt that the sort of men attracted to the Christian ministry also often showed a strong feminine element in their characters, an element which, he believed, would be obvious to everyone were not the taboo against seeing it so strong: "To come to more recent times, the frequency with which accusations of homosexuality have been launched against the religious orders and monks of the Catholic Church and even the ordinary priests and clerics, must give us pause." And Carpenter had no anti-Catholic bias on sexual matters; Protestants were as vulnerable on this point as Catholics: "Nor need we overlook the fact that in Protestant Britain the curate and the parson quite often appear to belong to some 'third sex' which is neither wholly masculine nor wholly feminine!"[80]

In this respect, the difference between the Christian church and many of the religions that preceded it in Europe lies only in the fact that homogenic love among the pagan priests or shamans was not disguised. To the early church, the homosexual or transvestite rituals of cults such as those of Dionysos or Antinous appeared abominable. In more recent times, missionaries all over the world have reacted similarly to non-Christian sexual customs. Carpenter quotes from the letters of Saint Francis Xavier, who, to his horror, found that the Buddhist priests of Malaysia took lovers from among the *Bonzes*, or youths, attached to the service of the temples. He could hardly believe his ears when they told him that such loves "were by no means execrable, but harmless and even commendable." Similarly, the Jesuits in South America could not quite grasp the fact that homosexual rituals featured prominently in native religion. "The Devil had gained such mastery in that, not content with causing the people to fall into mortal sin, he had actually persuaded them that the same was a species of holiness and religion," wrote one Fray Domingo of the Society of Jesus.[81]

Carpenter especially enjoyed the works of George Catlin (1796–1872), an early explorer of the Pacific Northwest, who described with great sympathy the life of the Native American *berdache* ("man-woman"), who as an adolescent receives a vision that instructs him to take a husband and become a shaman. Catlin records an experience he had while he was in a large meeting tent, painting portraits of some of the chiefs of the Mandans. He noticed at the door of his tent, apparently too shy to come in, three or four handsome and elegantly dressed young men who were not wearing the eagle's feathers of warriors. When he invited one of these men to come and pose for a portrait, "The youth was overjoyed at the compliment, and smiled all over his face." Catlin admired the soft white suede, embroidered with ermine, that the young Indian wore, and he explained that "with his pipe and his whip in hand, and his long hair falling over neck and shoulders, he made a striking and handsome figure, which showed, too, a certain grace and gentleness, as of good breeding." The young man astonished Catlin by introducing himself as the spiritual bride of a renowned warrior.[82]

Obviously Catlin's open-mindedness impressed Carpenter, rather than the moral outrage of Francis Xavier. Only our prejudices, Carpenter asserts, prevent us from recognizing in the natural dignity and refinement of the Mandan berdache a true moral superiority to the hypocrisy and brutality of many Christian missionaries.

Carpenter felt real fascination with sexually ambiguous or androgynous images of the divine—which, he felt, were both astonishingly common and by no means excluded from Christian iconography and poetry. Consider, for example, the famous legend of Saint Wilgefortis, a devout virgin. Her royal father tried to give her in marriage to the king of Sicily. Not desiring such a union, Wilgefortis prayed to God to disfigure her so that her suitor would marry someone else. Instantly, she grew a thick mustache and beard. Later, her humiliated father crucified her, making her another Christ (*alter Christus*)—an idea not at all offensive to medieval devotees. Saint Wilgefortis, the bearded virgin, has many predecessors in pre-Christian mythology. "In Cyprus there was a bearded and masculine image of Venus (probably Astarte) in female attire. In Egypt also a representation of a bearded Isis has been found,—with infant Horus in her lap."[83]

The conventional icon of Jesus as it has evolved in the West— from popular prints of the "Sacred Heart" to the "Ecce Homo" of such masters as Botticelli or Murillo—often has been decidedly feminine in expression and physiognomy. Sometimes (to twentieth-century eyes) this has been true to an almost embarrassing extent. For example, the model who posed for the once-popular "Light of the World" by Holman-Hunt in St. Paul's Cathedral, London, was the poet Christina Rossetti, wearing a costume beard.

To Carpenter, the androgynous image of the Christ was no accident of art history, no idiosyncratic lapse of taste without explanation or precedent. The love affairs of Apollo with handsome youths such as Admetus or Hyacinthus were celebrated in antiquity. Even the great Zeus, "Father of gods and men," was described in androgynous terms: "From him all things were created; Zeus was Man, and again Zeus was the Virgin Eternal." Dionysus is probably the best known of the bisexual gods of the Greeks; Aristides said of him, "Among young men he is a maiden, and among maidens a young man, and among men a beardless youth overflowing with vitality." Like many another critic, Carpenter marveled at the expressive Hellenistic bust of Dionysus, portrayed with full beard and shoulder-length hair, in the National Gallery at Naples, "which, though bearded has a very feminine expression, and is extraordinarily remindful of the traditional head of Christ."[84]

To Carpenter, the androgyny of Christ, like that of Apollo and Dionysus, has a profound significance. Androgyny was the core of Christ's nature, the hidden and yet obvious import of his message to the world. Christ is, in fact, the Divine Androgyne, "Thy Woman-soul within a Man's form dwelling. Lord of love which rules this changing world, passing all partial loves, this one complete—the Mother love and sex emotion blended." Like the many female mystics of the late Middle Ages recently studied by Caroline Bynum, Carpenter liked to think of Jesus as a spiritual mother and found particular poignancy in the idea of maternal love embodied in and expressed by a male figure.[85]

Carpenter insisted on the maternal nature of Jesus, and for him this was not simply the language of devotion. He believed that real spirituality led men and women away from the crippling, false stereotypes of conventional masculinity and femininity. He also thought that in the spirit of Plato, an essential fecundity is available by means of the union of masculine and feminine natures within one individual. Why are so many homosexual men and women so strikingly creative? For Carpenter, it is because this prolific union is embodied in them, also. Indeed such persons are more than creative; they have an innate tendency toward mysticism: "The double life and nature certainly, in many cases of inverts observed today, seems to give to them an extraordinary humanity and sympathy, together with a remarkable power of dealing with human beings."[86]

Carpenter thought he detected in the Gospel of John a hint that Jesus had had romantic relationships with his apostles and spiritual relations with women: "Women break their alabaster caskets, kiss and anoint thy feet, and bless the womb that bare thee, While in thy bosom with thee, lip to lip, thy younger comrade lies." In his crucifixion, Jesus becomes the prototype of all men misunderstood and persecuted because they love other men. In so far as Christ represents the highest spiritual ideal of humanity, he is an eternal reminder of the essentially androgynous nature of humanity. For Carpenter, as for most Christian mystics, the goal of the spiritual life is the realization of the Christ within. And when we discover the Christ within, we discover our own essential androgyny.[87]

In a famous metaphor, C. S. Lewis once described God as "One far more masculine than the male." This notion of God's masculinity has become a pivotal point in recent debates within the Catholic and Anglican churches over the ordination of women. Those who oppose such ordinations appeal to the notion of God as more masculine than the male to justify their belief that no woman can ever represent Christ to the church, as a priest must. Carpenter, who had some knowledge of Cabalistic literature, took great interest in the notion of the divine Sophia (or "wisdom") of God, thought of as feminine, imagined as the eternal shadow or spouse of God. A theory even more interesting, in this respect, was first suggested to him by Anna Kingsford, a close friend of Madam Blavatzky and a one-time president of the Theosophical Society, who described herself as a hermeticist and a Christian esotericist. Her theory was that the mysterious tetragrammaton (YHWH, translated with the vowel markings for "Lord" [*Adonai*] in the King James Version of the Bible, as "Jehovah," and more recently sometimes rendered as "Yahweh") might be expressive of the union of masculine and feminine. "The two words of which Jehovah is composed make up the original idea of male-female of the birth-originator. For the Hebrew letter *Jod* (or *J*) was the 'membrum virile,' and *Hovah* was Eve, the mother of all the living."[88]

Carpenter found equal opening from more-venerable theologians. For example, if Aquinas is correct when he says that God is called "Father" only because God is the progenitor of all things, then surely it is more correct to address the Deity (as Carpenter often did, echoing the words of Mary Baker Eddy) as "Our Father-Mother God, All Harmonious One." Indeed, Carpenter would have agreed with those modern feminists, such as Maralyn French, who identify the true message of Jesus by pointing out that "at its inception, Christianity, like most other religions, was a revolution against patriarchy. Jesus' doctrines were truly revolutionary."[89]

Carpenter came to believe that androgyny was virtually identical with the creative impulse—in humanity as well as in divinity. Men and women of this temperament, working as priests, poets, and philosophers, have given the human family virtually all that had enriched its life through the centuries: "We may almost think that if it had not been for the emergence of intermediate types social life might never have advanced beyond these primitive phases." Carpenter believed that when the man came along who did not want to fight, he necessarily discovered some other interest and occupation, such as composing songs or observing the qualities of herbs or the procession of the stars. "In this way, such men became students of life and nature, inventors and teachers of arts and crafts; they became diviners and seers, or revealers of the gods and religion."[90]

VICTORIAN LADIES AND A REBIRTH OF LOVE

The masculinization of culture, which Carpenter also saw as a hallmark of the capitalist era, necessarily appeared to him as human disaster, the ultimate death knell of all that made human life something other than nasty, brutish, and short. He would certainly have agreed with Maralyn French that "if we are to build a new morality, it is not enough to modify the value we place on power and other 'masculine' qualities. We must replace the ideal with a new one."[91] Carpenter wrote his last important work on homogenic love in support of the view that androgyny is a value humanity must rediscover if its future is to be any better than its past.

Carpenter's *Love's Coming of Age* relies heavily on Engels's *The Origin of the Family* for its analysis of the economic origins of conventional gender roles. But Carpenter also relies on the experience of his beautiful cousin and dear friend, Olivia Daubeney, for his conception of middle-class marriage. Daubeney was an ardent suffragist and the sole member of the family who sympathized completely with Carpenter's unconventional romantic interests. Having shocked the prim Carpenter family by divorcing her husband after discovering his many infidelities, she, rather than Carpenter's parents (who had been happily married), convinced her cousin that modern marriage was a prison and a trap. Even so, Carpenter went beyond anything that Engels or Olivia Daubeney could teach him. Engels had ended *The Origin of the Family* with a question: "What we can now conjecture about the way in which sexual relations will be ordered after the overthrow of capitalist production is mainly of a negative character, limited for the most part to what will disappear. But what will there be new?"[92]

Carpenter begins *Love's Coming of Age* by attempting to destroy the idea that some sort of essential beauty or spiritual inevitability exists in traditional notions of masculine and feminine. Christian theology had never had any doctrine comparable to the Eastern notion of yin and yang as the basic energies behind nature. Some Western philosophers—especially those concerned with problems of love and marriage—have resorted to similar theories. Erich Fromm, for example, quoted the Sufi poet Rumi in illustration of his own conviction that the masculine-feminine opposition was a part of the nature of things: "Heaven is man and Earth woman; Earth fosters what Heaven lets fall. When earth lacks heat, Heaven sends it; when she has lost her freshness and moisture, Heaven restores it." Man is the sun, woman the moon; man is fire, woman the water; and so on. C. S. Lewis expresses a similar notion: "The man does play the Sky-Father and the woman Earth-Mother" when they make love. "In Friendship each participant stands for precisely himself—the contingent individual that he is. But in the act of love we are not merely ourselves. We are also representatives."[93]

As poetry, this sort of thinking might have merit. Yet, even as poetry, traditional masculine and feminine roles are not genuinely complementary. Feminists have objected to such metaphorical construals because they usually turn out to be deeply prejudicial to women. Carpenter, although sympathetic to women, felt more concerned to show how these stereotypes limit men, the supposed beneficiaries of such heaven-and-earth hierarchies. Moreover, he talks most about the class of men he knew best, the men of the upper classes who were his friends at Cambridge, the men whom Matthew Arnold, in *Culture and Anarchy*, described as barbarians.

English Gentlemen and Victorian Ladies

In Carpenter's day, the English gentleman impressed most of the civilized world as the finest type of humanity on the planet. Matthew Arnold had seen things differently: "One has often wondered whether upon the whole earth there is anything so unintelligent, so unapt to perceive how the world is really going, as an ordinary young Englishman of our upper class. Ideas he has not."[94]

This was precisely Carpenter's view. With Arnold, he acknowledged that the young men he grew up with were commendable for their "vigour, good looks and fine complexion, chivalry, choice manners, and distinguished bearing." He admired also the "care of the Barbarians for the body, and for all manly exercises." What Carpenter chiefly regretted about this class, however, was its complete inability to understand or express love, sacred or profane: "The boy of this class begins life at a public school. He does not learn much from the masters; but he knocks about among his fellows in cricket and football and athletics, and turns out with an excellent organizing capacity." Even after graduation, his class privileges guarantee that "he glides easily into the higher walks of the world—backed by his parents' money." He has really no serious fights to fight or efforts to make, sees next to nothing of actual life. "Despite Victorian propriety, sex of course, is no problem, because he can marry pretty well whom he chooses, or console himself with unmarried joys; and ultimately settles down into the routine and convention of his particular profession—a picture of beefy self-satisfaction."[95]

Carpenter often joked that he, himself, would have become just such a pillar of society had he been heterosexual—or less innately honest. "I should easily have become a bishop," he told his friends, and had a "plump jolly little wife." As it was, however, Carpenter felt that he had seen the underside of all this polite Victorian complacency. For the British gentleman always remains essentially an adolescent, and adolescents trying to do the work of adults can do a great deal of damage: "It is certainly maddening to think that the Destinies of the world, the mighty issues of trade and industry, the loves of Women, the lives of criminals, the fate of savage nations, should be in the hands of such a set of general nincompoops." Behind the simpletons lay other more sinister forces that militated against humane feeling of any kind, the force of the "new economic order."[96]

Carpenter shows much more sympathy for upper-class women, whose oppression he readily understands. True, the Victorian lady of the upper classes suffered few physical hardships and little bodily discomfort. (Carpenter is a man of his time in not seeing childbearing as a hardship.) Her suffering was emotional and spiritual, as Carpenter's had been. As he saw it, the chief burdens of the lady-class were loneliness, guilt, boredom, and frustration—afflictions that Carpenter also knew well.

Olivia Daubeney had surprised him when she said that sexuality posed as serious a problem for the average upper-class woman as it did for gay men. Victorian prudery kept most girls astonishingly ignorant of sexual facts, whereas a double standard allowed their brothers to experiment with prostitutes in an environment not favorable to cultivating sensitivity or tenderness. The result was often a disaster on the wedding night. "The youth too is ignorant in his way. Perhaps he is unaware that love in the female is, in a sense, more diffused than in the male, less specifically sexual: that it dwells longer in caresses and embraces." In his eagerness, the groom turns the wedding night into something resembling rape: "Impatient, he inures and horrifies his partner, and unconsciously aggravates the very hysterical tendency which marriage might and should have allayed." Olivia Daubeney had felt that males, as a class, did not know how to make love to women. Still worse, as she saw it, they did not know how to talk to women. The average man, she told Carpenter, thinks of the women's role in conversation as that of "holding up a mirror for the Man to admire himself in." He hardly knows that she has opinions of her own, and, insofar as he becomes aware of this, he does not regard it as a desirable quality in a woman. In fact, the very ways in which society structures the lives of men and women necessarily entail "debarment of common interests [and] that fatal boredom which is the bugbear of marriage."[97]

Carpenter learned, too, that the average father took little interest in the nurturing and rearing of his own children. In this Victorian age which idealized and sentimentalized motherhood, most men knew little and cared less about what a woman experiences when she becomes a mother: "It is difficult for men to understand the depth and sacredness of the mother-feeling in woman—its joys and hopes, its leaden weight of cares and anxieties. What man really appreciates a women's most intimate experiences?" Most men dismiss out of hand or trivialize problems, such as "the burden of pregnancy, the deep inner solicitude and despondency, the fears that all may not be well. These are things that man can but faintly imagine." Carpenter well understood what today we call the "empty-nest syndrome": "a mother's sad wonderment and grievous unfulfilled yearning as one by one the growing boy and girl push their way into the world and disavow their home ties and dependence." The empty nest can mean terrible loneliness, "but for these things, too, woman can hope but little sympathy and understanding from the other sex."[98]

Women find that the men in their lives, sons as well as husbands, laugh at their troubles more often than they share them. After being talked down to in this way for a time, the mother's mind does, in fact, contract until all she can think about is triviality. "The parting word [to] the boy leaving home to launch into the great world has seldom risen to a more heroic strain than, 'Don't forget your flannels!'" Underneath the silliness, however, such women are frequently consumed by unacknowledged anger and a profound sense of alienation. "How bitterly alone such a woman feels."[99]

In her desperation, woman turns to the weapons of the weak: manipulation, deviousness, moodiness, jealousy, nagging. "Man, as owner, has tended to become arrogant and callous and egoistic; woman, as the owned, slavish and crafty and unreal." Many women soon learn how to lead their men around like children. "Certainly one of the rarest of God's creatures is a truly undesigning female," Carpenter wrote.[100]

The woman who lives by manipulation can gain considerable power of a certain kind. She can, "read characters at a glance, and know, without knowing how, what is passing in the minds of others." But even this sort of knowledge is limiting. "While her sympathies for individuals are keen and quick, abstract and general ideas such as those of Justice, Truth, and the like have been difficult of appreciation to her." Thus, he explained, reasoning with a woman can prove a frustrating experience for a certain type of excessively logical man: "A man, if he is on the wrong track, can be argued with; but with a woman of this type, if her motives are nefarious, there is no means of changing them by an appeal to reason."[101]

In her own way, the manipulative woman can be as destructive as the bullying male. The combination of the two is often lethal: "The frail and delicate female is supposed to cling round the sturdy husband's arm in graceful incapacity; and the spectator is called upon to admire the charming effect of the union—as of the ivy with the oak," Carpenter said. However, ivy is a parasite that suffocates life. "In the case of trees at any rate it is really a death-struggle which is going on."[102]

Carpenter espoused women's causes and deserves to be called a feminist. The cause of women's rights, however, is actually incidental to the real drift of his argument. Carpenter writes as a homogenic man, rather than as an oppressed woman. He judges the ordinary life of heterosexual couples as an outsider. And he does not judge it favorably. He felt alternately amused and depressed by the "weary couples that may be seen at seaside places and pleasure resorts—the respectable working man with his wife trailing along by his side, or the highly respectable stock-jobber arm-in-arm with his better and larger half." He wondered at "their blank faces, their lack of shared interests, the utter want of any common topic of conversation which has not been exhausted a thousand times already, and their obvious relief when the hour comes which will take them back to their several and divided occupations." All of this reflects poorly on the realities of middle-class marriage.[103]

Once again, Carpenter turns the tables on the society that has condemned him, saying in effect, "You ask me why I deviate from your standards; I answer that your standards don't impress me very much, and I ask you why you can't outgrow them." Carpenter had been labeled a freak because he was less than a man. In his view, the so-called real men and women of his culture looked freakish, at least to an outsider. "The bawling mass of mankind on a race-course or the stock-exchange is degrading enough in all conscience," Carpenter stated. "Yet this even is hardly so painful as the sight which meets our eyes between three and four in the afternoon in any fashionable London street. Hundreds of women—mere dolls—gazing intently into shop windows at various bits of colored ribbon." Even more discouraging was "the mob of women in these very same streets between twelve and one at night." Victorian prudery only aggravated the problem of prostitution.[104]

Far from being freakish, the average homogenic man impressed Carpenter as a much finer human type than the average, exclusively heterosexual middle-class male. Too often, Carpenter felt, gay men, as a class, are judged by the most offensive of their number. In *Love's Coming of Age*, Carpenter shows himself not overly sympathetic with the flamboyant queens or the butch numbers so vividly described by such popular gay writers as Jean Genet. "The extreme specimens—as in most cases of extremes—are not particularly attractive," he observes. But, their unattractiveness lies in their crude imitation of the equally unattractive heterosexual types whom they admire. Is Jean Genet's "Stilitano" really any more grotesque than such stock heterosexual heroes of contemporary times as Mike Hammer or Rambo? Is Genet's "Divine" less absurd than the sort of woman played by Jayne Mansfield or Madonna? In fact, the homosexual imitators are frequently much less pathological than their heterosexual models who pass for normal. (Genet liked to portray himself as a prince of evil, but, in fact, as Jean Paul Sartre points out, the most serious crime he ever committed was petty theft. Meanwhile, such authentic butch numbers as Mussolini or Hitler have seduced whole nations with their machismo.)[105]

Most homogenic men, however, do not at all resemble Genet's "Divine" or "Stilitano." "It is not an uncommon impression that most persons of the homogenic nature belong to either one or other of these classes," wrote Carpenter. "But in reality these extreme developments are rare, and for the most part the temperament in question is embodied in men and women of quite unsensational exterior." Carpenter rather thought of himself as a typical lover of the male, and his description of the homogenic personality type can be read as unbecomingly self-congratulatory: "Such men are often muscular and well-built but emotionally they are extremely complex, tender, sensitive, pitiful and loving, 'full of storm and stress, of ferment and fluctuation' of the heart." Carpenter might have been describing himself when he said of the typical gay man that "such a one is often a dreamer, of brooding reserved habits, or a man of culture, courted in society, which nevertheless does not understand him." Above all, the man who can love other men has an extraordinary capacity for love as such: "Indeed, it is possible that in this class of men we have the love sentiment in one of its most perfect forms."[106]

Although idealized, this characterization seems closer to the truth than the caricatures created by Genet and many other homosexual writers. Carpenter rather acknowledges that he was looking for the best, if only because so many others had looked for the worst. But in one respect, he is certainly right on the mark. Even in the twentieth century, homosexuals can be confused with misogynists—a type more often heterosexual than otherwise—and this confusion Carpenter was personally in a position to clarify: "That men of this kind despise women, though a not uncommon belief, is one which hardly appears to be justified." Quite the opposite seems to be true: "Such men are by their nature drawn rather near to women, and it would seem that they often feel a singular appreciation and understanding of the emotional needs and destinies of the other sex." Carpenter himself marked the tendency of women to fall in love with gay men: "There is little doubt that they are often instinctively sought after by women, who, without suspecting the real cause, are conscious of a sympathetic chord in the homogenic which they miss in the normal man."[107]

When Carpenter said that love between men could become a revolutionary force in society, he was not merely indulging in hyperbole. The fear of homosexuality had caused so much evil in the world that simply the ending of such fear should make an enormous difference in the way people feel about themselves. This alone should give people an enormous sense of freedom. But freedom to do what? Carpenter called for something more than an end to irrational fears or pointless anxieties. He energetically promoted the abolition of the irrational gender stereotype that had so crippled the emotional lives of most men, as well as of women.

The Fortress Family and Democracy

Some of the reforms that Carpenter proposed have become so commonplace that they seem almost quaint. For example, one of his most controversial ideas was the simplification of dress and the greater acceptance of public nudity. Today, it is the elaborate costumes of Victorian ladies that seem preposterous, and nude beaches—if not socially acceptable everywhere—are no longer uncommon. Most public school systems in America now mandate sex education, sometimes over the protests of religious fundamentalists, but even the fundamentalists no longer protest girls' sporting events in public high schools.

In contrast, some of Carpenter's ideas still seem, if not quite beyond the realm of possibility, at least wildly visionary. Of these, none is more startling than his ideas about sensual mysticism and the abolition of the family as European culture had come to know it. He believed that traditional family values no longer worked. The theological underpinning of the institution—among other things—was wrong, and a correct theology of sex would create new social forms far more spiritually liberating.

Advocates of family values in Carpenter's day (and even a century later) often have something of a fortress mentality. For example, Jerry Falwell asks, in *The New American Family*, "Why do families exist?" He can answer this question in one sentence: "The family is a shelter in time of storm." The shelter is, first, financial: "Most of us have had the experience of struggling together as families in times of real need. These hard times pull us together and help us grow." Second, insofar as families give "a sense of identity and belonging," they also provide emotional shelter. Falwell writes: "For me, home is a haven to which I run from the troubles of this world, a place of security and warmth, where each member belongs and knows it." In a heartless world, home provides the only refuge in a economic jungle: "A family is a place where people can be real with each other, laughing together, sharing hurts."[108]

Falwell's sermon apparently strikes a responsive chord in many readers. There is, however, a rather unpleasant corollary to his theories. He evidently assumes that outside the home, people feel that they do not belong. Outside the home, they do not feel they can be real or receive support or experience sharing. As the basic economic unit of society, the family provides the only security possible against the ruthless, cutthroat competition of the culture of greed.

Carpenter questioned the human feasibility of a social arrangement such as the sort of family proposed by Falwell—along with the rest of the Christian right. The burden of providing all the warmth and support people need proves too much for the institution of the family to carry alone. In the context of the culture of greed or raw capitalism, the Christian family seems destined to break down under the pressure. Maralyn French observes, "The extreme competitiveness of the masculine world teaches all men to fear and mistrust each other."[109] Increasingly, it is also teaching them to fear and mistrust their (employed) wives and their children as well.

"Marriage, by a kind of absurd fiction, is represented as an oasis in the midst of an arid desert," Carpenter wrote. "And when the desert is the heartless atmosphere of the current economic system, the hot wind is destined eventually to dry up the cisterns and the palms." "The essential fraternity of society at large was dwarfed now and contracted into the limits of the family; and this institution acquired an extraordinary importance (intensified by the darkness and chaos and warfare outside)." In theology, this led to the development of the cult of the Holy Family. So great was this importance, in fact, that the Holy Family became one of the central religious conceptions of the West: "It was commonly thought that society owed its existence to the Family—instead of, as was the case, the truth being the reverse."[110]

In short, the fortress family advocated by right-wing Christians such as Falwell does not hold society together; it is a symptom of the disintegration of the community spirit within society, a kind of last barricade against advancing disintegration. Carpenter believed that "bourgeois marriage, as a rule, carries with it an odious sense of stuffiness and narrowness, and that type of family is too often like that which is disclosed when, on turning over a large stone, we disturb an insect home that seldom sees the light." He felt that the only resolution was, "easy to see—that is, the expansion again of the family consciously into the fraternity of all society." The spirit of sharing, honesty, and concern, which Falwell wants to see in the Christian home, must be extended into the workplace.[111]

Opening of the Heart

Carpenter wanted something more closely resembling the cultural milieu of Periclean Athens—with the proviso that the Athenian democracy be extended to include the whole of society rather than simply an elite class of free males. As Pericles told his fellow citizens, Athenian democracy rested on the "confident liberality [and] the singular generosity" of Greek friendship. Marriage itself should resemble such a friendship: "Women are beginning to demand that Marriage shall mean Friendship as well as Passion; that a comrade-like Equality shall be included in the word Love."[112]

The purpose of marriage, however, is not to restrict love or to dam it back within the confines of a secluded family life. The point, rather, was to open one's heart to all sorts of relationships, romantic or merely intimate, with all sorts of people. He often spoke of the science of love, or even the astronomy of love. Friends should come in constellations, circling around each other like double stars with degrees of proximity determined by the gravitational fields of possible understanding and attempted intimacy.[113]

Distinct and inviolable inner forces bind each individual by different ties to different persons and with different and inevitable results according to the quality and the nature of the affection bestowed. These personal magnetisms can have an astronomical precision. "There is in fact in that world of the heart a kind of cosmical harmony and variety, and an order almost astronomical. It is no use to struggle against this law of emotional gravitation, against what may be called the planetary law of distances in the relation of people to one another. How marked and definite these personal distances are may be gathered from how largely the art of life consists in finding and keeping them."[114]

Carpenter perhaps expected too much of ordinary human nature. He himself chose to believe that society was poised on the brink of a new age of the spirit. Having learned George F. W. Hegel's philosophy through his father's early instruction, Carpenter thought of the modern era as a synthesis of the dialectical opposition between the periods of world history represented by primitive communalism and civilized individualism, which soon would come together so that most people would have access to the science of love. "Roughly speaking we may say that the worship of Sex and Life characterized the Pagan races of Europe and Asia Minor anterior to Christianity, while the worship of Death and the Unseen has characterized Christianity." Carpenter worked and prayed for a new birth of Christian humanism which would include all that was best in classical and medieval civilizations. "It remains for the modern nations to accept both Life and Death, both the Greek and the Hebrew elements, and all that these general terms denote, in a spirit of the fullest friendliness and sanity and fearlessness."[115]

The Roman poet Lucretius wrote, "Fear made God" (*timor deum fecit*). Allan Bloom has written that the essence of Platonic philosophy could be expressed by rewording the old formula. In a way, Plato wants to demonstrate that "Love made God" (*amor deum fecit*). Carpenter not only accepted the latter, but he also looked for the salvation of the world to come about as a general recognition of its truth. If religion and sex are two of the most powerful motive forces in human life, then the combination of the two should mean "the liberation of a Motive greater than Money, and the only motive perhaps that can finally take precedence of money."[116]

REDISCOVERING THE SACRED

Uniting sex and religion was, for Carpenter, more than a metaphor; he sought to elicit and develop their present ritual and cultic connections. He saw a certain beauty, for example, in the fact that the phallus had been honored as sacred in ancient religions—and still was as the *lingam* in the Shiva temples of India. He quoted with enthusiasm the prayers recited by Hindus during intercourse to consecrate their actions. It struck him as significant that "many early peoples regarded the semen as the vehicle and special condensation of the soul" and, therefore, sacred—not only as the symbol of life but as the literal giver of life, the original of the holy oils used for anointing in various Christian ceremonies. Carpenter, like modern sex therapists, stressed that regarding semen as a form of bodily waste material, like sweat or urine, is utterly mistaken. Semen, in contrast, contains the essence of man's life, and Carpenter enthusiastically endorsed the views of the fifteenth-century Italian humanist Marsilio Ficino when he wrote, "Lovers hungrily form one body, and join salivas, and pressing lips with teeth, they breathe from each other's mouths, but in vain, since they can rub off nothing thence, nor penetrate and pass over into its body with the whole body." A man's semen carries his spirit in it. "Since the genital semen flows down from the whole body, men believe that merely by ejaculating or receiving this, they can receive the whole body."[117]

Especially interesting to him was *maithuna*, or the "yoga of love," as still practiced in the India of his time. Carpenter first encountered this technique while visiting in the 1870s a colony of Christian perfectionists at Oneida, New York. They apparently discovered the practice on their own with no knowledge of its Hindu parallels. At Oneida, they called it "male continence," and, as this term suggests, the point was for the male to refrain entirely from climax, prolonging the sexual act considerably—often for as long as six or more hours. "In the course of an hour or more the physical tension subsides," Carpenter found through his own experimentation, "the spiritual exaltation increases, and not uncommonly visions of transcendent life are seen. The result of this is a more complete soul-union, a strange and intoxicating exchange of life." The whole point is to concentrate less on achieving a physiological release and more on savoring the beauty and the tenderness of the act itself. In the process, human love is mysteriously transfigured and becomes a symbol of the divine.[118]

This spiritualizing of love is the heart of the matter for Carpenter. He could be quite Victorian in his indignation at what he saw as the cold-blooded, cold-hearted hedonism of the sexual underworld of nineteenth-century London, whether homosexual or heterosexual. The outward prudery of society had the unintended effect of both intensifying and degrading sexuality until "the passion became one of fearful and compulsive power and fury." The sexuality of London's music halls, bordellos, gay bars, and opium dens had a kind of baroque extravagance and cruelty. It was the world of the Cleveland Street Scandal, Cora Pearl and Lily Langtry, Squire Abingdon and Frank Harris. "Sex today throughout the domains of civilization is thoroughly unclean. Everywhere it is slimmed over with the thought of selfish pleasure." But the selfish pursuit of personal gratification destroys the true spirit of eros. For Carpenter, hedonism destroys real eroticism. "Not for joy, not for mere delight in and excess of life, not for pride in the generation of children, not for symbol and expression of deepest soul union, does such sexuality exist—but for our own gratification." Genuine eroticism mean exactly the reverse of hedonism.[119]

The sort of anonymous, compulsive, guilt-ridden sexuality that characterized gay life in Carpenter's time (and that largely still characterizes it in ours) horrified him. A healthy sexuality begins with the acceptance of self, with the affirmation of the divine spark within each one of us. Hatred of self is the denial of the divinity within. "This, it must be supposed, is what is meant by sin—the separation and sundering of one's being—and all the pain that comes therewith." Self-hatred leads to a desperate and inhuman sexuality, a sexuality without intimacy and thus necessarily unsatisfying. "The dissatisfaction is not in the nature of the pleasure itself, but in the nature of the seeking."[120]

This more perfect love of which Carpenter speaks is precisely what he means by "sacred sex." He is not opting, as in the Christian tradition, for sacred love in preference to profane love. Rather, he rediscovers the meaning of profane love within the context of the sacred. "Sex is the allegory of love in the physical world. It is from this fact that it derives its immense power." Physical ecstasy, when combined with emotional intimacy, brings one close to the experience of divinity. "Therefore whoever has truly found another has found not only that other, and with that other himself, but has also found a third—who dwells at the center and holds the plastic material of the universe in the palm of his hand."[121]

The divine matrix unites all human souls in one embrace. The discovery of the divinity within makes human love possible, not as a compulsive or desperate search for an elusive self-fulfillment or ego gratification, but as a kind of overflow of happiness or celebration of life. The discovery of the divinity within the beloved unveils a new insight into the nature of the divine. Human love is, itself, a new revelation of divine love. Human love is a medium through which divine love comes to us. Because God is love, lovers unite only in God; this, in itself, makes completely exclusive relationships impossible.

The Spiritual Message of Falling in Love

To state matters the other way: All authentic love is open-ended in the direction of infinity and eternity. Carpenter had given a great deal of thought to that magical and excruciating experience referred to as "falling in love." Carpenter took this experience seriously, perhaps because, in his own case, it had caused him so much unnecessary shame and suffering. Carpenter came to believe that falling in love is a religious experience—perhaps the quintessential religious experience.

Certainly romantic love takes us out of everyday reality. It comes as a revelation and has been called a delusion. "Love is blind," as the proverb says, because it puts a veil over our eyes when we contemplate the beloved. We simply cannot see his or her human limitations and failings. The beloved appears as a god more than as a human.

Is romantic love a fantasy? Carpenter thought not. What is the real nature of the divine spark that constitutes our true identity as children of God? "If we do not recognize (which is naturally not easy) our own divine origin, it is certain that we cannot really love without discovering a divine being in the loved one—a being remote, resplendent, inaccessible, who calls for and demands our devotion." "Beloved, we are God's children now; what we will be has not yet been revealed. What we do know is this: when it is revealed, we will be like him, for we will see him as he is," wrote Saint John, the beloved apostle (1 John 3:2). For Carpenter, love reveals the promise of what we shall be when we realize our destiny in Christ. And when we shall realize our true identity in Christ—what Carpenter termed "our wonder-self"—then we shall realize that "the mortal form is most obviously a mere symbol."[122]

The religious significance of romantic love in all of its many and varied manifestations is that it introduces each one of us to the transcendent nature of our true nature and destiny. Because of this strong belief, Carpenter had nothing but scorn for the notion that the *only* purpose of sexuality is reproduction. To be sure, love has any number of purely human motives and biological purposes. Without negating any of these, however, he insisted that its inmost meaning is purely religious; it ushers us directly into the realm of the divine.

This is equally true of love between same-sex couples, which, because it adds to and embellishes the essential gift of love between a man and a woman, Carpenter loved to call a "gratuitous grace." "Friendship as an end in itself does not fit in the established order of things, for it is a law unto itself, one that is not easily deducible from the civil or divine law," Allan Bloom once wrote, commenting on Plato's symposium; "it does not point back to the claims of civil society in the production of children." For Plato, the gratuitous nature of love between men indicates its divine origin. Bloom thinks this also explains why it is so often banned and persecuted. "It is strictly on its own. It really knows no country and no family and frequently is the object of profound suspicion and the part of both."[123]

This summarizes the basic insight at the foundation of Carpenter's—and Plato's—understanding of homosexuality. Love between persons of the same sex is necessarily gratuitous; it has no obvious social or biological utility. For Victorians of every race and religion, this makes it evil. For Carpenter, as for Plato, the fact that it is humanly useless renders it morally divine. For, as Diotima told Socrates, men do not love the useful; they love the good. In proof, she cites the fact that men have been known to have parts of themselves amputated for a good cause. As Elizabeth Barrett Browning once wrote, in response to Gautier, "Art for art's sake, yes, and love for love's sake." Neither art nor love amounts to much if done for a reason. Love, like God, is its own reason for being. Homosexual love is simply a dramatic illustration of this point, and this is what makes it important as a key to the nature of the divine. In explaining this concept to Edward Lewis, Carpenter paraphrased Scripture: "[Love] is the 'I am.' It says with God, 'Before the world was, I am; and when time shall be no more, I am.' Love is the supreme good and the supreme goal of life."[124]

The *ascesis* of homosexual love lies in the equally unarguable fact that "it is strictly on its own. It really knows no country and no family." Carpenter found in his own life that the loss of social identity based on class or race can become an opportunity to discover one's true identity. This destruction of the merely surface ego constituted true asceticism—by contrast with the dramatic penances so ostentatiously practiced by the Anglo-Catholics of his time. It was real self-mortification and self-annihilation, and accepted in the right spirit, it had the desired result of revealing one's true identity in God.

The Social Self

Carpenter was no stranger to the groundbreaking research into the nature of the social self developed by such sociologists as George Herbert Mead in *Mind, Self, and Society* (1906), and Charles

Horton Cooley in *Human Nature and the Social Order* (1902). Carpenter would even have agreed with modern sociologists that the social self, by definition, is a social construct. He allowed that the local and external self, the social personal, the face we show the world—including "dress, facial outline, professional skill, accomplishments, habits of mind and body"—is a cultural artifact. "All these things depend on date, locality, heredity, surrounding institutions, social habits, current morality, and so forth."[125]

Carpenter breaks with sociologists' notion of the "looking-glass self" (the self that is revealed, as in a mirror, in the appraising stare of one's social peers and contemporaries) in his belief that beneath the myriad details of our surface personality there lies a deeper and more elusive reality. For whole decades of his life, Carpenter played a social role that was drastically at odds with his own inner feelings. Indeed, he came to understand that he was somehow able to hide those feelings even from himself. As a result, he inevitably thought of his painful search for his true identity as the major theme of his life. That he found that identity through the experience of love—homosexual love—struck him as significant. For this identity, he felt, is no mere social construct and has nothing to do with the limitations and restrictions of this particular cultural or historical moment: "The deepest and most central core of the man may survive, far beyond and above personality."[126]

Carpenter liked to compare the outer details of a person's social persona to plaster molds in which statues are cast. "Their outlines are the inverse of their true form; looking on them thou beholdest what thou are not." Humiliations, rejections, and persecutions chip away this false self, but what they leave uncovered is the true work of art: "As a mould for some fair form is made of plaster, and then when it is made and the form is cast therein, the plaster is broken and thrown aside." The soul transcends the social self infinitely: "For a form fairer than aught thou canst imagine, thy body, thy intellect, thy pursuits and accomplishments, and all that thou dost now call thyself, are the mould which in time will have to be broken and flung aside."[127]

Sartre believed (and much of twentieth-century philosophy has followed him in this) that any search for a person's true identity is inevitably futile, the essential self of anyone being a kind of nullity. Sartre illustrated his point by an extensive analysis of his own sado-masochistic experience. Carpenter, as a homosexual who had spent years being publicly secretive while struggling to find himself, could hardly agree. He felt that his own homosexual experience had disclosed to him important insights about the relationship between one's social persona and what can only be called one's soul.

Carpenter's sexual experiences had always been tinged with religious emotion; he thought of love as mutual worship, marveling that two beings, "half animal, half angel, shall see and wonder worshiping each other." In the act of love, a man discovers the god within his beloved and within himself. The language of love and the language of religion have overlapped for centuries, but Carpenter took such language with a startling literalness. When he spoke of his lover as a god, he really meant it, and he evolved an interesting theory of the soul to describe the experience. It is loosely based on the neo-Platonic theory of soul as a divine hypostasis, as it was modified by medieval theology and accepted by Anglican divines.[128]

The Self as a Divine Idea

In grappling with the then-already-ancient philosophical problem of the nature of human individuality, Plotinus taught that ideas or forms of particular human beings exist in the divine mind rather than simply one universal archetype or abstraction of humanity in general, as Plato had taught. "Might not one (archetypal) man suffice for all?" Plotinus asked. "No, one Reason-Principle cannot account for distinct and differing individuals: one human being does not suffice as the exemplar for many, distinct each from the other, not merely in material constituents but by innumerable variations of ideal type." Corresponding to every individual human being, then, an eternal idea of what that person was meant to be exists in God's mind. The scholastic philosophers call this divine idea the *Haecceitas* ("intelligible thisness") of the individual, his or her essential self. Aquinas postulates that the essence of anyone was perfectly complete and individual in the mind of God before the creation of the world. *What* a particular person is—his or her human essence—literally precedes existence, the fact *that* she or he is. (Sartre would later argue exactly the opposite position.)[129]

Our actual life in this world is never anything more than a rough approximation of God's eternal idea of us, because, in the words of Aquinas, "the divine essence comprehends within itself the nobilities of all beings according to the mode of perfection." The true person, according to God's idea, is never sinful and fallen, but always pure and perfect, mirroring God's perfection. "Our human height, scarce served from divine," wrote Edward Young, the Anglican divine, "who looks on that, and sees not in himself an awful stranger, a terrestrial God?"[130]

Meister Eckhart—the German mystic so beloved by Carpenter's father—wrote, in his own characteristically paradoxical fashion, of his intuition: "In that essence of God in which God is above being and distinction, there I was myself and knew myself as to make this man. Therefore I am my own cause according to my essence, which is eternal." Eckhart is only saying that a person's higher self is his or her true self, shaping the temporal self for its own purposes.[131]

For Carpenter, the mode of perfection described by Plotinus and Eckhart was not a theological concept, but a lived reality. At several moments in his life, Carpenter felt that he had a direct experience of the higher self—the self beyond the social facade most people use to hide their feelings. In each case, the experience came suddenly, a flash of revelation. But in each case, it changed him permanently.

In one instance, as a young man Carpenter had been deeply troubled by his emotional and sexual needs. An encounter with the poetry of Walt Whitman moved him profoundly—with the force of a divine revelation. "You have spoken the word which is on the lips of God today, and here dimly, I think I see the new open life which is to come," Carpenter would later tell Whitman in a letter he felt compelled to write. From the start, Carpenter felt a strange psychic bond connecting him to the "sage of Camden." Although hesitant to share this belief with a man he had as yet never met, Carpenter hinted at it in that first letter. "Whenever the most common desires and dreams of daily life are—wherever the beloved opposition is, of hand to hand, of soul to soul—I sometimes think to meet you."[132]

Interestingly Whitman reacted just as powerfully to Carpenter's letter. "It is beautiful," he told his friend Horace Traubel, "like a confession; I seem to get very near to his heart and he to mine in that letter." Whitman wrote back to Carpenter in the same intimate vein, assuring him that they were certainly destined to become "ardent friends" and inviting him to come to Camden for a personal encounter.[133]

Carpenter thought of his trip to America as a pilgrimage. And when he first set eyes on the man whom he now saw as his spiritual mentor, he was not disappointed. "In that first ten minutes I was becoming conscious of an impression which subsequently grew even more marked—the impression, namely, of an immense vista or background of his personality." During the days that the two men spent together, "a sort of spiritual intoxication set in; I felt that he was a god or in some sense clearly preterhuman." When the two men finally made love, Carpenter saw himself as worshiping the divine presence he sensed in Whitman's soul. "I was aware of a certain radiant power in him, a large benign effluence and inclusiveness, as of the sun." Afterward, Carpenter was reborn. His encounter with Whitman became in his mind an authentic conversion experience. Among other things, it led Carpenter to devote his life to promoting the political rights and the spiritual liberation of gay people.[134]

But Carpenter was to have this experience more than once in his lifetime—sometimes under rather unlikely circumstances. Once during a short stop in the middle of a long railroad journey, he stepped out of the car to stretch. "As it happened, just as we stopped at a small way-station, my eyes encountered those of a grimy, oil-besmeared stoker." Carpenter had been dozing in his compartment, and it took a moment for him to register what he was seeing. "Close at my elbow, on the foot-plate of his engine, the young man was standing devouring bread and cheese, and the firelight fell on him brightly as his eyes rested on mine." And in those eyes, Carpenter felt that he saw "an old divine light." "The quiet look, the straight untroubled unseeking eyes, resting upon me— giving me without any ado the thing I needed. For a moment, I felt the sting and torrent of Reality." As it happened, this momentary encounter became the basis for a lifelong relationship. Despite the worker's humble origins and lack of education, George Merrill fell deeply in love with the older poet, and the two lived happily together for over thirty years.[135]

Such dramatic experiences of erotic and spiritual intoxication became the foundation of Carpenter's philosophy of sex, as it did of his religious vision. He was convinced that erotic love had taken him out of the world of mundane experience and liberated him from the prison of his isolated ego. Sex discloses, though the medium of the flesh, what the psychiatrist C. G. Jung has termed the "undiscovered self," the deep spiritual reality that lies beneath the surface facade of social distinctions and that is the reality that bonds or unites the individual to others—and to the divine.[136]

Indeed, Carpenter came to believe that the experience of love—or even of desire—is essentially a response to some revelation, however dim, of the diviner phase of the soul. In the words of one modern philosopher, "sex exploits an embarrassing interest in organic detail in order to reach what is most central and secret in a personality. Sex is essentially symbolic, sacramental." Carpenter came to believe that the love of the mere surface person apart from the person within the person was a mistake. "Who loves the moral creature, ending there, is no more free—he has given himself away to Death," Carpenter wrote. A love that cannot see beyond the social persona eventually destroys itself, because it is based on superficial and contingent details which rapidly pass away. "If you must love me, let it be for nought, except for love's sake only that evermore thou mayest love on, through love's eternity," wrote Elizabeth Barrett Browning. The desire for love does not come from the surface self, and it cannot end there. The region of freedom lies in the infinite.[137]

Carpenter's logic is simple. On this earth, love (and especially erotic love) is as close as we come to heaven. "Everyone must have felt," he thought, "in all cases where the sense of Beauty is deeply roused, that strange impression of passing into another world of consciousness, where meanings pour in and illuminate the soul." He quotes enthusiastically from Giordano Bruno's *Gil Eroici Furori* that God is the true object of all desire. "All the loves have for their object the divinity, and tend towards divine beauty, which is first communicated to souls; and from them, or rather through them, is communicated to bodies."[138]

When their eyes meet, lovers behold the divine spark within each other. In the words of Bruno, "The more than mortal in him

beholds the more than mortal in her. " Like Dante, each of us can
find the vision of the mystical rose only in the eyes of our particular Beatrice: "With the eyes of the gods we see God." Marsilio Ficino
explained the idea this way. "This is how it happens that lovers
are so deceived that they think the beloved more beautiful than he
is." Love sees not though the eyes, but through the soul. "For in
the course of time they do not see the beloved in the real image of
him received through the senses, but in an image already formed
by the lover's soul." This soul vision has a divine origin. "In loving
[beautiful] bodies we are really loving the shadow of God; in loving souls the likeness of God."[139]

Love is the only real evidence we have of God and of personal immortality, Carpenter believed. "Love in some mysterious
way forbids the fear of death." Love guarantees that "every Self in
its essence is individual, eternal, perfect" and is proof "against
any mere doctrine of absorption in the Universal." God is in humanity and humans in God; the two terms of the dyad are never
identical, however, for love implies duality. "Perhaps in the outer
world we do not always see such relations quite clearly, and we
think that when death or other cause removes the visible form from
us that the hour of parting has come," Carpenter admitted. But
the experience of any profound love for another teaches us differently: "In the inner world it is clear enough, and we divine that
we and our mate are only two little petals that grow near each
other on the great Rose of Eternity."[140]

The vision of the mystic rose shown to Dante by Beatrice at
the end of the *Paradiso* became Carpenter's model of understanding the spiritual meaning of all human relationships. When human souls unite, they follow some occult law surpassing all human definition and all human power to control. That law acts as a
kind of gravitational force drawing souls together just as physical
gravity holds the galaxies—the flowers of heaven—together in their
own floral patterns. Carpenter taught that "there really is a Free
Society in another and deeper sense than that hitherto suggested—
a society to which we all in our inmost selves consciously or unconsciously belong." World religion has embodied this vision in
powerful metaphors: "The Rose of Souls that Dante beheld in Paradise, whose every petal is an individual, and an individual only

through its union with all the rest—the early Church's dream, even the New Jerusalem of St. John."[141]

For Carpenter, the essential role of homogenic love is to express this divine gravitational pull which draws people out of the double selfishness of the middle-class family and opens them up to larger influences. Homogenic love is not a threat to family values, but instead supplements and supports them. Homogenic love is strong precisely in areas where the family is weakest; it breaks down with impunity the barriers of race and class and religion that the family only works to reinforce. It violates all sexual stereotypes and unmasks their essential falseness. It hearkens back to the free sexual expression and communal spirit of the primitive gens (or confederation of tribes), and it looks forward to the more truly democratic societies of the future. The ideal of terrestrial society for which we naturally strive is that which would embody best these enduring and deep-seated relations of human souls; thus, it happens "that every society, as far as it is human and capable of holding together, is in its degree a reflection of the Celestial City."[142]

The idea of a society based on love, in which there is universal sharing and a sense of community reminiscent of early tribal societies (and of the primitive church) combined with the intellectual sophistication of high civilization, would strike many as an impossible dream. Yet Carpenter asks what the second petition of the Savior's prayer, "Thy kingdom come," implies if not such a dream. The Bible's last book ends with Saint John's vision of "the New Jerusalem, coming down out of heaven from God" (Revelation 21:10), a vision Carpenter interprets to mean, "Love is doubtless the last and most difficult lesson that humanity has to learn, but in a sense it underlies all the others."[143]

chapter three

THE CULTURE OF GREED AND
THE CULTURE OF BROTHERHOOD

From a Soldier to His Friend,
with an Identity Disc

If ever I had dreamed of my dead name
High in the heart of London, unsurpassed
By Time for ever, and the Fugitive, Fame,
There seeking a long sanctuary at last,—

Or if I onetime hoped to hide its shame
—Shame of success, and sorrow of defeats,—
Under those holy cypresses, the same
That shade always the quiet place of Keats,

Now rather thank I God there is no risk
Of gravers scoring it with florid screed.
Let my inscription be this soldier's disc.
Wear it, sweet friend. Inscribe no date nor deed.
But may thy heart-beat kiss it, night and day,
Until the name grow blurred and fade away.

—Wilfred Owen (1893 - 1918)

Urvashi Vaid, in assessing the current gay liberation movement, subverts the usual agenda: "Rather than asking how gay and
lesbian people can integrate themselves into the dominant culture,
what if, instead, we affirm that our mission is to assimilate the
dominant culture to us?" She does not mean that the rest of the
country should adopt the sexual mores of Greenwich Village. Instead, she lifts up the potential of gay and lesbian liberation to
change society in new, creative, and not altogether predictable ways:

"Unlike gay rights, gay liberation stands for a broader set of cultural values—such as political freedom for all, social justice, and the rebuilding of human community."[1]

The reason that Vaid has such faith in the redemptive potential of gay love is her equally strong sense of the boundless evil of what she calls the male-ego culture. The twentieth century—with its boundless faith in the productive power of male competition, with its fixation on male violence both in sport and in war, with its hero-worship of hypermasculine leaders such as Mussolini, Tojo, Hitler, and Stalin—is now passing into history as one of the most inhumane and destructive eras the human family has never known. Surely it is time to look for other values.

Edward Carpenter could not have foreseen the tragedy of modern history, but he did share Vaid's faith in the redemptive power of gay love. Throughout history, he demonstrates, gay people have functioned better than heterosexuals in professions that serve the common good—the priesthood and the military. "It is well known that Plato in many passages in his dialogues gives expression to the opinion that the love which at that time was common among the Greek youths had, in its best form, a special function in educational, social, and heroic work," he points out. "It is hardly needful, in these days when social questions loom so large upon us, to emphasize the importance of a bond that, by the most passionate and lasting compulsion, may draw individual men and different classes together."[2] In the modern world, the love of man for man might bring a new spirit of cooperation in a society rabid with ruthless competition and greed.

Carpenter liked to quote Walt Whitman's boast that, through the medium of poetry, "I will make inseparable cities with their arms bout each others necks, by the love of comrades." Carpenter, too, believed that "Democracy infers such loving comradeship, as its most inevitable twin or counterpart." But for Carpenter, oracular pronouncements were not enough. He felt that any authentic liberation of love between men required a detailed social program based on a careful analysis of the conditions of modern life. In the long run, the solution was spiritual. But the spirit of gay love had to be incarnated in an economic and political vision of a society reconstructed by the culture of brotherhood rather than the culture of greed. Without such a reconstruction, it is futile to talk about any form of gay liberation.[3]

Carpenter believed—along with such well-known modern historians as Kenneth Clark and Will Durant—that cultures which endorse love between men (classical Greece and medieval Japan are only the best known of these) fully integrate such unions and the fellowship they nurture into every level of their cultural life.[4] Greek art, Greek religion, Greek philosophy, even Greek sport and politics reflect their acceptance of love between men—and help to explain it. In the Japanese cult of Bushido, the arts of flower arranging and poetry evolved out of the rituals of male courtship, as did swordsmanship and the tea ceremony. Because among the Greeks, as among the Japanese, a man who might fall in love with another man was not seen as different or "queer" in any way, homosexuality would never constitute an impediment to marriage and certainly not an alternative to it. The Greeks never saw such male unions as a threat to family life—or a substitute for it.

Margaret Mead has defined culture as "the body of learned behavior" that a group of people who share the same tradition transmit in whole to their children; culture is an organic whole: "It covers not only the arts, religions, and philosophies to which the world culture has been historically applied, but also the systems of technology, the political practices, the small intimate habits of daily life."[5] Change one facet of culture—even something as comparatively trivial as the marriage ritual—and one necessarily affects the whole organism.

Thus the civil rights paradigm for gay rights needs to be rejected. Gay liberation, in contrast, means cultural transformation. To define gay people as a minority whose rights need to be established on a par with the dominant culture concedes that love or desire or cooperation between men is not normal. Carpenter, like Plato and Jesus, insisted that such love is normative for a society. An unhesitating endorsement of such love can change society. "We must supplement the limited politics of civil rights with a broader and more inclusive commitment to cultural transformation," Vaid writes.[6]

This is just Carpenter's point. But, unlike Vaid, he attempts to spell out in detail his vision of a society transformed by the manly love of comrades. Above all, his vision is never utopian. True, as a Christian minister, Carpenter often spoke and wrote like a visionary. But he was also a down-to-earth, practical man who, for years, had worked as union organizer, cooperating with the most uneducated and desperate of laborers in their often bloody struggles for economic justice. And as a trained economist, he wanted to prove that the culture of brotherhood was (to borrow a phrase from Theodore Roosevelt) a "realizable ideal," not under the historical conditions of ancient Athens or Jerusalem but under those of modern London or New York. His program for integrating gay love into a transformed yet modern and industrial society is both surprisingly pragmatic and astonishingly relevant a century after his death.

THE CENTURY OF MEGADEATH

In 1897, Edward Carpenter was invited, along with a handful of other prominent radicals of the period, to contribute an essay to a collection entitled *Forecasts of the Coming Century*. Now that the twentieth century itself is drawing to a close, and political pundits cast baleful glances at the twenty-first century, most of the essays in this 1897 volume make curious reading. In retrospect, it seems almost incredible that any group of self-proclaimed experts could have been so consistently wrong.

Carpenter's particular contribution reads rather better than many of the others; he is more tentative and less blithely optimistic than most, admitting freely that he is writing less about what he expects to happen than what he hopes will happen. And he enumerates candidly the forces that stand in the way of his hopes: "the corruption and imbecility of all governments generally," "the dangers of bureaucracy and officialism," "the vague and impossible theorizing of many on the left," "the apathetic routine and inertia of the human masses," and—above all—"the boundless greed and ruthlessness of the current ruling class." "It must not be blinked at, that in the growth of the modern millionaire we are face to face with serious evil," he said. What, after all, does it take for a man to make his first million? Carpenter answers: "Now that any man endowed with a little low cunning has a good chance of making himself enormously rich, Society is in danger of being ruled by as mean a set of scoundrels as ever before in history."[7]

Even with all these reservations and uncertainties, Carpenter was as wrong as any of his contemporaries about what the twentieth century had in store for humanity. In nothing does he seem so typically a person of his time than in his serene confidence about the immediate future: "For a century now commercial rivalry and competition, the perfectionment of the engines of war, and the science of destruction have sufficiently occupied the nations—with results only of disaster and distress and ruin to all concerned. Today surely another epoch opens before us—an epoch of intelligent helpfulness and fraternity." [8]

Carpenter's epoch of intelligent helpfulness became what many are now referring to as the century of megadeath. Hitler exterminated his six million, Stalin his sixty million, Pol Pot his two million—and all in peacetime. We have yet to consider all of the deaths caused by two world wars and all the dirty little wars in between.[9]

At the end of his life, Carpenter was still trying desperately not to believe the worst about the Bolshevik experiment—even when Lenin deliberately made civil war inevitable in Russia by rejecting outright the proposal of an all-socialist coalition designed to save the country from chaos.[10] By then, the sectarian bickering among socialist parties had been tormenting Carpenter for decades, and he noted with rueful irony the strange capacity for violence in many idealists and humanitarians of the left. Drawing on personal experience, Carpenter noted, "It is only such men—having the love of humanity in their hearts—who are able to believe in the speedy realization of an era of universal goodwill [and] being innocent enough to believe that the only impediment to the realization of this era is a certain wicked person (or persons)—who can spur themselves on to the bloody dispatch of such person."[11]

What Carpenter could not see, or refused to see, was that such so-called humanitarian murders would eventually number in the tens of millions. Zbigniew Brzezinski, former National Security advisor and Johns Hopkins professor, has observed that the twentieth century was born in hope, but contrary to its promise, it became humanity's bloodiest and most hateful century, a century of "hallucinatory politics" and monstrous killings: "There is a ghastly irony to this history. The contrast between the scientific potential for good and the political evil that was actually unleashed is shocking."[12]

Against such a somber backdrop, humanity now contemplates its own future with less optimism than it did in 1897. Maralyn French believes, for example, that humanity has difficulty imagining any future for itself. Journalist Allan May suggests that, given the facts of nuclear proliferation and ecological catastrophe, "the prevailing image of the future seems best summed up by the phrase 'nuclear winter.'" In light of such premonitions, why consider the political speculations of a Victorian idealist like Edward Carpenter, one intoxicated with the improbable dream of love between men and the salvation of the modern world? In fact, Carpenter could be portrayed—and has been portrayed, by Malcolm Muggeridge among others—as one of those whole hallucinatory politics helped create the grand failure that would be the twentieth century. "The ultimate significance of the totalitarian experience during the twentieth century," writes Brzezinski, "goes beyond the scale of the mortality deliberately inflicted in the name of the grand transcendental fictions so fanatically propagated. It involves the abortive attempt to coerce mankind into truly bizarre utopias."[13] But what utopia could be more bizarre than the homosexual fantasy world created by Edward Carpenter?

The Long Detour of Modern Times

There is another side to the story, however. Harvard historian Dominic Lieven has written that "at present much of European history between 1917 and 1991 appears to be merely an aberration, a detour." Between those two dates, Europe saw the rise and fall of the two great modern secular religions of fascism and Bolshevism. And when the great secular metamyths were gone, the world found itself much where it had been before they came. The words Carpenter wrote in 1915 could easily have been written yesterday: "For a century now commercial competition and the science of destruction have sufficiently occupied the nations—with results only of disaster and distress and ruin."[14]

Jean-Paul Sartre, at the conclusion to *Saint Genet*, wrote, "our age has a guilty conscience with respect to history. We are more aware of injustice than ever, and we have neither the means nor the will to rectify it." A half-century later, economics professor

Lester Thurow sees Sartre's worst fears realized as a handful of megacorporations take control of a "global village made up almost entirely of paupers." Malachi Martin, professor at the Vatican's Pontifical Biblical Institute and former Jesuit, speaks of the map of shame dividing the "have" nations from the "have-nots" and of the shooting war between desperate poverty and unlimited greed which erupts every day in the streets of such cities as Medellin, New York, and Los Angeles. Brzezinski expresses the consensus of opinion succinctly, that for most of world history, inequality was tolerated because continents were separated by huge distances and characterized by cultural remoteness. With the coming of the global village everything has changed. In a world that has become surprisingly small, and that is characterized by massive political awakening, inequality has become intolerable. In short, social injustice on a grand scale is a kind of time bomb. How that rejection of inequality will be expressed depends, however, on whether it acquires a defined sense of direction, whether the human family can evolve some universally accepted criteria of justice.[15]

All of this lands us right back in the moral dilemma once faced by Edward Carpenter and his generation. After the long detour of fascism and Stalinism, the world again faces the challenge of attempting to define the criteria for economic justice that will make the future once again seem livable. If Brzezinski is right, then the only thing that has changed in a century is that the mass media have made people around the world aware of the giant of global inequality in a way that was hitherto impossible. And as this inequality seems ever more intolerable, it becomes increasingly important for us to find "the means and the will to rectify it." Carpenter believed that the love of man for man might help to create both the means and the will to achieve real equality and real social justice. His contemporaries were hardly ready for this message. It remains to be seen whether or not the twenty-first century will be ready for it.[16]

Freedom and Equality

"The two words, Freedom and Equality, came to control all my thoughts and expressions," Carpenter wrote with respect to his book-length poem *Towards Democracy*. His poem, he said, was based on a vision granted him of "an absolutely common ground to all

individuals," where distinctions of class and race and temperament became irrelevant. In the opening verses of his poem, he announces this theme that "as the fish swim in the sea, the bird swims
in the air, so the soul of man swims in the ocean of Equality—
towards which all the other streams run." And he continues in the
style of Independence Day orations: "For this the heroes and lovers of all ages have laid down their lives. Where this makes itself
known in a people or even in the soul of a single man or woman,
there Democracy begins to exist."[17]

To twentieth-century sensibilities, this sort of rhapsodizing
can sound hollow. But just as Carpenter's religion was a religion of
the heart rather than of the law, so his politics was a politics of the
heart. He was less concerned with legislating equality than with
convincing people to want equality. He really did attempt to define new criteria for social justice, criteria that have a spiritual dimension and that speak to what is most profound in the human
soul. Moreover, Carpenter's special understanding of freedom and
equality clearly reflects his experience as a gay man—one who
(typically) endured years of repression and frustration and who,
when he broke free of crippling social restraints, found himself
deracinated from his class, his country, and his church. Certainly
Carpenter's political thinking is eccentric in the sense that it bears
no strong correlation with the great secular religions and
metamyths that have dominated the twentieth century. To this extent, his eccentricity may be a virtue.

In the 1930s, Adolph Hitler could still boldly say (and be
wildly applauded for saying it) that he completely rejected the
whole idea of human equality. "The belief in human equality is a
kind of hypnotic spell exercised by world-conquering Judaism with
the help of the Christian Churches," Hitler declared to the usual
hysterical throngs who followed him.[18] In the 1990s, many people
may quietly agree with Hitler that some religious groups promote
equality, but it is no longer fashionable to say so. Instead, politi-
cians prefer to dodge the whole problem of inequality. As George
Orwell prophesied, equality can be redefined in a way that makes
it look much like inequality: "Freedom is slavery."

For example, Francis Fukuyama, in his 1992 bestseller *The End
of History and the Last Man*, classifies equality as a strictly religious
and moral idea of limited applicability, arguing that all persons

"are equally endowed with one specific faculty, the faculty for moral choice." Fukuyama argues that people who are manifestly unequal in terms of beauty, talent, intelligence, or skill are nonetheless equal insofar as they are moral agents. "The homeliest and most awkward orphan can have a beautiful soul in the eyes of God," the otherwise secular-minded Fukuyama declares piously.[19] A lovely thought, but its implications for people such as Fukuyama's awkward orphan may not be so pleasant. If freedom and equality can be so narrowly defined, then such concepts can have little relevance to everyday life. In the name of freedom and equality, the grossest economic inequalities and the most confining social restrictions are defended.

For example, Cornell political scientist Clinton Rossiter accepts Fukuyama's basic postulate of moral equality, but he develops it in an interesting way. From the basic fact of moral equality come several secondary equalities: equality of opportunity, the right of each individual to exploit his or her own talents up to their natural limits, equality before the law. In this view, equality of opportunity necessarily entails inequality of attainment: "Beyond this men are grossly unequal—and, what is more, can never be made equal—in all qualities of mind, body and spirit." The good of society rests solidly on this one truth. "The public good actually demands not social equality, but social hierarchy. The social order should be organized in such a way as to take advantage of ineradicable natural distinctions among men" and women. In fact that hierarchy turns out to be rather inflexible. "Most . . . find their level early and stay in it without rancor, and equality of opportunity keeps the way at least partially open to ascent and decline."[20]

By this definition, freedom is reduced to the right to compete in the mad scramble for a rung on the economic ladder. Equality is reduced to the general right (sort of) to compete in the scramble. Fukuyama and Rossiter believe that most people accept their distinct level in the economic hierarchy without rancor, but this is not so obvious. Malachi Martin, for example, believes that the highest incomes recorded for a handful of individual Americans (more than forty million dollars) grossly exceed any commonsense notion of equality and justice. And even discounting such extremes of wealth, it is difficult to justify a system in which the average chief executive of a large American company is paid ninety-three times more than the average factory worker, and seventy-two times more than the average schoolteacher.[21]

The classic defense of economic inequality in the name of moral equality was penned a century ago by economist William Graham Sumner, who noted that projects designed to do away with poverty and misery, on further analysis, turn out to be projects for "making those who have share with those who have not." What justice requires, according to this line of reasoning, is not equality but gross inequality. "We cannot go outside of this alternative: liberty, inequality, survival of the fittest; not-liberty, equality, survival of the unfittest." Progress, in short, demands poverty for most Americans. Inequality carries society forward and favors all its best members, whereas an equality typified by the redistribution of wealth carries society downward and favors all its worst members.[22]

A BRIGHT FUTURE FOR THE CULTURE OF GREED

The name for rationalizing the unequal distribution of wealth as progress-building is "social Darwinism," coined by Herbert Spencer, the English philosopher usually acclaimed as the founder of modern scientific sociology. Spencer, like Sumner, was optimistic about the beneficial effect of the principle of survival of the fittest. It would create, they believed, a level of universal happiness hitherto unimagined. Rather surprisingly, such nineteenth-century optimism has been carried forward into the twentieth century by the disciples of Spencer, such as Fukuyama and Rossiter, who seem to share his confidence even in the face of much evidence to the contrary.

For example, well-known proponent of the equality-of-opportunity doctrine Richard Nixon liked to scold his fellow Americans for being too glum about the future of free-enterprise economics in a world cleansed of Marxism. "At a time when we should be celebrating victory, many observers are wallowing in Pessimism," Nixon contended. "Instead of pressing toward the mountain top and beholding a new vision of peace and freedom for the future, they are wandering in a valley of self-doubt."[23] The forced optimism of a person such as Nixon has a rather disingenuous quality, whereas his Victorian predecessors usually sounded sincere—if naive.

Edward Carpenter sought to expose the fraud, conscious or unconscious, at the base of this self-serving notion that an inequality in the distribution of wealth would lead directly to an equality of opportunity. He dismissed Sumner and Spencer alike as patently myopic in their vision and methods. As a Christian moralist, Carpenter found it impossible to accept morally "this bitter and continuous struggle for possession, in which the motive to activity is mainly Fear." To a gay man, the so-called capitalist man—whom Sumner termed the fittest and the best—seemed homophobic. Carpenter spoke of his incomprehension of "the covetous hard type of man [who] becomes the large proprietor, and (supported by law and government) is enabled to prey upon the small one."[24]

For Carpenter, hope for the future of humanity lay in another direction. To him, common sense seemed to dictate that love, whether sacred or profane, constitutes the chief joy of living. Why put so much energy into activities that cannot help but cause misery, while neglecting completely to cultivate those that alone can bring fulfillment? "Let us not pray the gods for any stupendous gifts for the coming generations—for towering genius or intellect or universal heroic character," Carpenter modestly suggested, "but only for a modest boon: to be able, namely, to conduct our own affairs with a little good sense—just a little, as much, for instance, as a sheep might have!"[25]

To Carpenter, it seemed plain that freedom and equality—if they were to have any meaning at all—had to mean more than the right to an endless competition for money and power. To him, the vision of peace and freedom cherished by a Herbert Spencer or a Richard Nixon seemed the most patent of chimeras. "It was a glorious dream, this apotheosis of Commerce! This vision of an international Brotherhood founded on trade and barter!" Carpenter wrote. Why, then, has it failed to materialize? "The reason why the dream has not been fulfilled is clear enough. Can international cooperation arise from the spirit of unbridled economic competition?" "You cannot make a silk purse out of a sow's ear. Out of Trade and Commerce founded on greed and self-seeking, and chicanery, and the law of devil-take-the-hindmost, you cannot get Brotherhood and trust and mutual help," Carpenter declared.[26]

No matter how one might attempt to dress it up or glorify it, the free-enterprise economy means pitting all individuals against their neighbors in continuous internecine competition—an only slightly less brutal form of Hobbes's war of all against all. In such a society, the only form of human intelligence or creativity that gains any wide recognition or respect is the sort of cunning or enterprise that serves to make a person rich. Spencer and Sumner, Fukuyama and Nixon, all social Darwinians use sweet names for what Carpenter terms "this cut-throat commercial warfare that we have been living." Nixon contends that the pursuit of excellence for its own sake is the motive force of capitalism. Borrowing a term from Plato, Fukuyama says that the motive force of capitalism is *thymos*, or "the striving to be recognized as superior." As such, thymos constitutes "the psychological seat of all the noble virtues."[27]

Earning a Living in the Age of Anxiety

Looking at the workaday reality of life for most people under the regime of the capitalists, Carpenter resolved to speak the truth. What compels the average person to the office or factory each morning is fear, not some appetite for excellence or passion for virtue. "Though it seems a hard thing to say, the life of modern society is animated first and foremost by Fear. In the case of working people living one pay check away from the street, anxiety often mandates a nightmarish of a way of living—as the wretched wage-slave rises before break of day, hurries through squalid streets to the dismal sound of the 'hummer,' engages for nine, ten, or twelve hours, and for a pittance wage, in monotonous work which affords him no interest." But one finds the same anxiety at the other end of the economic spectrum: "The big commercial man, who, knowing that his wealth has come to him through speculation and the turns and twists of the market, fears that it may at any moment take to itself wings by the same means."[28]

Carpenter firmly believed that "world history, except at rare crises, presents us with no such spectacle of widespread anxiety" as the social Darwinians assume. To a Richard Nixon, this would sound like the clumsiest sort of left-wing propaganda. Although not entirely satisfied with the tone of contemporary life in the West, he knows that "most Americans—poor, middle class, and wealthy—are fundamentally decent, patriotic, and enterprising." Only the intellectual establishment likes to bash America and portray our way of life as other than blessed. Fukuyama, too, finds real satisfaction in contemplating young America at work. "Those earnest young people trooping off to law and business school. For them, the project of filling one's life with material acquisitions and safe, sanctioned ambitions appears to have worked all too well." Which version of the story comes closer to the reality of modern life: Carpenter's anxious and compulsive workaholics, Nixon's decent and industrious householders, or Fukuyama's contented consumers? Perhaps it is a question of moral perspective. Carpenter is not blind to the material productivity of industrial capitalism, but his spiritual values focus on the passions of the heart.[29]

Consumerism as a Complication for Living

Carpenter made quite a reputation for himself in his own lifetime as an advocate of the simple life. He never preached poverty as a virtue in the Franciscan sense, but what puzzled him most about modern life was the mania for owning things—what we would term "consumerism." Carpenter took seriously Saint Paul's warning that people who through their worship of material wealth "pierce themselves through with many sorrows"(1 Timothy 6:10). He wrote that, in pursuit of material wealth, "vast numbers of people not only make miserable their own lives (which might not so much matter), but also the lives of thousands around them." Material possessions, for Carpenter, only have value to the extent that they enhance the spiritual life; beyond that, they become a burden. "Personally I like to have a few things of beauty about me, but I know exactly how much trouble each thing is and whether the trouble is compensated by the pleasure."[30]

Owning too much can make one a servant of one's possessions. Such possession can become a serious social as well as a personal problem—perhaps even more in the twentieth century than in the nineteenth. As modern economists Richard Barnet and John Cavanagh put it, "The itch to accumulate is not genetically programmed. Indeed, poor people the world over are often berated for their lack of acquisitive drive." But modern systems of mass communication, mass marketing, and mass advertising will soon change all this. "As the traditions of procapitalist societies fall away, visions of organizing social systems on values other than frantic consumption have dimmed." The message of the so-called global shopping mall is ascendant almost everywhere. For some, this future may seem entirely positive, but not for all. "Even for those who feel most alive when they are shopping, the message is neither inspiring nor ultimately satisfying. At times we all feel the inexplicable sadness of the child after all the presents are opened."[31]

Carpenter saw consumerism as a manifestation of universal anxiety in life under industrial capitalism. Compulsive shopping is a symptom not of the joy of living but of the obsessive fear of being dispossessed. An obsession with shopping offers the illusion of security; we build a wall of possessions between us and the desperate poverty that we all know to be the dark shadow cast by the material plenty of capitalism. It is what the anthropologists call an "atavism": "In the case of most of us, if not we ourselves, then our ancestors a few generations back, actually experienced real want of sufficient food or sufficient clothing," Carpenter notes. "The specter of such want still haunts us." As a result, many seize every opportunity to accumulate as much as they can in order not to repeat our own remote history. "Savages when they come across a good square meal—in the shape of a dead elephant—just stuff as much as ever they can, knowing it doubtful when they will get another chance."[32]

Carpenter thought that the whole business of this mania for ownership was "incompatible with Christianity; it gives a constant lie to the doctrine of human brotherhood." The meaning of his gospel of the simple life was perhaps best encapsulated by one of his disciples, Mohandes Gandhi, when he wrote, "Live simply so that others may simply live." Gandhi almost certainly derived this notion from Carpenter, whom he knew and loved.[33]

The Birth of Modern Advertising

The sudden growth in the advertising industry at the end of the century particularly annoyed Carpenter, as its later efflorescence would anger Gandhi. What Carpenter witnessed was the tenderest shoot of the jungle that would become the twentieth-century industries of publicity, promotion, and public relations. But even this mere seedling struck him as a moral travesty. "How near these various activities run to the line of Fraud we must leave to the parties concerned to judge, but of their signification as illustrating the intolerable Waste of our present system, every one can form an opinion." What does the advertising industry really create, besides artificial needs? "This vast expense of labor and treasure represents only the internecine warfare of firms with one another so that the total advantage or profit to the community is zero," Carpenter declared.[34]

Just as Carpenter's observations about compulsive consumerism and false advertising still have a timely ring, much of his writing about the social problems of his time also has relevance for our own. (This confirms Lieven's hypothesis about many of the political metamyths of the twentieth century being but an aberration and a detour.) When one looks through Carpenter's writings on social issues, one frequently encounters such topics as pollution, crime, unemployment, homelessness, racism, imperialism. In each case, however, Carpenter tries to analyze the problem in terms of his own special understanding of love between men.

ECOLOGY AND THE ILLUSION OF INDIVIDUALISM

Carpenter likely would not have been surprised to find that the problems of industrial capitalism are unchanged after a century. For him, these problems arise from a certain state of the soul, and a bad tree simply cannot produce good fruit (Matthew 3:10). The root cause of this errant growth is the profound belief, as Sartre put it, that a human being is "by nature a solitary entity" who enters into relations with other humans only "afterward." Carpenter agreed with Sartre, who wrote "the truth is that 'human reality' 'is-in-society' as it 'is-in-the-world,'" but the illusion of separateness has an enormous power. The cult of the rugged individual arises naturally and inevitably at a certain stage of evolution, bringing many blessings with it, but soon revealing its curse. "Competition, in fact, represented a portion of equality, but not the whole; insisting on individual rights all round, it overlooked the law of charity. Individualism, the mere separate pursuit each of his [or her] own good, on the basis of equality, does not satisfy the heart."[35]

Consider, for example, the spiritual connectedness of persons and the problem of industrial pollution. The fact that pollution is not ordinarily considered a spiritual problem is part of Carpenter's point, who claimed that it was. We contaminate and destroy nature because we do not recognize it as a part of ourselves—or, more accurately, we do not recognize that we are a part of it. We think that in desecrating nature, we do no harm to ourselves.

This separation from nature was not always held as true, however. Once, most people felt a reverence for the holiness of nature and acted accordingly. Carpenter liked to talk about the night when, while walking over the hills near his home in Sheffield, he saw one of those charming wayside wells or fountains, which he remembered as having been, years earlier, sparkling with pure water and overhung with ferns and mosses. Time had changed it. "I saw it neglected and shattered, dried up, and its place filled with broken pots and pans and old salmon tins. This sight afflicted me." Remembering how this was only one instance out of many, Carpenter asked himself, "Is the love of beauty and the sense of the sacredness of Life and Nature lost to this people? It is impossible (I thought) to imagine the Greeks of old permitting such a crime." Pagans understood the sanctity of nature. "For, for them, deities and spirits dwelt in the streams and fountains, and in the woods and to defile these things was an act of sacrilege." Even in the Christian era, the devout felt deeply the holiness of nature, as did Saint Francis of Assisi. As Carpenter pointed out that even our forebears, "a few centuries ago, had their well-dressings and festivals of gratitude to God for all creatures of beauty and use. But we—we have lost the sense of divinity in Nature and Life."[36]

Such disrespect for natural life corresponds, in Carpenter's view, to a still-more-fundamental disrespect for human life. The choked spring, like Jacob's well in the Gospel story of Jesus and the woman of Samaria (John 4:7–26), becomes for Carpenter a symbol of the living water of human spirituality, which is also choked and polluted with individualism gone berserk. Carpenter, a homosexual, did not anticipate being a progenitor of any children, yet he felt particular concern for the young, whose lives were being deformed and degraded by a increasing corruption and pollution of resources. Carpenter declared that his heart would sink when "I see the thin joyless faces of the children [of the slums], and the brick walls scarcely recognizable as brick for dirt, and the broken windows; when I breathe the thick polluted air in which not even plants will live."[37]

Gay Positive Family Values

Despite his heterodox views on human sexuality, Carpenter displays consistently throughout all his writing an intense concern for what today is termed "family values." To him, the most deadly feature of industrial capitalism was its breakup of traditional communities and family life. In his day, a pattern emerged in England, which is now usually associated with so-called Third World or developing nations. Dispossessed and increasingly pauperized agricultural laborers were being "driven from small holdings and the closure of all avenues of decent life in the country by the landlord class," drifting into urban industrial centers where they increased the vast army of unemployed and largely unskilled workers. "Saving becomes hopeless, long periods of unemployment occur; and the effect on the character of the man is most baneful," Carpenter observed. "The sufferings entailed in the process are so great," he explained, that each unemployed person "loses . . . courage, . . . loses hope and object in life." Carpenter often recalled an anxious unemployed worker who told him about a visit to a psychic. "When shall I get work again?" he inquired. "You will have bad luck for two or three years," said the old fortune-teller, "but after that you will get used to it!" Such was the good news of the day.[38]

In Carpenter's time, people had come to accept such conditions as inevitable, so that he felt it was important to remind them that life had not always been thus. "In the fifteenth century a landless, houseless family was almost unknown." It struck Carpenter that the right to work was every human being's basic civil right, which could not humanely be denied. "Some folk would deny that there can be any such right as a right to work," he acknowledged, but surely, in a society constituted as ours is, to deny that right is to deny the existence of any right: "If you have no right to work, you have no right to live. For a man can ask no more modest, no more reasonable, no more unassailable right than the right to support himself." Does a person have the right to demand charity? "Observe, it is not the right to beg that is claimed, though that to a starving man can hardly be denied; it is not the right to steal, or in some way to live on the labor of others." Carpenter saw the presence of Christ in the long lines of the unemployed. "The man who stands at the dock-gates asking not for alms but for a pittance of work is (though we do not see it so) the Christ knocking at the door of modern society, knocking at the door of our hearts."[39]

Unemployment and the Creation of a Criminal Class

Given this disparity of views on general equity between Carpenter and many of his contemporaries, perhaps it is not surprising that he viewed the criminal classes of his country more compassionately than many did. Despite its image of propriety, Victorian England experienced a crime wave comparable to the one now overwhelming modern America, as reflected in the works of such writers as Matthew Arnold and Charles Dickens. Because Carpenter's whole lifestyle was in violation of the contemporary vice legislation, because he had spent much of his life, if not in actual defiance of the law, then at least in the skirting of it, and because he made a practice of visiting prisons and of working with criminals, Carpenter knew more about the Victorian underworld than many of his opponents. Morally, Carpenter found most criminals to be no worse than the judges who sentenced them or the policemen who arrested them. "It is not uncommon to meet with professional thieves who are generous and open-handed to the last degree, and ready to part with their last penny to help a comrade in distress."[40]

He found that honor did exist among thieves—and rather more real communal spirit, equality, and freedom than among many respectable business people. The criminal underworld had a humanity of its own. "They have their pals in every town, with runs and refuges always open, and are lavish and generous to a degree to their own kind." True, they saw themselves as the enemies of society at large, which Carpenter would never excuse— nor yet entirely blame. "For if they look upon the rich as their natural enemies and fair prey many of them at any rate are really helpful to the poor."[41]

Carpenter would, I think, have viewed the rise of street gangs among modern ghetto youth with the same sort of rueful compassion. Whatever outrages they commit, they function as ersatz tribal communities in a society fragmented by a berserk spirit of rugged individualism. They provide the lost youth of the urban jungle with "the sense of self esteem, the feeling of belonging"—of being successful at violence, if nothing else. The larger society withholds such affirmation because capitalism needs a surplus pool of labor in order to keep inflation at bay and because it is poised only to affirm the successful. Carpenter also would have suspected that law-enforcement officials were themselves corrupted by the economic-political system and its violence. "We all know that the institution of the Law [enforcement] publicly sanctions and organizes violence, even in extreme forms; that it quite directly and deliberately supports vast and obvious wrongs in society."[42]

What passes for morality in such a society is often only codified greed. Carpenter made his Victorian audiences uneasy by pointing out that they lived by what had been known to traditional theology as the sin of usury. "There is nothing to show that the poor thief is really more immoral than the respectable money-grubber." Whereas the Victorians had made thriftiness and forethought the supreme virtues, Christ had advised his apostles to take no thought for tomorrow; he had cursed the rich and had spent his public life as one of the homeless, having nowhere to lay his head (Luke 9:58). "To have no settled habitation, or worse still, no place to lay your head, are [now] considered suspicious matters." Carpenter pointed out that we "close even our outhouses and barns" against the children of God, "and so to us the Son of Man comes not." Victorian respectability, Carpenter thought, is the enemy of Christ. "Respectability is the code of those who have the wealth and the command. There is nothing so respectable as being well-off. The Law confirms this: everything is on the side of the rich."[43]

Who, in our day, can lay greater claim to morality: the gang member with a distorted sense of community or the business person with no sense of community at all? What Carpenter saw as the fundamental criminal attitude of the nineteenth-century ruling class led him to expect the catastrophe of a world war long before it happened.

CAPITALISM, IMPERIALISM, AND THE CULT
OF MALE VIOLENCE

Historian Peter Gay, in *The Cultivation of Hatred: The Bourgeois Experience, Victoria to Freud*, has traced the increasing fascination of late Victorian society with violence and warfare. At midcentury, such eminent social leaders as Prince Albert (Queen Victoria's revered husband) and William Gladstone (theologian and leader of the Liberal party) gained enormous popularity by advocating diplomacy in the spirit of Christ and prophesying the imminent advent of an era of universal peace. By the end of the century, there arose a tendency to romanticize war as a noble and glorious adventure (as even Teddy Roosevelt promoted it in the United States). This culminated in the war hysteria that greeted the assassinations at Sarajevo in 1914. Literature and the arts of the day also became increasingly obsessed with violence and sadism, as evidenced in the writing of the Decadent movement.[44]

Carpenter viewed this whole trend as the outcome of the cruelty of daily life under advanced industrial capitalism. "What is the ruling principle of the interior and domestic conduct of each nation today—even within its own borders—but an indecent scramble of class against class, of individual against individual?" Carpenter stood against the sort of moral character the law of competition produces. "To rise to noisy power and influence, and to ill-bred wealth and riches, by trampling others down and profiting by their poverty is the real and prevailing motive of our peoples, whatever their professions of Christianity may be." When society admires cruelty in peacetime, what can it expect in war? "The brutality and atrocity of modern war [are] but the reflection of the brutality and inhumanity of our commercial regime and ideals."[45]

At the time that Carpenter was risking imprisonment by opposing the Great War (World War I), former U.S. president Theodore Roosevelt was appealing to a still-isolationist American public for U.S. preparedness. Roosevelt's foreign policy was predicated on the principle that "a just war is in the long run better for a man's soul than a prosperous peace." Kissinger explains what prompted Roosevelt to scoff at the pleadings of the peace movement of his day: "In his estimation, only mystics, dreamers, and intellectuals held the view that peace was man's natural condition and that it could be maintained by disinterested consensus." To him, the only peace was armed peace; peace could be preserved only by the arms of the strong. "Roosevelt lived a century too early," Kissinger believes.[46]

For Kissinger, Roosevelt, and many others, the outrageous violence so prevalent in every era of recorded history requires no explanation. Humans commit violent acts because humans are, by nature, violent animals. Sigmund Freud posited that a death wish lives in the human psyche, a principle of *thanatos* to balance the principle of *eros* ("desire"), which he had earlier thought explained all of human behavior.[47]

Carpenter belonged to that species of mystic, dreamer, and intellectual that, in the view of Roosevelt (and Kissinger), lacks sufficient common sense to understand the obvious. Kissinger (who regards himself as a practitioner of European *realpolitik* in the tradition of Bismark) also admits that all of the founders of the American nation belonged to this unrealistic and ineffectual class with Carpenter. Kissinger quotes, as an example of obvious idealism, the opinion of Thomas Paine, who believed that wars are made by governments rather than by humans: "Man is not the enemy of man, but through the medium of false systems of government." Kissinger wrings his hands in baffled sorrow over a nation that has, until his own rise to power, based its foreign policy on this really silly idea that humanity is not the enemy of humanity.[48]

Explaining the Killer Instinct

Carpenter confessed himself baffled on the topic of the supposed killer instinct inherent in human nature. He found no such instinct in himself and professed a quiet admiration for the kind of person "who did not want to fight—who was perhaps more inclined to run away." He was willing to concede that "fighting is obviously a pleasure to a very large portion of our male population." This explains the popularity of boxing matches and football games, but does it explain the mass carnage of a world war? "Those who know the artisans and peasants of this and other counties know well how little enmity they harbor in their breasts against each other," Carpenter observed. Tom Paine felt that "governments make war, not people—and certainly not a free People." "Wars to satisfy the ambitions of a military clique under a sensible Democracy," Carpenter believed, should "cease."[49]

Is this view too optimistic? Carpenter invites us to consider the issue from a biological point of view. Even granting without reservation the truth of the Darwinian model of evolution, what possible survival value for the human species could so hysterical an enthusiasm for mass murder ever have had? It has no parallel in the animal world; animals do fight their own kind, but almost never to the death. Why, then, in 1914 was the whole Western world seized by an insane passion for war? "How mad, how hopelessly mad, it all seems! With fifteen to twenty million soldiers already mobilized with engines of appalling destruction by land and sea, and over the land and under the sea," Carpenter exclaimed. "This war is the most monstrous the old Earth has ever seen. It is utterly senseless and unreasoning. But broken bodies and broken hearts and an endless river of blood and suffering are the outcome."[50]

Like Thomas Paine, Carpenter thought it made more sense to look for the cause of such madness in the observable facts of prevailing social conditions than in puzzling abstractions such as Freud's thanatos. "Because we cannot even explain why we are fighting," he said, "we are fain to adopt a phrase to condense complexity into a neat but lying formula which we call a Law of Nature." Instead, Carpenter favored an explanation for the war that involved economic realities such as class interest and imperialist expansion: "It is this Class-disease which in the main drags the nations into the horrors and follies of war."[51]

It was not difficult to discern in the supposedly enlightened and rationalist England or Germany of 1914, Carpenter thought, the special class interests that had led to one international crisis after another during the last decades of the nineteenth century. In England, for example, talk about "the Imperial Mission" to "take up the white man's burden" and civilize "the lesser breeds without the law" was common. But what was the British Empire? Carpenter points out that so august a body as the British Empire League, patronized by royalty, with Lord Rothschild as its treasurer, listed five principal goals as constituting the essence of the imperial mission. Carpenter noted with regret that all five had solely to do with the extension and facilitation of Britain's trade. The goal, at bottom, was simple: the "cooperation of the military and naval forces of the Empire with a special view to the due protection of the trade routes." Where, Carpenter asks, are the human and social responsibilities of the vast empire discussed?[52]

Carpenter's analysis of the events leading up to the crisis of 1914 placed particular emphasis on the leaders of then newly formed international conglomerates, such as Royal British Petroleum and Krupp Industries. "One must not forget to include the enormous powers exercised in the present day by individual corporations and individual financiers who intrude their operations into the sphere of politics. We saw that in our own Boer War." He stressed also that trade rivalries were at the bottom of international incidents, such as the Jameson Raid of 1895 (involving rights to huge African gold deposits) and the Algeciras Conference of 1906 (at which Persian oil had been a major issue).[53]

What really explained the war, however, was the logic of international capitalism—not a particular industrialist, a consortium of industrialists, a particular natural resource, or a combination of natural resources. "Early and primitive wars were for this—to raid crops and cattle, to carry off slaves on whose toil conquers could subsist; and the latest wars are the same." No greater economic sophistication is needed to explain the imperial conflicts of the previous century, Carpenter asserts, and he observes that the empire's current aims are not much more sophisticated than those of the ancient world: "to acquire rubber concessions, gold-mines, diamond mines, where colored labor may be exploited to its bitterest extreme; to secure colonies and outlying lands, where giant capitalist enterprises may make huge dividends." Such goals make war inevitable. "To crush any other Power which stands in the way of these greedy and inhuman ambitions—such are the objects of wars today. And we do not see the cause of the sore because it is so near to us, because it is in our blood."[54]

With giant German and British industrial conglomerates competing to secure "a field for the investment of capital under the protection of their own Governments, the two countries were committed to a mad race of armaments. The whole of Europe stood by anxious." Huge military budgets created "a defense establishment with an awesome power of its own." With reference to one of the more-prestigious luxury automobiles of the period, Carpenter wrote, "You cannot keep a 60-h.p. Daimler motor-car in your shed for years and years and still deny yourself the pleasure of going out on the public road." In the same way, "You cannot continue for half a century perfecting your military organization without in the end making the temptation to become a political road-hog almost irresistible."[55]

Even though, for Carpenter, there as nothing mysterious about the vested interest of the military-industrial complex engaging in an international war, the willingness of ordinary workers to support that war was mystifying. What was in it for them? In part, he realized, war fever was simply the result of a carefully orchestrated (although, by modern standards, rather heavy-handed) propaganda machine. "When the war first broke out no one could give an adequate reason for it. It all seemed absurd, monstrous, impossible. Then arose a Babel of explanations," Carpenter remembered. And all of these explanations amounted to slight variations on one overriding theme. "The newspapers had duly explained that the Germans were mere barbarians and savages, bent on reducing the whole world to military slavery." That is, Germany was the evil empire of its day.[56]

The Moral Virtues of War

As the death toll in World War I mounted to staggering proportions, Carpenter came to believe that there must be more to the violence than the simple chicanery of a ruthless military-industrial clique and the credulity of the average citizen. Here Carpenter parted company with the more doctrinaire Marxists, such as Lenin, in seeing the root cause of modern imperialist war as something more than simple class economics. For him, emotional, spiritual, and even moral forces were at least as significant. The working class did not go to war like dumb, driven cattle; they went eagerly, shouting and singing all the way. It was a real carnival of death. "I have been struck, since the outbreak by the altered look of crowds of young men whom I personally know, who are now drilling or otherwise preparing for it," Carpenter recalled. For many a wage slave, war meant freedom. He related his observation of the "gay look on their faces, the blood in cheeks when compared with the hangdog, sallow, dull creatures I knew before." The victimization of the working class, Carpenter concluded, resulted in its willingness to support violence. First, war provides the working class with the illusions of power and community—something their victimization made them hunger for. Second, the war was packaged by the capitalists as humanitarian sentiment in order to satisfy this hunger.[57]

Carpenter felt that war gives workers the illusion that their lives possess precisely that moral dignity which, in reality, they most notably lack and that workers really enjoy what the political propaganda promises—namely, freedom, community, and love. These factors combine, in military situations, with an opportunity to take violent revenge on the world for years of frustration and humiliation. "Many of the volunteers have only the vaguest notion of what it is all about, but for them to join the ranks means adventure, comradeship, the open air—all fascinating things." But the possibility for escape always means much to wage slaves. "They hail the prospect with joy as an escape from intolerable dullness— from the monotony of the desk and the stuffy office, from the dreary round and mechanical routine for the factory bench."[58]

For many young recruits, the realities of combat came as a bitter disillusionment, whereas others found that they were not disappointed. As opposed to a life of prolonged monotony and relentless poverty, the prospect of killing until one is killed became genuinely inviting—as many youthful members of modern street gangs testify. Carpenter once interviewed a newspaper correspondent freshly returned from the trenches, who told him that many men experienced real ecstasy in combat—"an actual lust and passion of conflict, a mad intercourse and ravishment." It was almost a sexual release for them to escape from an intolerable future into the risk of death under conditions that called forth the best they had to give. This explains the extraordinary ecstasy that more than a few soldiers experience on the battlefield, even amid all the horrors—an ecstasy so great that it calls them again and again to return. Carpenter cited a widely read war correspondent of the day. "'Have you noticed,' says M. W. Tomlinson of the Daily News, 'how many of our colonels fall? Do you know why? It is for the joy of riding, when the charge sounds, at the crest of a wave of men.'"[59]

RACISM, THE DEEP SHADOW OF PATRIOTISM

Carpenter never scoffed at the often naive patriotic emotions of his working-class friends. He allows that "patriotism often blinds a people to its own faults, and credits itself with all the moral virtues, while at the same time it gloats over every defamation of the enemy." Although based on a delusion, Carpenter thought that a positive side to this deliberate idealization of one's own people is the willingness of individuals to pull together for the common good. "If you look at the great majority of those who are enthusing just now about our country and patriotically detesting the Germans," Carpenter pointed out, "you will see their patriotism is pulling them together from one end of Britain to another, causing them to help each other in a thousand ways, urging them to make sacrifices for the common good." Carpenter drew an interesting conclusion: "Really, I think we ought to be very grateful to the Germans for doing all this for us."[60]

Shortly after the end of the Great War, Winston Churchill asked the British Parliament a thought-provoking question: "Why should war be the only purpose capable of uniting us in comradeship? Why should peace have nothing but the squabbles and selfishness and the pettiness of daily life?" What Churchill did not see was that the dark side of patriotism is racism. Given a society that, in Churchill's words, lacks "a common principle of action, a plain objective that everyone can understand and work for," the only possible force that can bring one people together is the hatred of a common enemy. And which enemy hardly matters. But Carpenter thought that, in every case and regardless of which brand of foreigner happens to be the target of patriotic hatred at the moment, the real enemy of every racist is his or her own people. Carpenter explained his insight in this way. "Verily I suspect that it is because we have not truly loved our own countries, but have betrayed them for private profit, that we have thought it fit to hate our neighbors and ill-use them for our profit too."[61]

Carpenter felt real anxiety for the increasing willingness of educated people to defend racism. He singled out Nietzsche for particular criticism on this score: "His blonde beasts and his laughing lions may represent the Will to Power, but one does not get a very clear idea what the strength which Nietzsche glorifies is for, or wither it is going to lead." Carpenter suspected that given the terms in which Nietzsche defines his race of Supermen, they could only turn out to be frighteningly dangerous: "If they have no common source of life, their actions will utterly cancel and destroy each other."[62]

In the middle of his discussion of the racism which the Great War had done so much to spawn, Carpenter, rather oddly, pauses to discuss the peoples of black Africa (oddly because the fate of these peoples was not really an issue at the moment). Did Carpenter somehow sense that, for white Europeans (and Americans), the ultimate butt of all racist emotion is black Africa?

"What a wonderful old globe this is, with its jeweled constellations of humanity," he begins. The so-called colored races spontaneously come to mind as prime examples of this jeweled beauty. He quotes "a shrewd vigorous old English lady" who had spent some forty years in Africa. "Ah! You British think a great deal about yourselves. You think you are the finest race on earth," she said to Carpenter, laughing. In her view, the black Africans were much finer: "They are splendid. Whether for their physical attributes, or their mental, or for their qualities of soul, I sometimes think they are the finest people in the world." He quotes explorer Alfred Russell Wallace, who wrote, "Their figures are generally superb; and I have never felt so much pleasure in gazing at the finest statue as at the living illustrations of human beauty [provided by] these copper colored natives." Carpenter also quotes Herman Melville and Robert Louis Stevenson on the beauty of the peoples of Polynesia and adds his own comments on the varied beauty of the Arabians, Hindus, Chinese, and Japanese he had seen in his travels through the Orient. His point is that racism has no obvious rationale; it certainly is not natural. Why should human beings naturally hate their own "varied and jewel-like beauty"?[63]

For Carpenter, the answer to this question seemed obvious; the Great War had provided it: whites hate other races because they hate their own kind as well. "Witness the endless and pointless slaughter proceeding on the fields of France," Carpenter observed. His point, however, was not simply to denounce racism or war as evil. He wanted to show that the root of racism lies not in some mystical principle of evil or thanatos, but rather in the simple human desire to feel a sense of belonging: "Verily I suspect that it is because we have not loved our own countries, but have betrayed them for profit, that we have thought it fit to hate our neighbors too."[64]

Racism and the Sense of Community

Racism provides an illusory sense of human community, of belonging to something larger than oneself. To fight for the white race or for the English people is morally wrong only because it is purely negative. Real community can never be built on hate; it can only be built on what Churchill called "a common principle of action, a plain objective that everyone can understand and work for." In war, people have the privilege of dying together rather than alone. What is needed is a common principle that will allow them to live together rather than destroy each other. "I think I now begin to understand why to thousands, and one may say millions, this War (even with all its horrors) has been a relief and an escape, why it has brought alertness of mind and brightness of eyes with it." Carpenter saw that, paradoxically, the war had brought real companionship and even love to millions of men. "It has meant to so many a life in the open-air; it has meant healthy, good food, a common cause, comradeship with others, and a dozen positive things, instead of the inhuman monotonies and negations of all life of slave labor."[65]

Carpenter's talk of comradeship suggests the main point he wants to make about the delusions of racism and militarism. "Why should war be the only purpose capable of uniting us in comradeship?" Churchill asked. But the term "comradeship" had a much deeper meaning for Carpenter than it could possibly have had for Churchill. Imprisoned by marriages all too often poisoned by the harsh economics and ruthless competition of the surrounding world, most people—in Carpenter's estimation—tended to feel emotionally starved by the conditions of modern life. Even the church could supply little in the way of true fellowship, he thought. A church built on the concept of sharing necessarily seems irrelevant in the culture of greed. Life in the lonely crowd can prove difficult, with or without access to the global shopping mall. Carpenter put it this way: "Our affections, our affinities, our passions, are not given us for nothing."[66]

The male sex, Carpenter asserted, suffers most from the emotional starvation of modern life. Thus, contemporary sociologist Warren Farrell describes males as the "suicide sex." Farrell attributes this fact to the two inconsistent demands that patriarchal society places on males, starting with adolescence. First, "the demand to perform without the resources to perform." Second, the result is escalating anxiety and despair. "It is adolescence during which boys' suicide rate goes from slightly less than girls' to four times girls."[67]

Patriotism, Male Bonding, and Homosexuality

In Carpenter's view, war frequently intervenes to resolve this impasse between the demand to perform and the lack of emotional support. The dangers of war provide men with a socially acceptable outlet for their self-destructive as well as for their aggressive impulses. But more importantly, war renders male bonding—otherwise strictly taboo—socially acceptable and even admirable. Indeed, Carpenter felt that the war hysteria of 1914 had an unmistakably homoerotic cast to it. For many men—perhaps even for most, Carpenter believed—the experience of combat was essentially a variant of homosexual sado-masochism.

The irony is that this sublimation of homosexual emotion into an obsession with violence and superpatriotism is highly respectable and widely admired, whereas actual love between men remains stigmatized as a public disgrace. Carpenter believed that war is as mad and unreasonable as love. In love, people desire to hurt each other; they do not hesitate to do so—wounding hearts, bodies, and even themselves with self-hate because of the pain inflicted on all. What does it all mean? "Are they trying the one to reach the other at all costs—if not by embraces, at least by injuries? Sex itself is a positive battle." In times of war, men get caught up in sexual emotions they scarcely can understand. They have only the faintest idea of what is really going on or what the warfare means. And the beautiful creatures in the trenches give their lives—equally courageous, equally justified, on both sides: "Such men fight fascinated, rapt, beyond and beside themselves, as though hating each other with a deadly hatred; seized with hideous, furious, nerve-racking passions; performing heroic, magnificent deeds, suffering untold indescribable wounds." In the end, we see them "lying finally side by side (as not infrequently happens) on the deserted battlefield, reconciled and redeemed and clasping hands of amity even in death."[68]

Carpenter made much of the fact, well-known to students of the period, that soldiers of warring nations often fraternized with the enemy during lulls in the endless and largely inconsequential trench warfare. "In the present war, there are hundreds of stories already in circulation of acts of grace and tenderness between enemies," he recounted. Sometimes the acts of love between combatants rose to the heights of true heroism. Carpenter liked to tell the story of a British officer who picked up a wounded German soldier and carried him across into the German lines. He saw that the man had been left accidentally when the Germans were clearing away their wounded, and he simply walked forward to save him: "But it cost him his life, for the Germans, not at first perceiving his intentions, fired and hit him in two or three places. Nevertheless he lifted the man and succeeded in bearing him to the German trench." One hardly knows how to react to such incidents, as Carpenter recognized. "How preposterous do such stories as these make warfare appear," he said. "The fraternization last Christmas between the opposing lines in Northern France almost threatened at one time to dissolve all the proprieties of official warfare."[69]

How much better, Carpenter thought, if love between men did not require the excuse of combat conditions to justify it. At the end of the war, the civilized world experienced an agony of revulsion at what it had done, a kind of prolonged hangover after the drunken orgy of killing and bloodlust. "Like a great cry these words today rise from the lips of the nations—'Never Again!'" Carpenter wrote, "The nations stand round paralyzed with disgust and despair, almost unable to articulate their shame. But how are we to give effect to the cry?"[70]

The Morality of a Just and Lasting Peace

Carpenter did not consider the desire for a lasting peace as hopeless. He did not consider the penchant for carnage an ineradicable instinct of human nature, not did he see imperial domination by one power as the only way to secure peace (as Henry Kissinger argues). On the contrary, people could be and had to be educated to love peace or they would never have it. In Carpenter's view, however, this lesson would not be easily learned. "We must not blink at the facts: And the fact is that it's a long way to never again, the causes of war must be destroyed first; and, as I have more than once tried to make clear, the causes are like the roots, pervading the body politic."[71]

In Carpenter's view, the demand for a lasting peace required nothing less than a complete moral revolution. It was not a question of a minor adjustment in our thinking to accommodate slightly altered social conditions. Carpenter did not believe that President Woodrow Wilson's League of Nations could accomplish this goal. Nor did he have much hope for Lenin's concept of an iron party pursuing permanent revolution. What he wanted, he felt, was a much deeper sort of change, a kind of religious awakening from the prolonged nightmare of bloodshed and hate. In particular, it was the fear of love between men that would have to go. "The present world which we see around us, with its idiotic wars its fears and greeds and vanities and its futile endeavors—as of people struggling in a swamp—to find one's salvation by treading others underfoot—is an illusion." The illusory nature of our fear of love bears a positive message, "but it is the blessed virtue of ignorance, or non-perception, that it inevitably—if only slowly and painfully—destroys itself."[72]

If war is the illusion of community through racism, if it is the illusion of freedom through adventure, and if it is the illusion of love through male bonding, then war can only be eliminated by establishing the reality in the world of true community, true freedom, and true love. For Carpenter—as for Saint Paul—the greatest of these is love, which always has a transcendent dimension. The failure to recognize this is what Carpenter means by "ignorance."

He understood the essential unity of all human life to entail much more than simply the sharing of a common language or culture heritage. For him, all persons are one in God, and the force of eros is the gravitational pull drawing all the many satellites of the divine sun toward their common center. His favorite image for this, which he uses over and over again, is the tree of life. "This Tree that is for the healing of the nations has its roots in the pure water of Life which flows from the great Throne" (Carpenter's paraphrase of Revelation 22:2). Jesus said, "I am the vine and you are the branches" (John 15:5). Carpenter explains, "Right down below all the folly and meanness which clouds men's souls flows the universal Life pure from its original source. The longer you live, the more clearly and certainly you will perceive it." Carpenter felt he could see the power of divine grace living in the eyes of the individual men and women he knew. "You will perceive it, and in the eyes of the children—aye, and even of the animals." This is not to deny the reality of evil. "Unclean, no doubt, will the surface be—muddied with meanness and self-motives. But those who take the time and make the effort to look beneath the surface will discover that the water of Life flows pure and free."[73]

Carpenter took seriously both the religious and erotic implications of his explication of this metaphor. For him, love between men is the one spiritual force capable of reforming the Christian church and renewing the body politic. The liberation of this form of love alone could end the obsession with violence inherent in patriarchal values. Only love between men could destroy greed and lust for power as the primary motives for masculine behavior. Only love between men could end racism and the fortress family. Until men are free to love and desire one another, social justice and human equality will remain a dream. When Carpenter speaks of the love of men for each other, he does not have in mind the sort of homosexuality visible in the pick-up bars and cruising the streets of modern Manhattan or San Francisco. He is thinking of the sort of emotion described in the early dialogues of Plato and in the romance tales of the Japanese Bushido.

With this sort of masculine love in mind, Carpenter calls for an army of lovers similar to the Theban band of classical Greece, only on a grand scale. Instead of a small troop, all of humanity is involved; instead of defending a city-state, the entire world is under watch; and instead of swords and spears, spiritual weapons are employed. In direct contrast to scientific socialists such as Lenin, for example, Carpenter believed that freedom cannot be forced on people through violence, and equality cannot be legislated by an armed elite. A sense of the common life can be shared only by people who know how to love. To those who admired him as a person or loved his work, he would say, "Here I give you my charge, that afterwards remembering and desiring me, You may find me again in these others. Slowly out of their faces I will emerge to you." Wherever men touch each other in love, a secret would be passed, a freemasonry of lovers established, a new culture created within the chrysalis of the old.[74]

It was inconceivable to Carpenter that such a union of gay men could ever for a moment entertain racist, militarist, or elitist thinking. What he would have made of contemporary organizations for gay conservatives is difficult to say. Certainly he would have felt that such men remained ignorant of their own best interests and courted the support of those whose nature made them the enemies of anything resembling authentic gay liberation. To him, homogenic impulses, simply by existing, ran counter to the whole spirit of a competitive, racist, and militarist society.[75]

THE JOURNEY OF SELF-DISCOVERY

Edward Carpenter's position is predicated on the personal as political. "There are few things as fascinating," Bruce Bawer writes, "than the psychology of a gay person who doesn't yet know he is gay." Carpenter would have broadened this observation in two ways. First, few things are more fascinating than any human being's search for his or her identity. (For a gay person, the search is more urgent and challenging.) Second, the gay community's effort to understand itself is a key to the salvation of the modern world.[76]

A great deal has been made in the history of Christian theology over the difference between religious freedom and political freedom, spiritual and legal equality, and so on. Not surprisingly, the consensus of received opinion is strongly against any attempt to equate the two, as Pope Leo XIII articulates in his encyclical on labor. All persons are equal before God, but in this world "the church recognizes the inequality among men, who are born with different powers of body and mind, inequality in actual possession also, and holds that the rights of property which spring from nature itself, must not be touched." To Carpenter, this sort of reasoning makes little sense. Equality before God and among humanity are correlative terms, each one implying and even requiring the other. Can a person who really feels joined in one divine life with others accept with equanimity the destitution of the majority of the human race? Persons who have really touched the divine ground of being, he thought, would never accept such a rarefied version of equality. "Those who say, 'I love God,' and hate their brothers or sisters, are liars; for those who do not love a brother or sister whom they have seen, cannot love God whom they have not seen"(1 John 4:20).[77]

For Carpenter, the humiliations attendant upon his love for his own sex had provided an avenue through which he discovered his essential unity with all sorts and conditions of persons. Carpenter had experienced the snobbery and acquisitiveness of his own family and their class as a burden. Perhaps his hope that, in time, other children of privilege would come to feel as he did was understandable. Yet nowhere does he seem more the wide-eyed idealist than when expressing his confidence that the English and American ruling class—the robber barons and the captains of industry, the generals and the bishops—might be susceptible to a conversion experience through the redeeming power of love between men. Given the experience of such love, it seemed incredible to him that any class of people, possessed of any intelligence at all, could persist forever in the pursuit of such self-defeating delusions. "As for the millionaire, having spent his life in scheming for Wealth, he cannot but continue in the web which himself has woven; yet is heartily sick of it, and longs in a kind of vague way for something simple and unembarrassed."[78]

In poem after poem, he portrays the complete spiritual bankruptcy and desperate boredom of a life devoted to consumerism. Through his work in the labor movement, Carpenter had known many sons of the aristocracy who, like him, had turned their backs on luxury and high living in order to find freedom in honest work among their friends and lovers.[79]

Bolshevism versus Industrial Democracy

Karl Radek once said of Lenin and the early Bolsheviks that "they hoped to force their way by a short cut, rifle in hand, into the classless society." Lenin thought of himself as a realist, and he had little tolerance for socialists of a more sentimental or mystical turn of mind. Carpenter tended to favor the sort of socialism denounced

by Lenin in 1921 when, in crushing the Workers Opposition movement within the party (led by Alexandra Kollontai), he branded
any proposal for industrial democracy or real worker participation in industrial management as "an anarcho-syndicalist deviation hiding behind the back of the revolution, a petit-bourgeois
anarchist element." In fact, any attempt to compromise the absolute dictatorship for the proletariat meant deviation, because "there
can be no talk of an independent ideology being developed by the
working masses of their own."[80]

In one of his more Orwellian pronouncements, Lenin summed
up the Bolshevik approach to socialism this way: "We recognize
neither freedom, nor equality, nor labor democracy if they are opposed to the emancipation of labor from the oppression of capital." Thus, instead of creating worker democracy, Bolshevism almost immediately turned Soviet factories into forced labor camps,
with the number of military guards almost equaling the number
of workers and the practice of spying taking on the sanctified aura
of a religious exercise.[81]

To a free spirit such as Carpenter, Lenin's approach to socialism made no sense at all. Carpenter believed in socialism from
below. He saw it as essentially a religious and sexual revolution
(the two being synonymous to him) in which persons would be
taught to share by their love and desire for one another.

Carpenter was nervous (in contrast to Fabian leaders Beatrice
and Sidney Webb) about direct government control of industry as
the only path to socialism. He knew too much about the evils of
government bureaucracy to feel overly optimistic about the nation-
alization of heavy industry. "It brings with it the very great danger of the growth of officialism, bureaucracy and red tape, than
which few things can be more fatal to the real life of a nation."
Carpenter foresaw the deadly social paralysis that state ownership
of the means of production might entail. "The multiplication of
officials strangles the spontaneous vitality of the people. It creates
a vast body of parasites and betrays the public into the power of a
class which is out of touch and sympathy with the needs of the
people." Not that Carpenter ignored the need for government to
guarantee basic economic rights, especially in a world that perse-
cutes love between men. "Thus, while we plead in many depart-
ments for more public administration of industry, it will be neces-

sary to guard against the great dangers of officialism."[82]

History has proved Lenin wrong (and perhaps Carpenter right?) to this extent. The tightly centralized and rigidly authoritarian socialism of the Soviet Union—established by Lenin and carried to nightmare extremes by Stalin—proved, in the end, to be an economic catastrophe. Economist Paul Kennedy sums up the seventy years of Bolshevik economics in Russia: "Seventy years of experience have demonstrated that 'scientific socialism' does not work." Responsibility and decision-making gravitated toward enormous bureaucracies. A rigid political ideology killed any creativity among the workers. New ideas and proposals had to pass the constant test of ideological orthodoxy: "In the spirit of Lenin, the CPSU [Soviet Communist Party] consistently made political control its top priority." Handicapped by bureaucratic planning, Soviet industry has steadily ossified. "Producing more steel or cement than any other nation was no help when a great proportion rusted or crumbled away in railway sidings." In the end, humane leadership became impossible under Leninist principles: "Management itself was a contradiction in a Soviet factory, where production targets were prescribed elsewhere and no deviation was permitted."[83]

Meanwhile, the West has had revolutions in sexuality and New Age spirituality (usually allied with the vanguard of that sexual revolution). Except briefly in the 1960s, neither movement has allied itself strongly with the interests of the working class—let alone with the idea of industrial democracy. Commenting on the spiritual bankruptcy of modern American life, Brzezinski has labeled New Age religion as a moral hoax. With its emphasis on self-actualization and quick-fix therapies, it often seems to amount to little more than "an increasingly fluid inner faith which, before long, becomes transformed into a self-serving justification for egocentrism." No wonder many working men and women see the cultural radicalism of the New Age as a masquerade for old-fashioned hedonism and a threat to traditional notions of responsible behavior, as *Washington Post* reporter E. J. Dionne points out.[84]

Does Carpenter's idea of a spiritual revolution leading to an economic and political revolution have any chance today? Does anyone really consider economic democracy a workable concept anymore? Do American workers want shared decision-making or some control in the management of the workplace? Are they capable of exercising it? Are our churches and spiritual leaders preaching this vision? Is real love among working men, in the classical spirit, anything but a demented dream?

Carpenter took the unlikely position that a true revolution was possible through the formation of a gay movement. In the 1960s, Harry Hay asked what positive or useful role gay people had to play in the life of society. Carpenter had tried to answer that question a half-century earlier. He borrowed a term from his friend Peter Kropotkin, the foremost theorist of philosophical anarchism. Kropotkin had said that the key to the social problems of capitalism was "mutuality," which he defined as the recognition that healthy human societies function like an extended family, "a new family based not on blood ties but on community of aspiration." But if what we need is a new sense of family, then surely gay people have a special interest and special insights in developing this, Carpenter asserted. Had not Plato said that if there were only some way of contriving a state or an army to be made up of (male) lovers and their loves, they would be the best governors of their own city. For such men, love would mean "abstaining from all dishonor, and emulating one another in honor; and when fighting at one another's side, although a mere handful, they would overcome the world."[85]

Carpenter believed that the important battles of modern life were fought between labor and management, between human and machine. In the ancient world, gay men had functioned most effectively as priests and warriors. In modern life, Carpenter thought they might function more effectively in the workplace, helping to create Kropotkin's community of aspiration. If the spirit of mutuality were to arise spontaneously among workers, and without coercion from the state, then surely the love of man for man could have a role in bringing this about.

To E. M. Forster, Carpenter's ideal seemed decidedly utopian. "What he wanted," Forster wrote, "was *News from Nowhere* and the place that is still nowhere, wildness, the rapture of unpolluted streams, sunrise, and sunset over the moors, and in the midst of these the working people who he loved, passionately in touch with one another." Forster refers here to William Morris's fanciful futuristic novel, titled *News from Nowhere*. In sharp contrast to later socialists such as the Webbs—and certainly to Lenin—Morris had attracted attention by his militant opposition to the whole process of industrialization. His Socialist League favored a neo-medieval utopia in which London would be small and white and clean.[86]

The Spiritual Blessings of Specialization

Forster seems to have assumed that Carpenter would advocate (given his well-known love of nature and the outdoors) the same sort of abolition of modern technology Morris advocated. But Carpenter was not a utopian; he tried to base his vision on the facts of industrial economy. Indeed, he taught that the world of the new technology might turn out to be conducive to the development of mutuality.

Carpenter was too concerned an environmentalist to entertain the sort of naive enthusiasm for heavy industry expressed by Lenin—and still more disastrously by Stalin and his successors. At the same time, Carpenter believed that modern industrialization had a moral advantage over earlier forms of society in that it created a complex division of labor and promoted what Emile Durkheim would describe as "moral density," a complex of web of relationships between people. Such moral density creates, at least potentially, what Carpenter called "the Supreme Life of a people— the life of Equality—in which each individual passes out of himself along the lives of his fellows, and in return receives their life into himself."[87]

The division of labor became a topic of vigorous debate among nineteenth-century radicals. Kropotkin thought of it as a bad thing (and so did Marx, at least during some phases of his thought). "The division and subdivision functions [have] been pushed so far as to divide humanity into castes which are almost as firmly established as those of old India," Kropotkin writes, "and with this class rigidity came a drudgery worse than that of the slave empires of the ancient world." The artisan who formerly found aesthetic enjoyment in handwork, for example, is replaced by the human slave of an iron taskmaster. Indeed, technology turns the worker into a machine cursed with the burden of consciousness. As the work required from the individual becomes simpler and easier, it thereby becomes in the same proportion more monotonous.[88]

Carpenter agreed with such criticism, and he insisted as loudly as Kropotkin on the need for variety in the workplace. But another side to the phenomenon of the division of labor exists, he insisted: "In the great industrial associations, folk [are] learning the sentiment of the Common Life—the habit of acting together for common ends, the habit of feeling together for common interests." The solitary artisan, solely responsible for the creation of a finished product, in spite of all the positive values that he or she represents, nevertheless becomes an anachronism in most industries. "But for all that is lost, something very important may be gained in humanity's learning to function in groups." "Co-operative work (provided the group were self-governing and not enslaved to any master) would be free and (through the group) the expression of each worker's will."[89]

Quite apart from any pleasure the individual might derive from feeling a part of a team, the division of labor in modern industry produces another consequence. Saint Thomas Aquinas stated the medieval understanding (which has been accepted as the basis of European property law) that an individual has the right to anything he or she makes or procures by his or her own efforts. John Locke, a seventeenth-century English philosopher, put it this way. "He that is nourished by the acorns he picked up under an oak, or the apples he gathered from the trees in the wood, has certainly appropriated them to himself."[90]

Given this principle, Carpenter asks to whom the products of modern industry properly belong. "The product is no longer the creation of one man, but of many; and as the process becomes more complex, ultimately of society. The product, therefore, is—or should be—the property of society." "For example," writes physicist Frank Tipler, "no individual human being has sufficient knowledge to make an automobile." The point is not just that modern cars are produced on the assembly line, but that no one person—not even an automotive engineer—understands, creates, or assembles all of the processes involved. "Considering the whole process from raw materials to finished product, no one human mind can grasp it all. No individual human being has this knowledge, and yet the human race collectively does." In short, if not sufficiently obvious a century ago, then it should certainly be obvious today that even something so routine and commonplace as the family car is a functioning monument to those principles so dear to Carpenter's heart: human community and mutuality. That this community had homogenic implications for him should go without saying.[91]

Sharing logically is the principle on which modern societies must be organized; the only question is whether economic wealth and political power will also be shared and, if so, to what degree. But this question, Carpenter thought, deals less with "ought" than with (to borrow a phrase from Lenin) who is doing what to whom.

CHRISTIANITY, PROPERTY RIGHTS, AND THE JOY OF WORK

Christian ethics would conclude that no small clique within society is entitled to the bulk of either wealth or power. For example, Aquinas (who did not consider private property a natural right) has written that "material goods are useful for certain ends, and we should seek them in a balanced way to the degree that they are necessary for us." Covetousness is, by definition, an immoderate desire for wealth that is not justly due to one. Carpenter did not believe in the classless society, but he did believe in a society without parasitic or predatory classes. "Class in itself as the mere formation within a nation of groups of similar occupation and activity—working harmoniously with each other and with the nation—is a perfectly natural and healthy phenomenon." Social class only becomes a curse when one class tries to subjugate and exploit another. "It is only when it means groups pursuing their own interest counter to each other and to the nation that it becomes diseased."[92]

The Joy of Work

Carpenter believed that work, freed from exploitation and coercion, could be a pleasure. "If any enthusiast were to preach in our factories about the pleasures of work, the men, I fear, would break out in scornful laughter," Carpenter admitted, adding that "they might even stone him with stones—even as they stoned Stephen at Jerusalem" (Acts 6:8–15). Carpenter believed, however, that workers had been taught to hate work by their employers, who humiliated them, taxed their energies to the breaking point, underpaid them, and made no provision for their comfort on the job or their security against unemployment. Such is a perversion of work, and here Carpenter borrows from Marx. Only through work can a person realize her or his individuality and learn to function as part of a community. To Carpenter, this implied the eroticizing of work, that all work should be a labor of love. Work necessarily brings persons together. Freely chosen and democratically organized, work creates an atmosphere ideally conducive to love.[93]

Carpenter concluded, on the one hand, that the desire to work together was as natural as the desire for love and, on the other hand, that forced idleness would be as painful as forced labor. "So great is the pleasure of free work that thousands and hundreds of thousands of folk after the day of leaden and slave labor in the factories, do, on their return home plunge into some sort of hobby of their own." Some of these hobbies could be quite arduous. Carpenter often remembered an amateur cabinetmaker he had befriended "who slaves in a dirty workshop for ten hours or so a day. When he gets home—and a very poor home at that—he actually begins work again, making little cabinets or corner-cupboards." To Carpenter, the lesson of this readily observable aspect of human behavior is obvious; the correct question can only be "What then are the necessary conditions for making Work a pleasure?" He answers, "They are so extraordinarily simple that it is a marvel that they have so far escaped attention. Work is a pleasure when it is free and creative in character." By "free," Carpenter means "freely chosen, compatible with the natural fits and talents of the worker, and, to some extent, organized and managed by oneself," rather than done on a whim or impulse. Carpenter recognized that all work, for whatever reason undertaken, demands discipline and commitment. And modern work must be as a contributing member of a team of equals.[94]

Carpenter was just as particular in his definition of the word "creative." Artists, in his view, were the only natural and healthy people and in line with the rest of creation—with the trees and animals. "But when people talk of art, they usually have in mind a very narrow understanding of its nature. But to confine the name to those who dabble in paints or letters or music is foolish. For the greatest of arts are the arts of Life." Indeed, real artistry can be observed in the humblest occupations. "The washer woman who takes real pride and interest in her work, to make it as perfect as she can, independently of any so-called profit or gain which she may derive from it, is an artist in her way."[95]

Producer Economics

Is Carpenter's position as unrealistic as critics such as E. M. Forster and Malcolm Muggeridge have suggested? Many economists, in attempting to forecast the future of American industry at the end of the twentieth century, have begun recommending what they term "producer economics," a concept pioneered by the Japanese. Carpenter would have found much to criticize in modern Japanese life, although he greatly admired traditional Japanese culture. But he would certainly recognize in producer economics a concept that he had spent his life developing.

Lester Thurow, dean of MIT's Sloan School of Management, refers to two different patterns in the animal world to describe the term. Some species, such as the American mountain lion, are solitary species—meeting only briefly to mate. In contrast, other species, such as the African lion, live in prides as a pack. Humans are individuals, but they share a good deal with herd-type animals. "In herd or pack species the desire for equal participation in group endeavors is not a perverse desire that has to be erased but a clue that can be used to generate solidarity and a willingness to sacrifice for the group." "Without this willingness, no army and no company, can really expect to win."[96]

Thurow believes that Japan's style of business management is producer economics, whereas the whole American (and English) style is little less than feudal. "A community is to be built in Japan," he says, whereas "money is to be made in the United States." Japanese companies nourish their workers, even in economic downturns; American companies lay off excess workers. Japanese companies set up retraining programs; American companies keep workers' salaries as low as possible while executive salaries are inflated. When times are good, American companies do not raise salaries, and, "when automation goes up in America, wages go down. In contrast, when automation rises in Japan, wages rise." Above all, the American conception of authority is different—and less efficient, Thurow believes. "No American becomes a boss to do less bossing. Participatory management may be an efficient way to cut white-collar overheads and raise productivity, but it requires a reduction in the boss's power." Thurow argues that American executives see themselves as tin gods. "The boss should 'Know Everything'" is the guiding rule in American companies: "In principle [the boss] should be knowledgeable enough to make every decision." Employees are reduced to the status of commodities to be bought as cheaply as possible and used as hard as possible. Loyalty is neither granted to them or expected from them: "Most [American] managers will argue that the sole purpose of the company is to maximize shareholders' wealth. Customers and employees are important only as they contribute to this goal." But this order of priorities is hardly written in stone: "If Japanese firms are asked the same question, the order of duty is reversed—employees first, with customers second and shareholders third."[97]

What all of this means for the comparative efficiency and productivity of American and Japanese industry is obvious to Thurow: "While there is some belief in the value of teams, the Anglo-Saxon shareholder wealth-maximization view of the firm explicitly denies the legitimacy of the group." Only the individual capitalist counts; employees are reduced to the status of things. Thurow points out that for a CEO to subscribe to such a view of the world is the same as announcing that the employees are not on the CEO's team. It is important to remember that Thurow does not speak here as a humanitarian or a moralist—still less as a mystic. His value system seems, at most points, almost the reverse of Carpenter's. Thurow acknowledges no values beyond productivity and never questions either the moral worth of economic competition as a way of life or free-enterprise capitalism as the best way to structure society. And yet, in the name of hard-headed practicality, he ends up endorsing much of Carpenter's program for industrial democracy. Thurow believes that the West is going to have a hard time learning the lessons of shared decision-making, participatory management, worker creativity, job security, community-building, and so forth. Carpenter also acknowledged that freedom and equality, as he understood them, would be no easy acquisition. As paradoxical as it seems, it is *hard* to be free: "It means education, alertness to guard against the insidious schemes of wire-pullers and pressmen, as well as of militarists and commercials." But Carpenter felt that he had discovered the one motive that would have the power to make men want to be free, the capacity of one man to love another.[98]

chapter four

THE REDISCOVERY OF SACRED SEXUALITY

To Tomasso Cavalieri

No mortal thing enthralled these longing eyes
    When perfect peace in thy fair face I found,
    But far within, where all is holy ground,
    My soul felt Love, her comrade of the skies:
For she was born with God in paradise:
    Nor all the shows of beauty shed around
    This fair false world her wings to earth have bound:
    Unto the Love of Loves aloft she flies.
Nay, things that suffer death quench not the fire
    Of deathless spirits, nor eternity
    Serves sordid Time, that withers all things rare.
Not love, but lawless impulse to desire
    That slays the soul; our love makes still more faith
    Fair friends on earth, fairer in death on high.

—Michelangelo (1475-1564)

That Jesus may have experienced typical sexual feelings of a healthy adult male still offends most people. The reason? The Christian ascetic tradition has prevailed for so long that most people now associate sexual purity, or abstinence, with holiness. For the same reason, many people still recoil at the concept of sacred sexuality, even though in many cultures throughout the ancient world and up to the present, nothing seems so sacred as sexuality. As for sacred homosexuality, the whole idea sounds like an oxymoron to modern ears—and, even in a secular age, still painfully blasphemous.

The ancient world knew many forms of sacred homosexuality. But the philosophy of Plato gave to the idea of sacred homosexuality its highest expression. "It was Plato's favourite doctrine that male comradeship, if properly conducted, led up to the disclosure of true philosophy in the mind, to the divine vision, and to remembrance within the soul of all the forms of celestial beauty," Edward Carpenter wrote. If God is love, then what could teach us more about God's nature than the experience of human love? "The image of the beloved one passing into the mind of the lover and upward through its deepest recesses reaches and unites itself to the essential forms of divine beauty long hidden there—the originals, as it were, of all creation."[1]

Edward Carpenter was a modern man, a trained scientist, and a professor of mathematics at Cambridge. He understood the need to translate ancient religious and philosophical insights into terms that made sense in the modern world. But on this one point, if on no other, Carpenter felt certain that Plato was correct: a careful examination of the subject would demonstrate the peculiar sanctity of love between men. Indeed, Carpenter was convinced that at a time when persons were losing their sense of the sacred altogether, the love of men might prove a key to a renewed sense of the spiritual meaning of life. Therefore Carpenter devoted much time and effort to defining this gay religious vision as well as demonstrating its cogency and value for the modern world.

Carpenter's own mystical experiences—which profoundly affected his personal life, specifically his sexual life—gave rise to his sense that others also needed this religious experience. Like the philosophers and sculptors of classical Greece as well as the humanists and painters of Renaissance Italy, Carpenter saw in human beauty—especially in the beauty of men—a reflection of a symbol of a yet more perfect spiritual beauty lying beyond the visible world. To his lover, George Merrill, he wrote of his experience of the presence of divine love in the act of making physical love. Human love made no sense except in the context of divine love, and vice versa.[2]

Any mystical experience must remain, at bottom, a subjective emotional state of mind which might, after all, turn out to be illusory. But Carpenter as a philosopher had learned from Schelling and Hegel that a person's sense of the sacred reflects the ultimate rational coherence of the universe itself, the sense that the universe has an intelligible meaning when considered as a whole. In this way, religion needs to address the head as well as the heart. He had learned, too, that the mystical is the key to social as well as personal transformation.

Every culture, Hegel had said, is "the incarnation of an idea . . . a moral whole, the actually existing realized moral life of a people." Saint Augustine expressed the same idea more simply when he defined a people as "a multitude of rational creatures associated in a common agreement as to the things that it loves." In the twentieth century, Paul Tillich defined religion as ultimate concern; a person's religion is what really matters to her or him. Thus religion is, as Hegel said, the well-spring of culture. The character of a people can be seen in their myths and dreams, the heroes they admire, the legends around which they build their lives. The most basic human values and insights arise not from metaphysical systems or political ideologies but from culture. Such cultures are propagated through a language that speaks directly to the imagination and heart—namely, the language of symbol, sacrament, and sacred story. Everything else rests on that foundation.[3]

Urvashi Vaid laments the lack of an empowering spiritual vision in the contemporary movement for gay rights. "Gay organizations stay small because they fail to convey a vision of what our movement seeks." Spiritual liberation should both complement and inspire political liberation. This spiritual liberation—so central not only to the Gospels but also to the various religions and disciplines of the East—is what Carpenter attempts to define. He wants a gay spiritual vision that is liberating rather than oppressive, that is both mystical and rational, that is modern yet incorporates the most ancient insights of the various spiritual traditions of the whole human family. Defining such a vision is an enormous task, but Carpenter tackles it bravely and with surprising degree of success.[4]

IN SEARCH OF A GAY SPIRITUAL VISION

After his first meeting with Edward Carpenter, Walt Whitman told Horace Traubel that "Carpenter is of a religious nature—not formally so, but in atmosphere." This was a rather perceptive statement because, at that time, Carpenter had recently decided to abandon his ministry in the Anglican church. He had a history of involvement with religion, but he felt far from sure that he wanted to continue that involvement.

As a lonely adolescent, Carpenter had experienced an emotional conversion, and the central conflict of his life since then had been between his religious idealism and his need for the love of another man. As a young priest, he had fallen under the spell of the Reverend F. D. Maurice, the founder of Christian socialism. As a union organizer and friend of the worker, Carpenter also felt compelled to hide his private life from his so-called liberal friends, whose liberalism had decided limits. Carpenter had begun to despair of ever reconciling his love for men with his sense of ethical behavior. He had traveled to America to confer with Whitman in much the same way as pilgrims go to some revered person for guidance. Perhaps Whitman carried for Carpenter the requisite holy aura; at a critical juncture, Carpenter had discovered the homoerotic poetry of Whitman and its revelatory effects. Here was the sort of spiritual vision Carpenter was seeking, and he felt compelled to make a personal confession to Whitman in order to garner the poet's advice regarding Carpenter's sense of vocation to the Anglican priesthood.

Although Whitman was deeply sympathetic, he hardly qualified as a spiritual guide. True, he had presented himself to his earliest admirers as the prophet of a new religious vision. Carpenter read Whitman's *Leaves of Grass* much as others among his contemporaries read Joseph Smith's *Book of Mormon* or Mary Baker Eddy's *Science and Health*. Carpenter was in search of viable religious convictions and, more importantly, of a way in which to reconcile his religious idealism with his love for men. Carpenter believed that he had found the key to that reconciliation in Whitman's poetry, although many had a difficult time pinning down Whitman's actual religious convictions.[5]

Marcel Proust once wrote that "literature, like life, should not so much give us thoughts as food for thought." By that standard, *Leaves of Grass* is an unqualified success. Most critics of Whitman's poetry have commented on his highly allusive use of language. Whitman himself admitted to cultivating a certain deliberate obscurity, which he preferred to call "suggestiveness." "I round and finish little, if anything. The reader will always have his or her part to do, just as much as I have mine." In a poet, deliberate obscurity may be a virtue; in a prophet, it is probably a vice.[6]

Whitman also had proclaimed himself a social reformer. However, before the Civil War, he had completely refused to give even the slightest support to the abolitionist movement. After the war, this friend of the worker refused just as adamantly to support the burgeoning labor movement. Although an enthusiast for the manly love of comrades, Whitman would never identify himself publicly with Carpenter's organized movement for gay liberation. Whitman's religious dedication proved similarly diffuse and undirected. Carpenter told Whitman that religion had to amount to something more than mere emotion, that it necessarily required some coherent philosophical support. "There are thoughts which cannot be stated in downright language and yet they may be passed from mind to mind by Poetry and Parables," Carpenter conceded. But "if no thought can be extracted from the Poem, then damn the Poem! Thought need not be definite, but *there must be thought*." Whitman replied by suggesting that Carpenter was perhaps overly intellectual. "I must seem like a comical, a sort of circus, genius to [persons] of the severe scholarly type," he quipped.[7]

Behind Carpenter's annoyance with Whitman lay an unspoken demand for what an earlier generation would have called a "philosophy of love," a rational understanding of the relationship between love and spirituality and of both to the pursuit of happiness, which can be considered the goal of every human life. Still Whitman was a poet, not a philosopher; and with the best will in the world, he could not satisfy Carpenter's demand. In effect, he only reiterated his often stated position that all love is a mystery— and especially the love between men. But Carpenter had already experienced the mystery of love between men. He felt the need for some sort of clarification.

Carpenter's questions remain pertinent today: Why do so many men need one another's love as much as they need the love of women? Why do some men feel sexual desire for each other? Is such desire morally right? What purpose does it serve? Can it ever lead to lasting happiness or personal fulfillment? Such questions tormented Carpenter's waking hours and kept him from sleeping at night. He wanted definite answers, not oracular pronouncements. Carpenter only said to Whitman what Socrates had said to Phaedrus centuries before: "We ought to agree upon a definition of love [between men] which shows its nature and its effects, so that we may have it before our minds as something to refer to while we discuss whether love is beneficial or injurious."[8]

Whitman's love and sympathy strengthened Carpenter's resolve but increased his sense of bafflement. On the twin subjects of love and religion, Carpenter found himself in a state of greater turmoil than ever. Never had he felt so completely alienated from the whole Christian enterprise and yet never more in need of some positive spiritual vision. As it happened, his disillusionment coincided with a vast cultural change in Anglo-American culture regarding this very subject.

The Death of God and the Birth of Agnosticism

Friedrich Nietzsche, in an oft-quoted aphorism, pronounced that the death of God was the most important event of the nineteenth century. The sense of break with the past was keenly alive. For example, Matthew Arnold wrote in the conclusion to his influential 1875 study *God and the Bible*, "We live at the beginning of a great transition which cannot be accomplished without confusion and distress." For this transition, Carpenter, as professor at Cambridge, had something of a box seat. He had heard lectures on the philosophy of science by the great Thomas Huxley, who had coined the term "agnostic" ("any ultimate reality, such as God, is unknown and likely unknowable") at a dinner party in 1867. He had heard Darwin in defense of evolution and Bishop Colenso in defense of the historical criticism of the Bible. Moreover, because of his interest in radical social causes, Carpenter came to know well the Marxist critique of religion in all of its devastating incisiveness.[9]

Even in such turbulence, Carpenter rejected Marx's materialism as decisively as he did Huxley's agnosticism—thus proving the truth of Whitman's observation about his essentially religious nature. He did so, however, not in the name of Whitman's obscure mystical divagation, but because of his own increasing sense of the inadequacy of scientific rationalism to explain to him his own situation as a homosexual.

As late as the 1950s, so great a humanist as Erich Fromm was still announcing that no such thing as homosexual love existed, that what might look like love in homosexuals had to be something else because, by definition, "the homosexual deviation is a failure to attain this polarized [male-female] union." From his own experience, Carpenter felt that he knew otherwise. For him, the problem of love between men is only a particular instance of the larger problem of love itself—and a poignant one at that. Love is not simply *a* religious problem; it is *the* quintessential religious problem. For him, attempts to explain the existence of homosexuality are, however veiled, attempts to explain the existence, the nature, and the meaning of love.[10]

Fromm had found that even when one is doing scientific psychology, any serious discussion of love is apt to end in a discussion of religion. Plato had made the same discovery. For Carpenter, the impersonality of science, the much-vaunted objectivity of scientific rationalism as a philosophy of life, rendered it a clumsy instrument for the exploration of the workings of the human heart. This perhaps explained also the essential futility of the medical literature on homosexuality pouring out of Germany throughout Carpenter's lifetime. Such literature, in its attempts at complete scientific objectivity, made even sex somehow barren.

Like the unnamed hero of Fyodor Dostoyevsky's *Notes from the Underground*, Carpenter rather felt that mathematical certainty regarding love is something insufferable. Dostoyevsky's hero frankly admits that for him, "twice two makes four is simply a piece of insolence. Twice two makes four is a pert coxcomb who stands with arms akimbo barring your path and spitting." It is as though scientific reasoning had become the enemy of the human spirit. "I will not be put off with a recurring zero, simply because it is consistent with the laws of nature and actually exists," Dostoyevsky wrote.[11]

That is not to say that Carpenter was naively romantic in his attitude toward science; he did not believe, as Whitman did, that dissecting is murder. Carpenter objected to the arrogance of many nineteenth-century scientists. Many physicists during Carpenter's lifetime actually believed, Stephen Hawking points out, not only that science could explain all of reality but also that it was on the brink of doing so.[12]

The history of science in the twentieth century has turned all such optimism on its head. Carpenter could not foresee Einstein, but he could see through the hubris of his contemporaries. As a professor of mathematics and astronomy, Carpenter always stressed the limitations of the scientific method as a tool by which humans try to understand themselves and their place in the general scheme of things. "It is one of the difficulties which meet anyone who suggests that modern science is not wholly satisfactory, that it is immediately assumed that he wishes to restore belief in the literal inspiration of the Bible," Carpenter complained. Although no obscurantist, Carpenter would never worship at the shrine of the natural sciences, interpreted as a religious faith. While admitting that "science has done a great work in opening the path to saner views of the world yet her methods may be of limited applicability."[13]

Carpenter's criticism of scientific rationalism anticipates, in important respects, the work of Thomas Kuhn's 1962 epoch-making study, *The Structure of Scientific Revolutions*. Like Kuhn, Carpenter felt that "The positivist conception admitted humans into the process of science only grudgingly and admitted humanness not at all if it could be helped." Carpenter predicted that the science of the future would much more freely acknowledge its own subjectivity than did the (to him) arrogant positivists of his own time. It was a prediction that Kuhn fulfilled. The Kuhnian movement has placed humans and human subjectivity (in the form of values of the community of scientists) firmly in the center of science. So thoroughgoing has been the revolution in the philosophy of science initiated by Kuhn that some of Carpenter's most radical observations now sound like truisms: "Science in searching for a permanently valid and purely intellectual representation of the universe has, as already said, been searching for a thing which does not exist."[14]

For Carpenter, the real danger of scientific positivism lay in its denial of the personal—what Ashley Montagu has termed the "dehumanization of man." True, Carpenter did not quite foresee that a time would come when eminent psychologists (such as behaviorist B. F. Skinner) would deny that human consciousness exists at all (because it is not scientifically observable). But he could see in what direction the main trends in scientific psychology were moving—and already had been moving for some time before Carpenter's day. And he was as convinced, as Montagu would be a century later, that this psychology was becoming increasingly inhumane.[15]

For Carpenter, the point was that the scientific method, with its emphasis on putatively objective and value-free universals and abstractions, could never explain the personal feelings of individual human beings. Carpenter wrote that there have been persons "who declared that consciousness itself was a mere incident of the human machine—as the whistle of an engine—and thus the matter stands." How long would it take before this merely incidental consciousness vanished altogether, the concept of the soul being classified—along with angels, devils, and hobgoblins—as metaphysical nonsense? Gilbert Ryle once lampooned Descartes's concept of mind as the theory of the ghost in the machine. Already in Carpenter's time, several philosophers of science were trying to exorcise that ghost.[16]

Carpenter writes that, historically speaking, "we know that early and primitive folk, letting their imaginations run loose, peopled the 'spirit world' rather promiscuously with all sorts of fairy beings and phantom processions." The progress of philosophical reasoning inevitably destroyed primitive animism because "the growing exactitude of science made it impossible to accept these imaginings; and it may be said that about the middle of the last century these cosmogonies finally perished." In the nineteenth century, however, scientific materialism also questioned the actual existence of the human soul itself: "It was allowed that intelligences and personalities (human and animal) moved on this side of the veil, and were visibly distinguishable as operating in the actual world; but they were accidental products of a mechanical universe." This rendered problematic the whole concept of mind: "That mechanical arrangement of atoms was the universe, and somehow or other it included everything. Any intelligent existence behind or on the other side of this veil of mechanism was mere nothingness and vacancy." Carpenter suggested that the more commonsense way of viewing the situation was "to see such clean-cut infallible systems and immutable and everlasting laws as proclaimed by the science" of his time for what they were—namely, "simple 'working hypotheses' of limited applicability and destined to be overturned with time." Push them beyond their limits and make of them a rigid system (as Kuhn may have done with his concept of "paradigm") and one gets into serious trouble.[17]

Positivism portrays reality as a medley of material objects and forces—more or less orderly and distinct from humans—in the midst of which humanity is placed, the purpose and tendency of human life being adaptation to this environment. Carpenter described this situation with the homely metaphor of a certain Mrs. Brown in the middle of Oxford Street. "Buses and cabs are running in different directions, carts and drays are rattling on all sides of her." This is her environment, and she has adapted herself to it. "She has to learn the laws of the vehicles and their movements, to stand on this side or on that, to run here and stop there." This is well, Carpenter concluded, but Mrs. Brown has a destination. "Indeed, how would she ever have got into the middle of Oxford Street at all, if she had not had one? The question is, What is the destination of Man?"[18]

Carpenter felt certain that the attempt to apply the scientific method to religion was like thinking that "by studying the laws of cabs and buses sufficiently you will find out where you are going." Nor could he, as David Hume advised, abandon questions about the meaning of life and love as unanswerable and, therefore, unprofitable. His own situation, which placed him so much at odds with his environment, did not permit him this luxury. To drift along with the generally accepted moral assumptions and social prejudices of his time and place, as skeptical philosopher David Hume recommended, was simply not an option for Carpenter.[19]

Annie Besant and the Theosophical Movement

In the midst of these spiritual struggles, help came to Carpenter from a somewhat unexpected quarter. Among his colleagues in the Fabian Society was a beautiful, intense young woman who proclaimed herself an advocate of militant secularism and (even more outrageously) planned parenthood. Mrs. Annie Besant had been the wife of a country parson, but like Carpenter himself, she had found the Anglican church a spiritual prison. Now an ardent radical, she seemed without fear, proclaiming unpopular causes on streetcorners in the most dangerous sections of London. Public ridicule and violent threats only whetted her appetite for controversy. The gospel of planned parenthood she preached all her life—in the face of the law. But militant secularism she shed early in her career. Because both suffered from the same gnawing spiritual restlessness, Carpenter and Mrs. Besant gravitated toward each other.

The revelation came suddenly for Besant, through the vehicle of one of the most flamboyant personalities and dramatic storytellers of the nineteenth century. Helena Petrovna Blavatsky—known to her disciples as H.P.B. or simply Madam—gave the most amazing account of her own early history. The daughter of a colonel in the imperial Russian army, she had been forced into marriage at the age of seventeen (in 1848, that year of revolutions). Within months she had run away from her husband in order to preserve her virginity, she said. She became a wanderer over the face of the earth, sojourning over four continents, getting lost in a desert, being abducted by bandits, and ending up in a Tibetan lamasery disguised as a monk.

Here she contacted the ascended masters, mysterious adepts of occult science who had transcended the dimension of time-space, and who (although unknown to the world) were now in control of its spiritual destinies. The ascended masters informed Madam Blavatsky that all of the great religions of the world, beneath their surface differences and peculiarities, had the same core of hidden truth. But now, history was about to take a new turn. The masters had chosen her as their vehicle for revealing hitherto concealed mysteries and thereby initiating a new world religion.

Sometime in the 1870s, Madam Blavatsky settled in New York City and was already a familiar figure on the seance circuit when she encountered an ambitious journalist named Henry Olcott. By this time, H.P.B. was a large, middle-aged woman who dressed in the style of a gypsy fortune-teller (or a Parisian bohemian). Her electric blue eyes and hypnotic speaking style rendered her claims to extraordinary psychic powers almost believable, and with Olcott's help, she began turning out her now well-known mystical tomes. "Theosophy," teachings of mystical insights that echo Buddhist and Brahmanic theories on such subjects as pantheistic evolution and reincarnation, was born in 1875 as a modern religion.[20]

Whether taught by the ascended masters or not, Madam Blavatsky did possess a surprisingly extensive knowledge of the world's mystical literature—from Orphism and Cabala to Sufism and Vedanta. Moreover, either she possessed amazing psychic powers or she was a talented actress. When Carpenter was introduced to her by Annie Besant, he rather thought she was both. Her conversation, he reported, contained "some shining jewels of truth, but mixed at the same time with a huge mass of rubbish."[21]

Annie Besant adopted theosophy rather uncritically and traveled to India in order to study Vedanta firsthand and to crusade against the British Raj. Her politics made her a national hero to the Indian people (who have never forgotten her). In time, Carpenter would make his own pilgrimage to India, and like Besant, he reacted violently to the odd contrast between the horrors of the caste system and the profound spirituality of individual gurus and rishis. His reaction to Theosophy, however, was much more qualified. Of Madam Blavatsky's magnum opus, he wrote, "No words can describe the general rot and confusion of Blavatsky's *Secret Doctrine*." Although often described as a theosophist, Carpenter did not so much embrace theosophy as employ it in his own philosophy.[22]

Especially important to Carpenter was the fact that Annie Besant (who rapidly became Madam Blavatsky's second-in-command and heir apparent as leader of the movement) accepted his homosexuality without reservation. Besant was one of those women—there had been several in Carpenter's life—who possessed an instinctive understanding of his male love affairs and who felt at home in the company of gay people. She found Carpenter's love poetry refreshing and saw his sexual orientation as no barrier to his spiritual development.[23]

CARPENTER'S SPIRITUAL ODYSSEY

Much in the theosophical spirit, Carpenter embarked on a course of eclectic philosophical and religious reading, practicing at the same time a variety of spiritual disciplines. In particular, he devoted himself to mastering the fine art of meditation as taught by various masters of both East and West. Meditation, as he practiced it consisted of two exercises: "(a) that of concentration—in holding the thought steadily for a time on one subject and (b) that of effacement—in effacing any given thought from the mind." For him, the goal of meditation was to find "in the very midst of the cyclone of daily life a resting place," to gain through consistent practice "the power of stilling Thought, that ability to pass unharmed and undismayed through the grinning legions of the lower mind into the very heart of Paradise."[24]

Carpenter never aimed in his study and meditation at what Madam Blavatsky and Colonel Olcott described as "the mystic potencies of life." In what are ordinarily described as "psychic powers," Carpenter had only a limited interest. He was willing to believe that at least some of the cases validated by the London Society for Psychical Research were genuine examples of extrasensory perception (ESP). But the psychics best known to him—such as Madam Blavatsky or her almost equally famous friend, Anna Kingsford—struck him as unpleasantly inflated and ultimately quite foolish. Carpenter's meditation practice cultivated mysticism in a different sense, the sort of mysticism that the sixteenth-century Spanish mystic Saint Teresa described as an "interior journey to the center of the soul." [25]

The Nature of the Ego

In direct opposition to the spirit of British empiricism and logical positivism, Carpenter believed that the key to understanding humanity's place in nature lies in understanding the self and that this self is best understood through introspection. For Carpenter, meditation means just such an interior journey in order to understand, first, the nature of the self and, only then, one's position in the world. This places Carpenter squarely in the Cartesian tradition, because he sees conscious thought as the only indubitable reality, from which all other realities must be deduced. This relationship with the French philosophical tradition also gives Carpenter a curious affinity with such twentieth-century philosophers as Husserl and Sartre, for whom the introspective analysis of the nature of consciousness also provides the key to any understanding of humanity's place in the world. Whole passages in Carpenter's book on the nature of the self, *The Art of Creation*, seem interchangeable with Edmund Husserl's *Cartesian Meditations* or Jean-Paul Sartre's *The Transcendence of the Ego*.[26]

Carpenter wrote that we are aware of the ego only in the act of perception or knowledge—which at the same time involves the consciousness of the non-ego. Without an act of knowledge, no consciousness of the ego can be obtained. Thus consciousness, or mind, always means a relation implying the dyad of subject and object. Apart from its object, the knowing subject becomes enigmatic. "The consciousness of the ego, present in the act of knowledge, seems to be the most real thing in the world. It pursues us everywhere; we refer everything to it. Yet it remains curiously simple and unanalysable." Carpenter describes the problematic nature of mind this way: "We cannot avoid the ego; but we cannot analyze it, for the simple reason that as soon as it is envisaged, it becomes the Object, and the real Ego is found to be again at the hither end of the stick."[27]

For Carpenter, as for Descartes, the self is "the most real thing in the world" but also the most paradoxical. The "I think" is what accompanies every perception and conception. Even though linked to every observation, it cannot ever be observed directly; its existence can only be inferred. For Descartes, the essential nature of this *res cogitans* ("thinking thing") is doubt, uncertainty. And out of this self-awareness of uncertainty, Descartes evolved (by a dialectical process) the concept of a Divine Mind, whose essential nature is absolute and unqualified certainty, omniscience. For Sartre, the essence of the self is anxiety, from which he evolves the concept of radical freedom. For Carpenter, the essence of the self is loneliness, and out of this existential loneliness he develops his notion of infinite love. "The great mystery of human Love," he wrote, "is the firmest, most basic and indissoluble fact that we know." Carpenter's position can be stated as a play on Descartes's: *Amo ergo sum* ("I love therefore I am").[28]

Love as the Key to the Enigma of the Self

The irony is that the reality of love is first confronted in experiencing its absence. In the modern literature of homosexuality—from Arthur Rimbaud to Jean Genet—loneliness has been the central theme. Compounded by shame and guilt, this loneliness isolates one not only from society at large but also from would-be lovers and even from God. Carpenter experienced this loneliness as the essence of the human condition—perhaps more acutely felt by homosexuals, but endemic to human nature as such. "Some folks say they remember the moment when, as quite young children, to them with a sense of alarm, self-consciousness suddenly came," he wrote. "They were suddenly terrified at the thought of self, as of a separate item or atom in this vast world. The self is suddenly face to face with an alien world."[29]

For most homosexuals, no change in outward circumstances could alter or affect this sense of existential isolation, Carpenter found. As long as the self misunderstands its own nature and regards itself merely as an isolated monad in the midst of a dead and senseless world, it will discover only its own loneliness in every attempt at human contact. In particular, the sort of anonymous and promiscuous sexuality characteristic of the gay underworld only has the effect of further enclosing the individual inside the prison of his or her own ego. For Carpenter, the only alternative to this sort of anguish was the interior journey of meditation, which is composed in more or less equal parts of detachment from desire, quieting of the mind, and philosophical reflection. "Slowly and resolutely—as a fly cleans its legs of the honey in which it has been caught—So remove thou, if only for a time, every particle which sullies the brightness of thy mind," Carpenter advised. "Return into thyself—content to give, but asking no one, asking nothing." Silence and solitude become tools that the soul uses to explore its own nature.[30]

Sartre said that the individual, insofar as absolute autonomy is recognized, necessarily also discerns radical freedom. This recognition demands, however, that the individual recognize the freedom of others as well. In choosing to be oneself, one chooses what one believes one ought to be and becomes "thereby at the same time a legislator for the whole of [hu]mankind." Carpenter, who had little interest in legislating anything for another, felt that in exploring his own aloneness he realized also the aloneness of others—and thereby the possibility of the creation of love. "There are millions of selves which are or think themselves separate," Carpenter wrote, observing that this illusion of separateness itself constitutes a kind of oddly unifying force. "The self, hitherto deeming itself a separate atom, suddenly becomes aware of its inner unity with these other human beings. It is the great deliverance from the prison-life of the separate self."[31]

The realization of existential loneliness as a universal of the human condition paradoxically unites all persons in a shared need.

But if this need creates the first suggestion of a possible escape from the prison of ego, then it does not in itself create the fact of love. Indeed, the individual who has a sense of isolation is often given to panic. "Fear, in fact, is an inevitable accompaniment of the consciousness of self." This fear creates enemies. "The images of fearful things in the brain are already beginning the work of destruction which the real things in the outer world are accused of." In this state, the isolated ego is more likely to classify the other as an enemy (actual or potential) who can be dominated but never trusted. "The ego sense is called forth and descends into operation" within the individual. "It desires as its food, the applause of others." Loneliness can create hate and manipulation as well as love, as one inner void attempts to extort what it needs from another inner void. "I sometimes think that this is the explanation of those strange cases in which a man, mad with desire, and unable to satisfy his passion, kills the girl he loves," Carpenter said, meditating on sexual sadism. The prison of ego tortures a person more horribly than any other type of prison. Somehow, a person so imprisoned must pierce the wall of indifference that separates one from the beloved. "I don't think it is hypothetical jealousy of a possible other lover. I think it is something much more direct than that—the blind urge to reach her actual self, even if it be only with a knife or a bullet."[32]

This is the sort of sado-masochistic situation that Sartre defines as the bottom line of all human attempts at love. It is also the human reality that Genet found on the streets of Paris. In Carpenter's view, ordinary consciousness can never solve this problem, "because clearly the evidence of ordinary consciousness, however long we work at the problem, can never carry us one step farther than it does now." As long as the only thing human beings have in common is need, they will never have anything substantive to give one another. We may all be in the same boat, but if that boat is sinking, then all we can share is our desperation.[33]

THE LOVE AT THE HEART OF THE UNIVERSE

Human loneliness requires something larger than a merely human resolution. Like many Christian theologians, Carpenter felt that reason points in the direction of faith. In showing humanity its need for faith, reason can lead persons a good way toward receptiveness to an experience of the divine, "because the indirect evidence of the ordinary thought and consciousness all point in the same direction."[34]

Reason can wend its way toward the divine in two ways, Carpenter contends. One moves outward in the direction of other people; the other moves inward in the direction of the true or transcendent self. In this first way, Saint Paul did not speak metaphorically when he said that "we are all members one of another"(Eph. 4:25). Any self, as an I, could not even conceive of its own existence as a person if it were reared in isolation. Personal thought presupposes a culture of thought and thinking selves. "My soul," each person can say in this sense, "is only a part of the larger soul (or mind) of my culture, which itself is only a phase of the evolution of the mind of humanity." Individual experience, even at its most private, always presupposes the gradual unfolding of the totality of the human experience as it evolves through history, so that all human beings participate in one communal and all-embracing Mind. "If A knows his essential identity with objects a, b, c, etc.; and B also knows the same; then A and B know their essential identity with each other. And so on. All our selves must consequently be one, or at least united as branches of the One." Carpenter theorized that all separate, finite human minds necessarily connect as they gradually expand in the direction of infinity; they are all fragments of absolute mind, the infinite consciousness toward which each infinite mind reaches in its ongoing transcendence of itself. Carpenter uses a biblical metaphor to explain this: the divine mind is the heavenly city, the new Jerusalem. "The ground of the universe must be one universal self or one Eternal City of selves, ever united and ever arriving at the knowledge of their union with each other."[35]

In Carpenter's second approach to God, reason operates not by expanding consciousness but by intensifying it inwardly to see what it might be within itself. Like the ancient neo-Platonists, Carpenter explains individual consciousness by deducing it from an absolute consciousness, a "constituting hyper-consciousness." The self, for Carpenter, is the Kantian "I think" that accompanies every perception. One's perception, insofar as it is one's own, is defined by its limitations, by the ways in which it is limited by one's personal idiosyncrasies, the qualities that make one not another. To the extent that one truly empathizes with another, however, one moves beyond one's limitations and grows as a person. By turning inward, to see what one is in oneself, apart from one's social context and the personal qualities that define this self, one wanders into what Sartre refers to as "the infinite series of reflected consciousness." "If the ego appears as beyond each quality, or even as beyond all qualities, this is because the ego is opaque, like an object: we would have to undertake an infinite plundering in order to take away its powers."[36]

Carpenter expresses the same idea in less-philosophical terms. Suppose that this question of the nature of the self is put to a boy. He might reply, "I know well enough who I am: I am the boy with the red hair what gave Jimmy Brown such a jolly good licking last Monday week." At an older age, he might describe himself as a good ballplayer or a successful student. Yet his method is practically the same. "He fixes his mind on a certain bundle of qualities and capacities which he is supposed to possess and calls the bundle Himself." And in a more elaborate way, all of us do the same. Soon, however, with more careful thought, we begin to see difficulties with this view. "I see that the 'I,' the Self, is not that bundle, but is the being inspective of the same—something beyond and behind." "I may imagine an inner being, or 'Soul,' inhabiting the body and perceiving through its senses, but quite capable of surviving the tenement in which it dwells—and I think of that as the Self." But no sooner has one taken this step than one perceives that one is committing the same mistake as before—Sartre's "infinite regress of reflected consciousness." For Carpenter, as for the ancient neo-Platonists and Sartre, this is a regression toward infinity. Its only limit is the ideal one of an absolute consciousness. Thus, Plotinus taught that "every human soul is a spectrum of possible levels of life, on any one of which one may choose to live until for the perfect sage, the [soul] is the One itself."[37]

This Neo-Platonic concept of an infinite mind may seem remote from the spirit of modern philosophy, but Carpenter is eager to demonstrate that this is not necessarily so. For example,

Descartes, at the beginning of the modern era, made the problem of God an aspect of the larger problem of mind and of the relationship of mind to the material world. Modern philosophy has struggled with that problem ever since. Modern materialists think that they follow Cartesian insights when they understand nature as a vast unthinking mechanism, the random interplay of unconscious forces.

The place of mind in such a universe is itself problematic; Einstein once said that the most mysterious thing about the universe is that it is understandable. Descartes, however, saw the laws of nature as the manifestation of one transcendent reason-principle, of which the human intellect is only a partial manifestation. In an oft-quoted aphorism, Hegel said, "Ultimately, Being and Thought are One." In this view, the variety of limited human intellects presupposes the existence of one infinite intellect that both subsumes and transcends them.

To be sure, no finite mind, and no collection of finite minds, can understand the meaning of the universe as a whole. Only omniscience can do that. But Hegel would argue that no logically coherent thought is possible without the assumption that the universe, as a whole, is logically coherent. When we read a sentence, for example, we read it one word at a time, but no one word would make any sense by itself unless we assumed that, when we got to the end, the sentence as a whole would have meaning.

For Carpenter, as for philosophical idealists generally, each limited human intellect resembles one word in the complete sentence that is the mind of God. Considered apart from each other, or from God, we appear meaningless, absurd. In our true context, we abound in meaning, a meaning that transcends itself in the direction of infinity.

Carpenter has consciously allied himself with modern philosophical idealism, particularly in the style of Hegel. The difference is that for the philosophical idealists the unifying soul is a logical deduction whereas for Carpenter it is a mystical experience. "These conclusions were not so much the result of the analysis of the mind and the following out of strict argument," he admits. "They were flashes of intuition and experience." Because his philosophy rests so firmly on mysticism, its statements often read like poetry. "This solid earth, and the great liquid sea, and even the midnight sky with its wonderful starry systems is a panorama of a conscious life ever pressing forward toward Expression and Manifestation." For Carpenter, "these dots and scratches in the divine handwriting, these stones and stars and storms, are words appealing to us continually for our loving understanding and interpretation." Carpenter considered this not poetry but common sense. "We conclude the intelligence of our friends because we should find it absurd and impossible to place ourselves on a lonely pinnacle and look upon those we love as automatons." The face of nature is to be read like the face of a lover. Thus Carpenter's understanding of truth reflects his experience of love. "In proportion as we come to love and understand the animals and the trees and the face of Nature shall we find it impossible to deny intelligence to these."[38]

Gay Mysticism

Carpenter often sounds like a typical English Romantic in the tradition of Wordsworth; in one sense, this is what he is, but with a key difference. If Carpenter's philosophy rests on his mysticism, then his mysticism just as surely rests on his homosexual experience. The phrase "we cannot look upon our friends as automatons" is significant. Carpenter's attitude toward the natural world grows out of his attitude toward the human world. His sense of social isolation gives him a powerful sense of the supreme importance of the category of the personal. As William James felt was true of all Christian mystics, the category of the personal is absolute. God, the ultimate reality, is an infinite person. As Robert Flint, Carpenter's associate and a widely read contemporary theologian, writes, "Reason, if honest and consistent, cannot in its pursuit of causes stop short of a Rational Will. That alone answers to and satisfies its idea of a cause." Carpenter agreed. Even the universe can only be rendered intelligible if in it "we feel the overshadowing of a universal mind."[39]

The animism of primitives, Carpenter said, is closer to the truth than the mechanical, clockwork world of the positivists. The dead matter of the materialist hypothesis is an abstraction, after all, and an enigmatic one. To explain all of human experience in terms of this hypothesis is, in effect, to explain the known in terms of the unknown and (by definition) unknowable. In contrast, to explain experience as a participation in minds (or a mind) like our own is to render it perfectly intelligible, or so Carpenter thought. "I do not for a moment deny that 'matter,' or the objective basis of external experience has an independent existence but I deny that it has an independent non-mental existence, and I say that, if it has, then such an existence cannot be imagined."[40]

This denial saves Carpenter from the philosophical embarrassment of postulating a reality that can never be experienced by any mind, but it also sets the stage for his conviction that all reality is essentially spiritual. "If we conceive that 'substance' as having subjectivity, as a self of some kind, then I say we can imagine it." For Carpenter, as for Baruch Spinoza, God is the only substance, spirit the only enduring reality. No finite being exists by itself or is understandable in itself. The infinite, then, when taken in its true nature, is the only complete reality. The finite always requires a context that accounts for it. Once again, on the analogy of love, which always understands physical or sensual facts sacramentally, as outward and visible signs of an inward and spiritual grace, Carpenter sees God in the world "just as it is possible to know something of our invisible friends who lie behind the voices and faces of daily life." After studying the rather abstract theological speculations of Descartes, Pascal responded with his well-known one-liner: "The heart has its reasons that the reason knows not of." Carpenter, too, felt passionately interested in this logic of the heart, which (for him, as for Pascal) pursues not so much perfect knowledge as perfect love.[41]

But then, Carpenter, like Plato, identified absolute reason with absolute goodness and absolute beauty. Omniscience, after all, must know and understand the nature of the good—unless one assumes that human notions of goodness are purely subjective and arbitrary and hence not, properly speaking, objects of knowledge at all. With respect to the theology of Saint Anselm, Simone Weil once observed that "the Ontological argument is mysterious because it does not address itself to the intelligence but to love." Carpenter through meditation came to view nature, in the words of Thomas Traherne, "as the most perfect gift given in the most perfect way from the most Perfect Lover to the most perfectly be-loved." And through the spiritual discipline predicated on this theology he learned to approach people in a different way. Love became a genuine human possibility for him only so long as it was seen as an aspect or manifestation of the divine. "We can none of us boast, at any point, of a rounded, definite and stationary self, apart from all others; but we are all approaching the universal from different sides." Yet our apparent separation from others does have its value. "Through the very obstacles that surround us, and through the things that seem to divide us from others, first simple consciousness and then self-consciousness are born." After all, the discovery of self makes love possible: "Then comes a time when the limitations and the barriers become intolerable. Then in each of us the Divine Soul is born; a vista of glory and splendor opens in front and on all sides barriers fall to the ground."[42]

Carpenter's point is that the too often joyless and compulsive search for love between men, in a context of persecution and ano-nymity (which is the essence of gay life as it has been lived for a millennium), becomes unnecessary to those who understand the nature of the divine. Through meditation and spiritual discipline, every individual can understand that she or he is already loved, already understood, already an integral part of the natural and the human world that surrounds him or her. The truly isolated self, cut off from its divine ground of all being and from human nature as a whole, does not and cannot exist. Rejection, hatred, isolation, loneliness are all, in one way, delusional and, in another, necessary steps on the path to the realization of infinite love. Sexual experience that does not transcend these delusions never can be anything but self-defeating. But for those who understand that all human love comes from God as its first cause and returns to God as its final cause, sexuality becomes a celebration of the divine. Carpenter's close connection of sexuality and the divine stands in the face of millennia of Christianity. Sexual experience is not only not essentially opposed to religious experience; it is essentially identical with it. The essential meaning of both is the desire for personal union and escape from the prison of ego. [43]

In a famous passage of his *Apologia Pro Vita Sua*, John Henry Cardinal Newman told his readers that, in his quiet moments, the material world itself often took on an air of unreality for him: "I thought life might be a dream, or I an Angel, and all this world a deception, my fellow angels by a playing device concealing themselves from me, and deceiving me with the semblance of a material world." Carpenter's sense of the reality of the spiritual world was easily as vivid as Newman's, so that for him also only the spiritual is real. Matter he defined as "a surface of contact" through which "one spirit encounters another." In a way that anticipates the modern phenominalist reduction of matter. Carpenter wrote, "The body in any state is, I repeat, a surface of contact. Wherever one intelligent being comes into touch with another there immediately arises a body. There arises the sense of matter, which is in fact the impression made by one being upon another." In a way, the simple physiological facts of sense perception indicate this. "The actual world which we know is built up out of the material of our physical senses, but if these were altered even slightly in their range, the whole world would be different." They would create for us another world. "At the death of the physical body, the soul will create other senses, so, if these present end-organs of sense were destroyed, the soul, furnished with the inner faculties corresponding, would create another world." In fact, the sense perceptions of the spiritual body will outshine those of the physical. "When we understand ourselves, and what we are, and when we understand others, and what thy are, Time and Space and Estrangement will no longer avail against us; they will no longer hinder us from recognition of each other." Love will be easier in the next life and more complete. "Those we love are ours already, in the deepest sense—and one day we shall wake up to know that they are ever present and able to manifest themselves out of the unseen."[44]

Transformative Sexuality

Carpenter came to believe that Mary Baker Eddy was right, to a degree, in her concept of Christian Science. "Divine science" became a favorite phrase of his, which he used in roughly the same sense as Eddy used it—as a reference to the power of the conviction of divine love to heal broken bodies and broken lives. Carpenter had befriended Eugene Sandow, a famous physical-culturist of the period, who gave nude physique exhibitions in the 1890s and is now considered the father of modern bodybuilding. Carpenter, who was something of a nudist anyway, was impressed when Sandow told him that "the bones and muscles are affected by thought." Sandow, Carpenter reported, "has particularly insisted on the great influence which concentration of the mind exercises on the growth of the muscles."[45]

If Sandow could demonstrate the ability of the mind to condition the body, then certainly it ought to be possible to use spiritual power to transform our emotional lives. Like Eddy, Carpenter believed that only the consciousness of infinite love can really heal broken bodies and sick minds. The realization of humanity's essential unity with God is like the lifting of a veil from a new world full of new possibilities. The revelation of these divine realities, for Carpenter, can come only through love. "The soul is born through love," he said, "and through love it grows and expands." "For the reason that the Love itself (like Beauty) belongs to another plane of existence than the plane of ordinary life and speech." Thus Dante had discovered the beatific vision in the eyes of Beatrice. Carpenter writes in his *Art of Creation*, "It is seen by lovers in each other's eyes—the One, absolute and changeless, yet infinitely beautiful and intelligent—the Supreme life and being."[46]

Seen from the divine perspective, human beings no longer appear as fearfully limited creatures, full of their petty cares and their own absurd self-importance. Love cleanses away the pretensions of the surface personality in a dramatic way. Carpenter writes, "One often thinks what divine and beautiful creatures—men and women—there are all around, how loving and lovable, how gracious in their charm, how grand in their destiny!" Thus, love perceives a spiritual beauty in persons which their surface personalities might believe. "And then alas! one of these divinities begins to talk—and it is like the fair woman in the fable, out of whose mouth, whenever she opened it, there jumped a mouse! The shock is almost more than one can bear." What disturbs Carpenter here is not human stupidity but human folly. Not that the shock proceeds from the ignorance displayed (because "the animals and even the angels are deliciously ignorant") but from the revelations that speech unconsciously makes of certain states of the soul—in the strange falsity that too often is heard in the words and in the tones of the voice. "Only when human nature transcends itself through love can this folly be overcome. Love burns this falsity away. That is why love—even rude and rampant and outrageous love—does more for the moralizing of poor humanity than a hundred thousand Sunday schools."[47]

A recurrent theme in Carpenter's thought is that love, especially between men, obviates distinctions of class and race. On the other plane of existence where love and beauty are found, such mundane and essentially superficial human distinctions lose their meaning. He had learned by experience that his love for other men could create intimacy for him with individuals whose race and class ought to have made them his natural enemies. "When two strangers of different race and tongue meet, they usually eye each other with suspicion and misunderstanding," he observed, calling upon his own experiences as a world traveler. "Instantly a word or a glance of the eyes, in the external world, reveals abysmal depths in the two selves, and a sense of age long union."[48]

On his Indian voyage he had just such an experience with a young Cinghalese cooley, to whom he gave "a part of his soul." Although the basis of this experience might be sexual, the revelation brought by love can change even the whole configuration of daily experience. "There are times when this strange illumination falls on people at large and we see them as gods walking." All too often, however, these human gods act in ignorance of their high destiny. "Yet of what is really nearest to them all the time these folk say nothing, and we are astonished to find them haggling over halfpence or seriously troubled about wire-worms." For Carpenter, this human forgetfulness of our divine origin corresponds to the Oriental doctrine of Maya. "It is as if a play, or some kind of deliberate mystification, were being carried on—with disguises a little too thin."[49]

The real mystification involved, it could be argued, is Carpenter's own romanticizing of these essentially mundane sexual encounters with uninspiring individuals. Bruce Bawer, among others, has written of the general tendency of promiscuous homosexuals to romanticize squalid behavior and attribute existential meaning to conduct that is only irresponsible. Bawer writes that "it is often claimed that gay bars, where members of upper-class WASP [white Anglo-Saxon Protestant] families mingle with Puerto Rican janitors, are the perfect democracy." Such is an illusion, however, because "mingling in a pickup bar is hardly a good example of the sort of mutual respect that democracy seeks to encourage, and one-night stands do not erase socioeconomic barriers." Carpenter would insist that sexual desire is seldom merely trivial. When the upper-class WASP finds beauty in the Puerto Rican janitor, something important has happened between them. They have, if nothing else, recognized their common humanity. And if, outside the bar, they become strangers to each other again, does this invalidate what they felt inside it? Perhaps what it invalidates is the hypocrisy and bigotry of the surrounding culture.[50]

IN SEARCH OF A RATIONALITY OF LOVE

In the hard-headed twentieth century, the whole idea of romantic love has come under attack, and the possibility of romantic love between men has been all but denied for centuries. Carpenter does his best to defend this ideal. But as a philosopher, he was eclectic. Although not without originality, his reasoning is apt to seem interesting rather than compelling—and as a mystic who had demitted from his ordination in the Anglican church, Carpenter belonged to no sharply defined religious tradition or tightly organized church. He had no generally recognized religious authority, no bishop or caliph, to whom he could appeal to authenticate his mystical experiences. (In contrast, in 1915, Pope Pius XII had authenticated the visions of the eight-year-old shepherdess Lucia dos Santos at Fatima, Portugal.) If this mysticism seems bogus, then it raises an interesting question: How does one authenticate a mystical experience? How does one separate genuine contact with the divine from fraud or delusion?

Carpenter attempted to validate the truth value of his own mysticism in two ways. First, he never claimed any privileged status or special authority for his own experiences—no special visionary powers or psychic gifts, as both Madam Blavatsky and Annie Besant had claimed. He felt that anyone who practiced meditation, who simply tried to quiet her or his mind and concentrate on the things of importance, would come to the same mystical awareness as he did: "Of all the hard facts of Science: as that fire will burn, that water will freeze, I know of none more solid than this: if you inhibit thought (and persevere) you come at length to a region of consciousness different from ordinary thought in its nature."[51]

Carpenter felt this was especially true of meditation practiced in connection with sexual experience. Sexuality only makes sense, Carpenter claimed, if one sees it as a spiritual quest for essential beauty and spirituality. To those who might feel skeptical about such a possibility, he simply suggests that they test it in their own experience. This process works itself out through love. "From point to point through union with others, by absorbing something from their experience, by sharing a wider life, the spirit's manifestation grows." Echoing Plotinus, Carpenter defined human love as the struggle of finite consciousness to transcend itself in the direction of eternity. "Each soul is a gradual rising to the consciousness of the All-soul; a gradual liberation and self-discovery of the divine germ with it."

Again, like Aldous Huxley a century later, Carpenter also felt driven by the logic of his position to posit the existence of some sort of universal mysticism—what Huxley called the *philosophia perennis*. Like Evelyn Underhill somewhat earlier, Carpenter felt that he could describe the characteristics of this objective mysticism and use them as a criterion by which to test the authenticity of any putative mystical experience on the part of an individual. "It will of course be said, and often is said that those phenomena are only hallucinations, and have no objective existence. But the sufficient answer to that is that the things also of our actual world are hallucinations in their degree." Beginning students in philosophy are often asked if color is in the flower or in the eye, if a tree falling in a remote jungle makes a sound. "The daffodil in my garden is an hallucination in that degree that, with the smallest transposition of my senses, its color, its scent and even its form might be quite altered." How do we differentiate the real from the illusory? Obviously, the one has a logical place in the space-time continuum. "What we call its objectivity rests on the permanence of its relations—its visibility to different people at one time, or to one person at different times, and so forth. Religious experience meets that criteri[on]. But if that is the definition of objectivity, it is obvious that some forms [of mysticism] have been seen over and over again."[52]

Comparative Religion and the Study of Mysticism

In defending his position, Carpenter had an obvious problem: many of the world's most revered mystics were ascetics and, as such, rather suspicious of sexuality in general and homosexuality in particular. Even so, Carpenter took the position that all mysticism is either overtly or covertly erotic—and frequently homoerotic as well. In order to make his case, he relied heavily on the known myths and rituals of pre-Christian pagan religions, especially those that adapted themselves to Platonic philosophy. In addition, he worked hard to show the covertly erotic content of many Christian symbols, legends, rituals, and customs.

The myths and symbols of religion, Carpenter hypothesized (in a way that seems to anticipate Jungian psychology), originate deep in the human subconscious or semiconscious mind. Although social and economic conditions affect the formation of these symbols, their essential meaning transcends historical conditions because it originates in an area of the psyche that touches the eternal. "The gods and creeds of the past are essentially projections of the human mind," Carpenter allowed, "and no doubt those who are anxious to discredit the religious impulse generally will catch at this, saying: Yes, the history of Religion is a history of delusion and illusion; why waste time over it?" Such a conclusion was, to his view, premature. Carpenter possessed a pre-Freudian sense of the importance of dreams and fantasies. What, after all, were the magnificent creations of literature and art if not dreams and fantasies? And where did these dreams come from? Why did humanity need them so desperately? Carpenter looked to his own experience of meditation for guidance. "We have only to indulge in a few moments' rest, and immediately we become aware that our mind is peopled by a motley crowd of phantoms. We seem to see them springing up of themselves, and almost at random, from the background of consciousness when we daydream or let our minds wander." Where does it all come from? "Yet a moment more and we realize that the crowd is not a random one, but that it is inspired and given its forms by the emotions, the feelings, the desires, lying deep and half-hidden within."[53]

Carpenter believed more or less, as Freud did, that the natural language of the deepest layer of the mind is symbol. Carpenter also believed that most individuals have only a dim awareness of their own motivations and are, as often as not, surprised and puzzled by their own behavior and emotions. While we puzzle over the mystery of our own inner conflicts, "all the time in silence thought has been busy within, making ready the channels; and so one day when a great rush of feeling comes [desire] flows down, and our purpose in an instant, as it were, before we have time to Yea or Nay, has flung itself forth into our actions." Carpenter parts company with Freud over the latter's commitment to philosophical materialism and the exclusively biological nature of libido. As we have seen, Carpenter believed in the reality of the spiritual world, both on philosophical and experiential grounds. If each self is "a rising toward the All Self," then the deepest layers of the individual psyche will touch closely on the psychic realities of other selves—ultimately merging in the All Self, like thousands of separate streams flowing into rivers which, in turn, flow into the sea.[54]

The symbols and myths of religion have more than a private meaning because they express the collective, albeit unconscious, experience of the whole human race. "Yes, the gods and creeds are only projections of the human mind. But all the same, materialism misses the essential fact. It misses the fact that there is no shadow without a fire, that the very existence of the shadow argues a light somewhere." For Carpenter, each of the figures of world mythology expresses in its own shadowy way the beauty of the divine ground of being. "Deep, deep in the human mind there is that burning, blazing light of the world-consciousness—so deep indeed that the vast majority of individuals are hardly aware of its existence."[55]

Pursuing suggestive insights he found in the thought of theosophists such as Anna Kingsford (who, unlike Madam Blavatsky, took a greater interest in Western mysticism than in Eastern), Carpenter evolved his own version of the neo-Platonic theory of the divine *henads* ("shape or cause" in Greek), as first developed by ancient philosophers such as Iamblichus and Proclus. Most people have at least a general idea of what Jung meant by the archetypes of the collective unconscious, as a key to the meaning of world mythology. In a much earlier period of history, the idea of the divine henads functioned similarly to explain traditional religious beliefs to a generation that was losing its sense of their meaning. The henads were understood, roughly speaking, as the Platonic forms identified with the traditional gods of Pagan pantheon. On the one hand, as divine ideas, the henads were thought of as a part of God, or as aspects of the infinite and eternal mind—corresponding roughly to the divine attributes in Christian theology. On the other hand, as divine hypostases, they had a real existence of their own and could be worshiped or loved as separate personal beings—rather like angels in Christian theology. Thus, Proclus writes, "All [of the gods] are in each other and are rooted in the one."[56]

The idea of the divine henads has an interesting history in Western mysticism. In Cabalistic thought, God's wisdom becomes God's companion and even a feminine consort, as the divine Sophia. Similarly, the divine name itself has been thought of as an angel, sometimes called *Metatron* ("before the throne") and sometimes simply Michael ("God's glory"). Dionysus the Aereopagite associates the hypostases of the Trinity with the neo-Platonic henads, and at a much later date, Leibniz developed his monadology from neo-Platonic roots. Carpenter also accepted the traditional doctrine of panpsychism as first enunciated by Thales when he taught that all things are full of gods (*omnia animata*). Carpenter used Leibniz's version of this idea, according to which scientific laws can be thought of as divine ideas—or henads.[57]

Is the Universe Composed of Dead Matter?

Panpsychism seems to be staging something of a comeback with modern philosophers of science, even though it still might seem completely alien to modern physics or biology to think of scientific laws as conscious personal forces. Thus, Sir James Jeans says of the impression created by modern physics that "the universe begins to look more like a great thought than like a great machine." Philosopher Paul Weiss observes that "matter for the [modern] philosophical materialist is quite immaterial. The space-time continuum in the geometricized physics of modern relativity is somewhat closer in nature to Plato's pure receptacle than it is to the hard atoms of Democratus or Lucretius." Frank Tipler rejects out of hand, as totally incompatible with the most recent advances in physics, the nineteenth-century view that "the universe is a cold unknowing place, that human beings are accidents of evolution, that when we die, consciousness disappears into oblivion."[58]

Carpenter, with his consistent emphasis on the personal, simply argues that the natural forces that shape our lives can usefully be experienced as personal. "This enables us dimly to see how the great panorama of creation has come forth, ever manifesting itself from within through the disclosure from point to point and from time to time of ever-new creative feelings or ideas." And as creation expresses the divine artistry, so it points back to God by the light of its reflected glory, "the whole forming an immense hierarchy, culminating in the grandest, most universal, Being and Life." Like much neo-Platonic theology, this all may sound abstract. But actual experience shows it as simple and personal. The deep mind functions like an artist, giving concrete form to every abstract idea. Thus, the goddess Aphrodite represents "the sense of Beauty taking some definite form." Below the idea of beauty lies the human reproductive instinct, which might be considered an impersonal law of nature. Taken as a personal force, is the goddess real? In some sense she is.[59]

Carpenter was fascinated by ancient theophanies as well as medieval and modern visionary experiences. Consider Pheidippides, who was sent by the Athenians to Sparta to ask for aid against the Persians. He was exhausted by the journey, for he covered, it was said, the 150 miles in less than two days. As he rested for a moment in some quiet valley beside a spring, "the great god Pan suddenly appeared to him, and his voice was heard promising victory to the Athenians." In gratitude, they dedicated a temple to Pan after the battle of Marathon and honored him thenceforth with annual sacrifices and a torch race. "We cannot but feel that whatever was the actual occurrence, the popular belief in the reality of the apparition and the voice was irresistible," Carpenter concluded.[60]

Christian Mysticism and Ancient Mythology

Carpenter applies the same principle to both Christian mysticism and ancient (he terms it "pagan") mythology. For example, without being Roman Catholic, one can accept as valid and genuine the visions of the Madonna (Mary, mother of Jesus) experienced by figures such as Saint Francis and Saint Teresa. Yet one would not expect Mary to appear to a Hindu, or the goddess Kali to appear to an Irish Catholic. But perhaps Mary and Kali are, allowing for cultural differences, manifestations of the same spiritual power. This is also true of Christ. "Allowing for cant and custom," Carpenter observes, "there are thousands and thousands round us to whom the figure of Christ is an intense, a living, and an actually present reality." It is difficult to suppose that all these people are merely deceiving themselves. "Obviously, this figure is much more than imagination or a fairy tale, and represents a real power there present and acting within the [person]."[61]

For Carpenter, then, the gods of all mythologies, along with the angels and saints (and devils) of the traditional Christian pantheon, are all real because they are aspects of the divine ground of being—God's attributes or ideas, whichever one prefers—but they are apprehended through the medium of the collective unconscious. "Through the gods, divine ideas become personal forces transforming human lives by a power, whose essence is eternal but whose form is apparitional and dependent in some degree on outer circumstances." By studying the spiritual visions of every great culture or religion, "we may be lifted for a moment out of our work-a-day existence and touch upon that which is eternal."[62]

The gospel story must be read as an allegory of love, Carpenter asserted, as well as the central doctrines of the Christian faith (incarnation, atonement, and the resurrection) along with its central sacraments (Baptism and Holy Communion). These can only be understood in the context of the ancient religious beliefs that preceded them. Pre-Christian religion knew of many incarnations and many atoning sacrifices. Even the word "Christ" itself—in the sense of "savior" or "anointed one"—antedates Christianity and was used as a title for such deities as Dionysus and Mithra. Of baptismal washings and divine communions (frequently involving bread and wine), the ancient world also knew many. And these facts have a special significance of their own.[63]

Christianity, the Religion of the Heart

Christianity had assumed a special role in the evolution of the human spirit, Carpenter maintained, although he denied the claim that Christianity was absolutely unique among the religions of the world—a claim still routinely put forward in his time. Here the influence of pioneer theosophist Anna Kingsford, who (unlike her friend Madam Blavatsky) considered herself a Christian, can be seen. For Kingsford, it was the message of suffering and redemptive love as taught in the Gospels that gave Christian mysticism its special significance. "The Buddha, great as was his Renunciation, underwent not such extremity of ordeal as that ascribed to his counterpart of the Gospels. Suffering is not of the mind, but of the heart." In the worldwide development of humanity's religious consciousness, "Buddha represents the intellect. Jesus represents the affections." Thus, if Buddha taught us renunciation, Jesus teaches us love. Kingsford maintained that "in the figure of Jesus, as its highest typical expression of the love element, Humanity fulfills the divine injunction, 'My son, give me thine heart'. Thus, then, in Christ Jesus the holy systems of the past find their maturity."[64]

For Carpenter, this fundamental message that God is love made Christianity valuable and even indispensable, although not necessarily unique or in any sense exclusively true. The message of Christianity can be realized only if it is seen as one member of the whole family of human religions, a fact routinely ignored by dogmatists and fundamentalists of every sort. But dogmatism, by its nature, violates the spirit of love. Kingsford wrote that students of Christian theology will learn to understand and appreciate the true value and significance of the symbols familiar to them only by the study of Eastern philosophy and ancient idealism. "Christianity does not cancel the old law but fulfills it. For Christianity is the heir of these and draws her best blood from their veins."[65]

Carpenter's originality is in the specifically sexual and homoerotic meanings that he finds in these ancient mysteries and their Christian reworkings. For him, the spiritual life is always and everywhere grounded in the body. The most basic mysteries of religion reflect the still-more-basic mysteries of biology. Why are we born? Why do we love? Why do we die? For those who accept the God-hypothesis, then these questions can be rephrased in theological terms. Why did God create the world, and why this kind of world? Why do the innocent suffer? Why does evil prosper? Carpenter accepts one traditional view that God creates because God is love, and love is by nature creative. Human sexuality is a reflection of this fact. "In God, to love, and hence to will all creatures, is simply to extend outside Himself His infinite Perfections," Aquinas taught. Although no pantheist, Carpenter does take issue with the idea that anything can be in any sense simply outside of God. With Hegel, he insists that it is contrary to the whole nature of a mystical absolute that anything should have a completely independent nature or do or be anything entirely on its own. For Carpenter, the whole drama of creation takes place within the divine nature. Carpenter is no process theologian in the modern sense of the word. Yet his understanding of creation resembles that of some process theologians, such as Charles Hartshorne, for example, who understand creation as God's concretizing God's own timeless perfection in an endless series of finite beings, each perfect in its own limited way, for instance, a perfect rose.[66]

God's concretizing is necessary because the paradoxical nature of love is that while it unites all things in harmony, it is the most individual of all our emotions. This is the odd duality of love. Its first phase is the discovery of one's own identity through self-expression; its second phase is that separate identity is transcended through union with another. "There is nothing vague and general and undifferentiated about that passion [of love]; on the contrary, it is most strongly personal and sharply outlined." Carpenter believes, as did the great American philosopher Josiah Royce, that only the idea of divine love finally explains the significance of the individual. What else could? "Why is it that out of the hundred thousand people that a man may meet, only one will arouse this tremendous response? Why is it that every great love in its depths seems different from every other?"[67]

Like the ancient neo-Platonists, Carpenter takes great interest in trying to define the exact nature of the principle of individuation in humans. Carpenter favored the view of Proclus that the principle of individuation is the order in which, through infinite time, the individual realizes the nature of the divine. "Each individuality in the end would reach the totality of experience, but in a different manner from any other; and all individualities would all the time—though changing themselves—remain within the unchanging intelligence of the absolute."[68]

LOVE AND SPIRITUAL REGENERATION

Carpenter's favorite metaphor for this individuation was the mystic rose envisioned at the end of Dante's *Paradiso*. "Each petal converges on the divine center from a different direction." Through love, the individual both expresses and transcends her or his own identity. The individual becomes more intensely herself or himself to the extent that she or he is subsumed into a larger beauty. Divine love expresses itself through us, as God's ideas. We participate in God's love for Godself to the extent that we realize God's presence in one another. But this realization can also be accompanied by much suffering.[69]

On the question of theodicy (if God is all powerful and good, then why does evil exist in the world?), mainstream Christianity, from Augustine to Leibniz, has insisted that God permits evil in order to give rise to greater good. But at the same time, it has also insisted that the existence of evil is in no sense necessary to God's plan. Thus, Aquinas believed that the variety and diversity of created beings did not necessarily entail conflict. Diversity, in itself, is entirely a good thing, "for the goodness which God has whole and together, creatures share in different ways, and the whole universe shares and expresses that goodness better than any individual creature." Carpenter, in contrast, asserted that varieties of experience and diversities of viewpoint among human beings do inevitably result in conflict. "It seems as if when two naked souls approach, or come anywhere near each other, the one inevitably burns or scorches the other. The whole process is by no means only joy, but agony also, even as childbirth is."[70]

It is this inevitability of suffering in connection with love that constitutes for Carpenter the essential meaning of the mystery of the atonement (God in Christ's death reconciling the world). In orthodox theology, sin often appears as purely factitious, even accidental. God did foresee it but never intended it. There is no necessity for it to have happened. The unintended corollary of this view is that salvation also becomes factitious, the cross itself thus appearing as a tragic accident. For Carpenter, working broadly in the Hegelian tradition, with its emphasis on absolute reason, evil is not a contingency. It necessarily arises in beings that have the contradictory need, first to assert their individuality, and then to overcome it through love. Love carries with it at least some suffering, and to the puny, self-centered human ego, love always comes as a kind of saving death. "The connection of Love with Birth is of course obvious. And the connection of Love with Death, though not so prominent, can similarly almost everywhere be traced. The whole of poetry in literature teems with this subject; and so does the poetry of nature!" Carpenter often alludes to the universal myth that in the male, each expenditure of semen—regarded as a man's vital essence—hastens his death. Although not biologically accurate, it suggests a deep spiritual meaning. "The expenditure of seed in the male animal is an incipient death; the formation of seed in the male animal is an incipient death, and the glory and color of the flowering plant, are already signs of its decay."[71]

This intimate, essential alliance between love and death means to Carpenter that any formation of new life necessarily means the death of the old self. In this sense, the child must die so that the adult may be born. The selfish ego—the Old Adam in traditional Christian parlance—that dies in the birth of love gives way to the risen Christ who brings life eternal. "Surely the world we know through our material bodies is not designed to encourage love; might we be destined to another world yet more 'personal' than the one we know?" On the principle that "it is the mind that sees and the mind that hears [that] the faculty of sight clearly does not reside in the cornea of the eye and [the ear] in itself is deaf," Carpenter was willing to consider the neo-Platonic notion of the astral body, also then being enthusiastically preached by Madam Blavatsky. "Nor is there any call to think of a bodiless heaven or bodiless state of being in any plane of existence. The external senses, of sight, hearing and the rest, are modifications of or limitations of more extended faculties with a finer range of sense."[72]

A central theme for Carpenter is that human sexuality exists more for spiritual regeneration than for biological reproduction. "Regeneration is the key to the meaning of love—to be in the first place born again in some one else or through some one else; in the second place only, to be born again through a child." But for Carpenter, spiritual regeneration implies rebirth into an undying life. Jesus said, "Whoever lives and believes in me shall never die" (John 11:26). As regards the possibility of life after death, love is the only real evidence for it, the only hint granted to mortals that we might be intended for something beyond this world. "Difficult as this conception of a continued individual existence after death may be to hold to in view of the terrible and eternal flux of general Nature yet, as I say, it is Love which compels us to the insight of its truth." Love has the clear conception of uniqueness of the beloved, "it is love which positively refuses to believe in [the beloved's] annihilation." Why? Because only love reveals the unique value of the individual. Every genuine experience of falling in love takes place in the timeless moment of eternity. "And it is in the meeting of lovers' eyes that the heavens open, allowing them to see—if only for a moment—the eternities to which they both belong."[73]

The heavens opening in the meeting of lovers' eyes is the meaning of the resurrection for Carpenter—not only of Christ but also of Osiris, Orpheus, Dionysus, and many others. To the collective unconscious, the Savior is necessarily the first fruits of those who sleep, the firstborn among many. Resurrection to eternal life through the experience of love is the central fact of humanity's life in this world. After all, death is a moral evil only insofar as it appears, to our limited experience, as a temporal defeat of the purposes of human love.

Thus, Carpenter believed that eternal life begins not at the moment of death but in the midst of life through the experience of love—or prayer. In these moments of exaltation, we already touch the eternal. It is truly astonishing to hear him talking matter-of-factly, and in the manner of the great mystics, about his almost daily contacts with the heavenly life. "I saw eternity the other night, all calm as it was bright, like a great ring of pure and endless light," wrote Henry Vaughan, the seventeenth-century Anglican divine. Similarly Carpenter advises his readers to overcome the fear of death by practicing the art of dying every day. With reference to Plato's *Phaedo* (where the practice of philosophy itself is described as a kind of death), Carpenter maintains that the art of dying can be practiced: "It is really possible to pass through Death on the mental plane, by voluntary effort." Even the simple experience of falling asleep is a kind of little death. "Most people regard the loss of ordinary consciousness (apart from sleep) with something like terror and horror. The best way to dispel that fear is to walk through the gate oneself every day—to divest oneself of that consciousness, and mentally speaking, to die from time to time."[74]

Carpenter alludes to the experience of union with the divine, which is the goal of all meditation. In such union, the ego does die and rises again to a larger life. "If you inhibit thought [through meditation] the ordinary mental self, with all its worries, cares, limitations, and so forth, falls completely off, and lies (for the time) like a thing dead; while the real [human being] practically passes onward into another state of being." The experience of the divine carries its own certainty with it: "So great, so splendid is this experience, that it may be said that all minor questions and doubts fall away in face of it."[75]

The Mystical Body of Christ

The experience of love shares with meditation or prayer the common effect of lifting the individual out of ordinary reality and placing him or her in touch with the real self. "The real self—conscious, logical, argumentative personality" drops away, and its petty preoccupation no longer cloud the soul's vision of reality. The center of the soul, for Carpenter as for Saint Teresa, is the throne-room of Christ. "The inner personal soul of [the human being] is surely already conjoined to the universal, and must cling to it by its very nature." The individual is usually not exactly conscious of this union. Like some magic spell, some thin film may yet divide one from the all-redeeming Presence; yet nonetheless, that Presence is there and is the core and center of one's being. Through meditation and sexuality, the soul "sprouts its wings," as Plato said. Suddenly, ancient myths and religious symbols take on a new reality and poignancy, but even these point beyond themselves. A person must die completely to the old Adam (or old Eve) in order to be born again in Christ.[76]

The significance of Christian initiation—the first of the two great sacraments of the Christian church—is Baptism into Christ. In ritual form, Baptism enacts the second birth of the soul to the depths of reality which lie within itself. Carpenter took great care to explain to his readers what most educated people now take for granted—namely, that the Christian rite of Baptism has a long pre-history, both within Judaism and outside it. Symbolic cleansing, lustration, and bathing formed an important part of almost all of the religions of the ancient world—and for reasons that are not difficult to see. "Our Baptismal and Confirmation ceremonies clearly correspond to the ancient ceremonies of Initiation, which are, or have been observed in almost every primitive tribe over the world." An initiate is one who enters in. The initiate enters into the tribe as well as the revelation of certain mysteries. The initiate becomes a member of a new society—the church of Mithra or Dionysus or Christ. "To do any of these things, he [or she] must be born again, and . . . must pass through ceremonials which symbolize the change. One of the ceremonials is washing. As the new-born babe is washed, so must the new-born initiate be washed."[77]

The sacrament of Holy Communion only extends this notion of the new or shared life first begun with Baptism. Carpenter explains this sacrament in much the same terms as he explains Baptism. The idea of sacred communion with a divine saving victim is an ancient one in human history. He cites, with interest and respect, examples of quasi-philosophical cults and mystery religions in the ancient world that practiced such communions. Orphic congregations solemnly partook of the blood of a bull, which was by a mystery the blood of Dionysus himself, the bull of God, slain in sacrifice for the purification of humanity. The Egyptian mysteries were still older. "The old Egyptians celebrated the resurrection of Osiris by a sacrament, eating the sacred cake after it had been consecrated by a priest, and thereby becoming veritable flesh of his flesh."[78]

Carpenter does not regard these parallels with primitive religion as in any way disparaging, still less disproving the truth of Christian sacraments. Quite the contrary. The fact that the Christian rituals of Baptism and Holy Communion are only variations of rituals far more ancient and more universal establishes even more firmly their timeless value and their spiritual necessity. As Freud once observed, the whole of the ancient world yearned for salvation and spiritual healing. "Who then was this 'Christos' for whom the world was waiting three centuries before our era (and indeed centuries before that)?" Carpenter asked. "Who was this thrice Savior whom the Greek Gnostics acclaimed?" In the world of the ancient Hebrews, the dream of salvation expressed itself as the myth of the Messiah. "What was the meaning of that 'coming of the Son of Man' whom Daniel beheld in a vision among the clouds of heaven? or the perfect man who, Paul declared, should deliver us from the bondage of corruption into the glorious liberty of the children of God?" For Carpenter, ancient and Hebrew dreams of deliverance have the same meaning. "It is the blossoming indeed of this new life in the deeps of our mind which is salvation." It is this presence which down through history has been hailed as Savior and Liberator: "The experience of salvation means, the daybreak of a consciousness so much vaster, so much more glorious, than all that has gone before that the little candle of the local self is swallowed up in its rays."[79]

The search for the historical Jesus was already well under way by the time Carpenter came to maturity. The question interested him only casually because he did not attach to it the importance that it had in the eyes of most of his contemporaries. Matthew Arnold captured the sentiments of many. "Our religion has attached its emotions to the fact [of Jesus' historical ministry including miracles and healings], and now the fact is failing it." Carpenter concedes that the facts of the four Gospels are, at best, historically doubtful and probably in large part legend. For Carpenter, however, such doubts about the historical accuracy of the Bible have little or no religious significance. Whatever the real facts of Jesus' career, he became the vehicle for a divine henad, a revelation in human terms of a divine idea. Carpenter would have said that, wittingly or unwittingly, Jesus manifested both for his own time and for eternity the henad of the divine mercy.[80]

Even so, in spite of Carpenter's heterodoxy, he was surprisingly pastoral. "There is no doubt that after the destruction of Jerusalem [in c.e. 70], little groups of believers in a redeeming Christ were formed there and in other places," Carpenter said. These groups in many respects resembled other cults of the period, satisfying the spiritual hunger of the age. Just as there had certainly existed in the first century b.c.e., groups of Gnostics, Therapeutae, Essences, and others whose teachings were similar to the Christians, so "the early church soon discovered a need to record in writing its beliefs about the Savior." Carpenter acknowledge the historical need for such writings, but reserved judgment as to their veracity. "Just how far these accounts of Jesus of Nazareth are reliable history is a question which is a difficult one for skilled critics to answer, and one on which I certainly have no intention of giving a positive verdict." Indeed, Carpenter stated that he rather preferred the mythic interpretation of the Gospels to historical literalism. "Personally I must say that I think the 'legendary' solution in some ways more satisfactory than the opposite one." Carpenter had more faith in the redeeming Christ within than in the historical Jesus. "It seems much more encouraging to suppose that the story of Jesus is a legend which gradually formed itself in the conscience of [hu]mankind, and thus points the way to humanity's future evolution."[81]

Rudolf Bultmann's call for demythologizing the Gospels would come later. Rather, Carpenter is simply following the example of Anna Kingsford by appealing to the centuries-old insight of mystics such as the Germans John Tauler and Meister Eckhart. The true incarnation of Christ does not take place in "the external world in which the [Savior] ate and drank with us, but . . . it applies to the inner world in the most inward part of the spirit." The early Quakers echoed this idea when they wrote that it is not the "carnal Christ that died at Jerusalem" who saves us, "but the Christ within, who is the hope of glory." Yet, the Quaker mystics did not understand this Christ within as a mere metaphor for some entirely human ability or idea: "We understand not this divine principle to be any part of [human] nature for we certainly know that this inner light is not only distinct, but of a different nature from the [human] soul . . . and its faculties." Neither did Carpenter understand the Christ principle as mere metaphor. Christ is a supernatural power manifesting itself within human nature and thus making possible a new type of saved humanity. Anna Kingsford had written that "the falsification generally, has consisted in removing the character described under the name of Jesus, from its true function as the portrait of that of which every [person has] the potentiality."[82]

Carpenter also saw in the advent of true Christianity the real promise of a new type of human being, of a new way for ordinary people to live together. Christianity brought into the world "an unprecedented sense of humanity." The appearance of Christianity on the scene signaled a new era in the history of the West. "There was growing, in the races which gathered round Imperial Rome a new plexus among the nerves of Humanity. A wider sense of humanity was growing up. Hospitals, orphan schools, for animals even, began to be founded. It was a great step forward in the evolution of the human spirit." A new type of human being demanded new gods. Carpenter attached much importance to the humble origins of most of the early Christians. "Men and women whose hearts began to respond to the power of gentleness, who, as slaves and the descendants of slaves, knew well what it was to be despised and rejected, began to see the glamour of figures of a different complexion from those who had dominated their predecessors."[83]

The social gospel of F. D. Maurice may have colored Carpenter's historical vision in this description of ante-Nicene Christianity. But interestingly, Carpenter saw the same forces at work in shaping the cult of Marianism at a somewhat later period in church history. "The Madonna links very closely to Isis, Demeter, Ceres—the virgin, yet ever fertile goddesses of the elder world; yet her motherhood has more of human feeling in it and less of Nature-symbolism than theirs." Carpenter really believed that Marianism has a positive message for modern feminists. "Her worship marks perhaps a growth of filial worship and respect for Woman." Like some modern feminists such as Maralyn French and Mary Gordon, Carpenter saw in the Jesus of the Gospels the real promise of rebellion against the values of patriarchy. Jesus and Mary represent the culmination of an ancient tendency in human religion—they are the supreme expression of the myth of the suffering Savior and the great Mother. They are also the promise of a new spirit of humanitarianism.[84]

The Divorce between Christ and Christ's Church

The main question remains for Carpenter, as for most feminists: What went wrong? Why did Christianity fail so drastically to fulfill this promise? It was not just the usual catalog of horrors from church history that distressed Carpenter—the crusades, inquisitions, pogroms, witch-hunts, book-burnings, the woman-hating, the heresy-hunting, the Jew-baiting, and so on. He felt real astonishment at what looked like the systematic opposition of the institutional church to every stirring of the authentic spirit of gospel Christianity. Its official theology, its moral code, its hierarchy, its organizational procedures, its code of morality—they all seemed in flagrant contradiction to the whole spirit of Christ and at a fundamental level. Carpenter detected a certain bloodlessness in much Christian theology after the apostolic period. "Its Scheme of Salvation through Christ takes on the character of a rather sordid and huckstering bargain by which man gets the better of God by persuading the latter to sacrifice his firstborn son for the redemption of the world!" Every period of church history had moments of authenticity. "There were the noble brotherhoods and sisterhoods of Friars and Nuns, dedicated to the help and healing of suffering humanity (and these manifestations can hardly be claimed by the Church, which pretty consistently opposed them)." But on the whole, he thought that after about the fourth century, the real spirit and light of early Christian inspiration had died away.[85]

Most painful of all the church's sins, and most inexplicable, was its hatred of sexuality. This, Carpenter felt sure, lay at the root of all its other outrages. The Gospels—perhaps more emphatically than any other document in the history of religion—placed love at the center of the religious life. The whole Jesus story is predicated on love. "Greater love hath no man than this, that he lay down his life for his friends" (John 15:13). Based on such texts, one might have assumed that the church would have encouraged the love between men even more passionately than had Plato. The truth is that the church had done as much to spread homophobia as any other force in history. What is there in the gospel story that explains or justifies this sort of hate?

Mainstream Christian mysticism is based on the gospel metaphor for Christ as the bridegroom of souls. This bridal mysticism, borrowing its imagery from the biblical Song of Solomon, often uses strongly erotic language. Famous mystical writings, such as *Spiritual Canticle* by John of the Cross or *The Divine Espousals* by Saint Gertrude echo this same imagery. Based on such texts, one might infer that the church had sanctioned some form of the sacred sexuality that had been so routine a part of the mystery religions of the ancient world. Instead, one finds the opposite. In the words of one historian of the subject, "their erotic mysticism seldom moved beyond the theological and emotional level." This is a serious understatement.[86]

What the Christian love mystics taught was that the divine eroticism presumed a total renunciation of the human. In the church's view, sacred and profane love are not on friendly terms, but are mortal enemies. So great is this enmity, in fact, that any association of sexuality with Christian religious symbolism seems grossly sacrilegious. In the ancient world, the separation of the sacred and the sexual would have seemed equally astonishing. "The Pagan cults generally made a great deal of all sorts of sex-rites, laid much stress upon them, and introduced them in what we consider an unblushing and shameless way." After Emperor Constance's reformation of the church in the fourth century, however, orthodoxy formally embraced asceticism. "The Christian Church took quite the opposite line—ignored sex, condemned it, and did much to despise the perfectly natural instincts connected with it."[87]

Carpenter felt sure that, in this respect, orthodoxy betrayed the spirit of Christ. "I say 'the Christian Church' because there is nothing to show that Jesus himself (if we admit his figure as historical) adopted any such extreme and doctrinaire attitude." The early church was diverse, and even had room for sexual, not to say homosexual, mysticism. "In fact, as is well known, strong currents of pagan usage and belief ran through the Christian assemblies of the first three or four centuries. The followers of Jesus were at times accused of celebrating sexual mysteries at their love feasts."[88]

Today, the evidence is stronger than ever that Carpenter was correct in believing that the rituals of sacred sexuality had an important place in the life of the early church—either in spite of the influence of Paul or over his objections. Second-century texts, or fragments of texts, have actually been found that portray Jesus as the ideal homosexual lover, who is best understood and worshiped by male lovers. Much Christian symbolism clearly reflects this type of Christian spirituality. Consider, for example, the symbol of the cross. Christ is only one of many savior figures who died on a tree, and the tree is always a symbol of life. In the case of Dionysus and Adonis, the pine tree is specifically involved, and the pine cone fastened at the tip of a pole becomes the symbol of their life-giving death. As shocking as it seems to Christian sensibilities, the cross as a religious symbol has phallic overtones. "The well known T-shaped cross was in use in Pagan lands long before Christianity, as a representation of the male member, and also at the same time of the tree on which the god (Attis or Adonis or whoever it might be) was crucified." To the ancients, it did not seem blasphemous to suggest that the Child of God might have died on a symbol of life and love; it seemed inevitable because to deny this would be to divorce Christ from Christ's church.[89]

SACRED SEXUALITY AND CHRISTIAN HUMANISM

The notion of sacred sexuality is undergirds Christian religious symbols. Carpenter believed that the loss of this notion was significant because, without it, the Christian psyche is divided, pitting one's spiritual yearnings against one's emotional needs and physical well-being. "This corruption of Sex led (quite naturally) to its denial and its denial led to the differentiation of it from Love." And love that denies sexuality can kill the spirit. "Love relegated to heaven as a purely spiritual affair, became exceedingly dull; and sex, remaining on earth, but deserted by the redeeming presence fell into the wretchedness of unclean living."[90]

Carpenter agonized over this strange divorce between Christ and the church. On the whole, he followed Hegel in understanding ascetic Christianity as the painful adolescence of the human spirit. Its rise coincided roughly with this breakup of the old unity of the spirit characteristic of classical cultures. Humankind, he said, "haunted by the sense of loneliness and the sense of guilt associated with [its] new-found sense of individual separateness, needed a religion that would stress individual salvation in another world." The result was a cultivation of a purely spiritual love—"a morality whose inspiration was a private sense of duty to God rather than a public sense of duty to one's neighbor and to society generally." This insistence on the importance of the individual at the expense of the community only increased over time, resulting in alienation from nature and the body. Carpenter believed, with Max Weber, that "Capitalist economics exploited Protestant individualism and vice versa. Religion, and Morality too, under the commercial regime became, as was natural, perfectly selfish."[91]

With characteristic Victorian optimism, Carpenter believed that this spiritual adolescence of the human race would come to an end in his own lifetime. The "unhappy consciousness" (Hegel's term) had plumbed its own depths, and history was about to turn a corner. Carpenter did not doubt this, but he had his own ideas about what this new age might be like. What he most wanted to see was a religious revival, an honest rediscovery of the sense of humanity introduced by Jesus, but with an open sense of the sacredness of sexuality that was only implicit in the Gospels. The new Christian humanism would be a Hegelian synthesis of all that was best in ancient and medieval civilizations.

Carpenter's own religious writings were an attempt at promoting such a synthesis. Carpenter even toyed with the idea of founding his own church. For him, any movement for liberation of love between men would, almost by definition, have to be a religious movement. In any case, Carpenter took an intense interest in the study of liturgy, in its ancient as well as its modern variations, its Christian as well as non-Christian forms. He never made an attempt to create rituals of his own. The rituals of the churches best known to him struck him as hopelessly empty, whether of the "mawkish milk-and-watery" Protestant variety or of the ceremonious high Anglican and Roman Catholic variety, with "its genuflexions and mock oblations and droning ritual sing song."[92]

In contrast, Carpenter read with deep appreciation the liturgical writings of Father Alfred Loisy, the eminent French biblical scholar whose efforts to harmonize historical criticism of the Bible with Catholic doctrine earned him the respect of Pope Leo XIII and excommunication by Pope Pius X. "In this direction [understanding liturgy], M. Loisy has done noble and excellent work; but the dead weight and selfish blinkerdom of the Catholic organization has hampered him to that degree that he has been unable to get justice done to his liberalizing designs."[93]

Loisy did influence Carpenter to witness an Easter vigil service in Seville that made a great impression on him. "In Spain, some ancient Catholic ceremonials are kept up with a brilliance and splendor hardly found elsewhere in Europe," Loisy told him. The resurrection service really impressed Carpenter. "In the Cathedral at Seville the service of the Passion, carried out on Good Friday with great solemnity and accompanied with fine music, culminates on the Saturday morning—i.e. in the interval between the Crucifixion and the Resurrection." Carpenter had learned that traditional Spanish liturgy also included sacred dancing. "There is also held at Seville Cathedral and before the High Altar every year, the curious 'Dance of the Seises' (sixes), performed now by sixteen instead of (as of old) by twelve boys, quaintly dressed." Carpenter saw astrological elements in the dance. "It seems to be a survival of some ancient ritual, probably astronomical, in which the two sets of six represent the signs of the Zodiac."[94]

Carpenter's good friend Annie Besant, in cooperation with her (homosexual) companion Charles Leadbeater, put a great deal of effort into designing a liturgy for the Theosophical Society. A creative blend of esoteric Masonic ritual with high-church Anglican ceremonial, Besant's liturgy—for which she built chapels around the world—aroused great dissension among theosophists. Even today, the society is divided over this issue.[95]

Perhaps it was these dissensions that dissuaded Carpenter from making efforts in liturgical or new-church creation. Or perhaps he felt that his ideas were too radical for his time; they certainly would have included ritual expressions of love between men. What he said was that a more important challenge than liturgy was the building of community. Sacred sex would remain largely an impossibility so long as the world remained so divided by race and class. While the ethic of universal competition remained in force, religion would have to remain something of an illusion, a "talking always of altruism and self-sacrifice while in reality one's heart is entirely occupied with the question of one's own salvation." In any case, a new religion—even when designed by so large-hearted and original a thinker as Annie Besant—would only be one more church among many others. As Camus had said, "So many churches, so much loneliness."[96]

chapter five

GAY SUFFERING AND THE PROMISE OF IMMORTALITY

Poem CXX, from *In Memoriam to Arthur Henry Hallam*

Thy voice is on the rolling air;
    I hear thee where the waters run:
    Thou standest in the rising sun,
And in the setting thou art fair.

What art thou then? I cannot guess;
    But though I seem in star and flower
    To feel thee some diffusive power,
I do not therefore love thee less:

My love involves the love before;
    My love is vaster passion now;
    Though mixed with God and Nature thou,
I seem to love thee more and more.

Far off thou art, but ever nigh
    I have thee still, and I rejoice;
    I prosper, circled with thy voice;
I shall not lose thee though I die.

—Alfred, Lord Tennyson (1809-1892)

"If what my soul doth feel sometimes, My soul might ever feel," wrote George Herbert, the seventeenth-century Anglican poet and theologian. As every serious Christian knows mystical "highs" are only a part of the spiritual life. The most exalted of visionaries must return to the problems and the struggle of everyday life. For many modern readers, Carpenter's erotic mysticism will seem wildly visionary, a trip to Herbert's fortieth heaven. For Plato, the love of one man for another may have opened heaven's gate and disclosed "a vision of wondrous beauty, a beauty absolute, separate, simple, and everlasting," just as Dante saw the "Beatific Vision" reflected in the eyes of Beatrice. But what has all that to do with the pick-up bar on the corner, where loneliness and paranoia and anonymous sex are the norm? What has it to do with the church where (in many so-called Christian denominations) AIDS is preached as a divine visitation and families are praised for disowning gay children?

Carpenter was a nineteenth-century optimist. But unlike his famous mentor, Walt Whitman, Carpenter did have a profound sense of sin—and his own version of the doctrine of the cross. He knew well that in a sinful world, love often means the cross. Few people know more about the human capacity for cruelty than gay men. Carpenter understood what it means to be the object of unreasoning, unrelenting hate; he often wrote about it. "Are you laughed at? Do they gaze at you and smile to each other as you pass by? Do they despise you because you are peculiar—and you know it's true? Does no one think of you except with contempt?" Carpenter asked, remembering his own bitter experience. "Have you sinned? Are you tormented with clutching lusts which you dare not speak? Are you nearly mad with the sting of them, and nearly mad with terror lest they should betray you?"[1]

Carpenter liked to say that "a man who loves unsuccessfully knows himself to be a god"—that is, he knows the suffering of love. When the object of one's love betrays that love, one realizes that love needs to become its own object, its own justification. To search for a perfect love is to search for the perfect lover. Whether we know it or not, this means the search for God, the one Being entirely worthy of our love. Thomas Traherne wrote, "Love is deeper than at first it can be thought. It never ceaseth but in Endless Things."[2]

As a theologian, Carpenter is less concerned to explain (or explain away) the cross—the innocent sufferings of Jesus, understood as a gay man, than to taste deeply of the grief and the glory which it represents. The gratuitous evil of human nature constitutes a kind of inexorable surd in a philosophy that aspires to complete rationality. It can be encountered but not rationally explained or rationally justified. The cross, however, is God's answer to the puzzle. If humanity could be truly happy in this world, truly at home here, then the cross would be the worst tragedy imaginable. It would mean that we are much less than we imagine ourselves to be. Traherne wrote that it is the nobility of the human soul that persons are "Insatiable. . . . You must want like a God, that you may be satisfied like a God."[3]

For Carpenter, the doctrine of the cross means that human suffering is the seal of a divine promise. In trying to understand the intensity of the hatred of gay love, he was, at the same time, exploring the depths of the promise entailed by that suffering and love.

THE DEFEAT OF LOVE

Most of the young people involved in the Stonewall riots were keenly optimistic about the future. At that time, we were a generation of visionaries. We saw the age of Aquarius dawning in our lifetimes, and we knew that the future would not repeat the mistakes of the past. We were building a new civilization, and we would settle for nothing less that the complete victory of revolutionary love. We quoted Plato's maxim with total confidence: "An army of lovers cannot be defeated."

For those of us who lived through those first exciting days of gay liberation, the events of the last quarter-century have come as a sobering experience. We thought we could change the world, but now many of us wonder what, if anything, has changed. Can any of us really expect a better life because of what the gay liberation movement has accomplished? To be sure, the conspiracy of silence surrounding homosexuality has been broken, but sensational publicity does not necessarily promote human understanding among ordinary people.

Gay Liberation and Cultural Paradoxes

Has it really become any easier in the last quarter-century for men to care for one another than it used to be? Does a teenager confused about his identity find it any easier to reach out to friends or teachers? Is he or she apt to get better advice or more acceptance?

Are male friendships more supportive and enduring than they once were? Are females—sisters, girlfriends, wives, and mothers—better prepared to talk openly with the men in their lives about the true nature of their feelings? Such questions are not easily answered.

Chapter 1 analyzed contemporary American attitudes toward homosexuality in terms of four paradoxes. These same paradoxes might make convenient tools for evaluating the comparative strengths and weaknesses of the current gay movement. First, many Christian churches preach universal love but then confine it to the home and make it "women's work." Second, American democracy is theoretically based on brotherhood/sisterhood but actually promotes ruthless competition. Third, the sports industry purports to teach team spirit and fair play but actually glorifies superstars and emphasizes winning by any means. Fourth, the U.S. Constitution recognizes the full equality of women and others, yet white males still define manhood as the capacity for violence, domination, and control. Has gay liberation helped in any meaningful way to resolve—or even relieve—these paradoxes?

Two Recent Political Developments

A strong case could be made that the efforts of gay liberation may only have aggravated these four paradoxes. Consider, for example, two important recent political developments that ostensibly promote the liberty and well-being of gay people. The gay movement has claimed both as victories for revolutionary love, yet both victories have come to look much like defeats.

The first is President Clinton's 1993 executive order to eliminate the fifty-year-old ban on homosexuals in the military. "During the Reagan presidency, and on his direct orders, the military spent as much as $500 million dollars trying to identify homosexuals in the armed forces, and it discharged more than 16,000 people on charges of homosexuality." When Clinton condemned this policy as an insane waste of taxpayers' money, he faced with a full-scale revolt of his generals against their commander-in-chief. Joint Chiefs of Staff chairman General Colin Powell described himself as having an almost mystical love for the armed forces and denounced the president's order specifically for humanitarian reasons. "You've got to see our armed force as a human living organism," Powell declared, adding, "I care about structure. I care about doctrine. I care about all the papers that come out of think tanks telling me what to do. But what really counts . . . is the quality of the force." It bothered him, Powell contended, that men and women in the armed services were never asked their opinions of having homosexuals in their ranks—implying that the army should be run as a democracy.[4]

Apparently Powell believes that prejudice and paranoia are their own justification. He reasons that because the average soldier (or sailor or marine) does not like or trust gay people, gay people should be uncovered and expelled from the military. (Thankfully, a similar form of bigotry—namely, white soldiers resenting blacks because whites do not like or trust them—has actively been opposed since World War II.) "The presence of homosexuals adversely affects the ability of the Military Services to maintain discipline, good order and morals; to foster mutual trust and confidence among servicemembers . . . who frequently must live and work under close conditions affording minimal privacy," Powell said. Thus, the general illustrates another cultural paradox. Male bonding is indispensable to the successful functioning of an armed force, and homosexuals, he maintains, undermine such bonding because they cannot love their fellow men.[5]

Fittingly, the president and his generals resolved this absurd conflict in an equally absurd compromise: "Don't ask, don't tell." The immediate result, however, was a dramatic increase in the number of men discharged from the military on charges of homosexuality. Gay-bashing also increased dramatically among servicemen. The sensational murder of an inoffensive sailor was most shocking. He was beaten beyond recognition for having made the mistake of admitting to friends that his homosexual tendencies worried him.[6]

The Supreme Court 1996 decision in *Romer v. Evans* has been touted as a significant step toward the toleration of homosexual people. One lawyer for the Lambda Legal Defense and Education fund, Suzanne Goldberg, described the decision as "the most important victory ever for lesbian and gay rights."[7] In fact, the Supreme Court specifically denied that its decision gave any legal protection to homosexual behavior as such, and the justices deliberately avoided commenting on the status of the antiquated sodomy laws still enforced in many states.

What the court did was strike down a provision of the Colorado State Constitution that not only nullified existing civil rights protections for homosexuals in the state but also barred the passage of any new antidiscrimination laws at any time in the future. The justices objected as much to the clumsy wording of the Colorado law as to its substance. "A state cannot so deem a class of persons a stranger to its laws," Justice Anthony M. Kennedy said, complaining that such a sweeping denial of human rights to any group of people was inexplicable on any other basis than animus. "It is not in our tradition to enact laws of this sort," Kennedy argued.[8]

Although the Justice claims to have no animus against gay people, he makes it clear that his ruling does not provide any affirmative rights for them, and it does not require states to offer any new civil-rights protections. The Court simply affirmed that even so-called sexual outlaws have civil rights (even criminals are entitled to some legal protection). At the same time, Justice William H. Rehnquist warned of the insidious *Kulturkampf* of homosexuals who plot the "piecemeal deterioration of the sexual morality favored by a majority." He asked that states take carefully aimed measures to protect themselves against this without violating federally guaranteed civil rights.[9]

Sports Icons in Popular Culture

The ambivalence of the men who rule America is clearly reflected in the ambivalence of popular culture. Consider, for example, the fate of two sports icons who have made headlines in the last few years. One is the notorious bad boy of the NBA, Dennis Rodman, who knows how to promote his own personality more effectively than any athlete since Muhammad Ali. But unlike Ali, Rodman is no gentleman. He makes a point of violating every rule of fair play and good taste, even flaunting his penchant for cross-dressing and casual homosexuality. The other is Mr. Universe 1983, Bob Paris— until recently very much the golden boy of the International Federation of Body Builders (IFBB). Fans and promoters loved Paris until he shocked everyone by publicly marrying his male lover at a formal church service. The different careers of the two men illustrate perfectly how contradictory public attitudes toward homosexuality have become.

In many ways, Bob Paris is Dennis Rodman's polar opposite. Looking every inch the ex–Eagle Scout and ex-marine that he is, Paris has the kind of open-faced, all-American appeal often associated with midwesterners. He speaks with the boyish charm of Jimmy Stewart and moves with the gentle masculinity of Mickey Mantle. In fact, Paris did grow up in rural Indiana, and he radiates small-town family values and grassroots Protestant piety. And in most respects, Paris does have traditional values. He finds casual sexual adventures distasteful and believes strongly in fidelity. Paris remembers that even as a young man newly arrived in southern California, "my romantic ideal was someone who was as concerned as I was about political and social injustices in the world, who had a high level of compassion, who could keep up intellectually, and who was athletic." As an athlete, Paris neither drinks nor smokes, and he is one of the few professional bodybuilders who do not abuse steroids. "I hated the direction bodybuilding was headed in," Paris wrote, commenting on the high mortality rate among professional competitors in recent years due to serious drug abuse. "I saw bodybuilding as a road toward the perfect physical specimen." He expressed sincere regret that "the dominant culture of the sport for the last ten years has been grotesque freakiness for the sake of freakiness."[10]

Paris feels very strongly about the integrity of his sport. "It is misunderstood, under-appreciated, corrupted by petty greed, and considered to be the realm of freaks," Paris concedes, "but it is also beautiful and can be graceful and thrilling and lifted high above the dull thud of conformity." Bodybuilding, he contends, enabled him to bring together opposite sides of his own personality, his athletic prowess and his artistic sensitivity: "I knew—with the sort of instinct that reveals itself only in rare moments—that I could have both. I could be the artist I'd always dreamed of being and I could . . . exert my physical presence in a way that would demonstrate to all the world that I was truly a man." Paris especially resents any comparison of his sport with "strip-tease" shows such as those of the Chippendale dancers. What he does is art, "not sleazy burlesque": "I believed that through athletic effort, I could build a work of art; I would carry that work around with me—I couldn't leave it in the studio, as a traditional artist might."[11]

"The fact that I was gay was no secret in bodybuilding circles," Paris recalls, but this was not a problem "because I was allowed to stay in the sport as long as my gayness wasn't made public. The fact I was gay was kept absolutely quiet." Other gay bodybuilders had no problem staying in the closet, so why should he? When Paris asked Arnold Schwarzenegger how best to promote himself with the fans, "he said that I should find a really attractive woman and go to all of the Hollywood parties and have our pictures taken together and get them in the newspaper."[12]

But deception did not come easily to Bob Paris. "I was miserable keeping secrets," he admits frankly. Moreover, he sincerely believed in the importance of good citizenship, in social concern and personal involvement: "Deep down I thought I had a responsibility to change the world and maybe could use my position as a successful professional athlete to make a positive difference."[13] And when he fell in love, Paris felt a natural inclination to tell the world; secrecy was now out of the question: "I wanted to be married because in our culture that's the highest level of commitment we could make together." Nothing but a church wedding would do. "We wanted to be married in church, before God," he explains simply.[14]

Needless to say, the mass media had a field day. Sports journalists tended to dismiss bodybuilding itself as freakish; here was the biggest freak show of all. Bodybuilding enthusiasts themselves reacted with embarrassment and hostility. "Right after I came out, my appearance bookings dropped by seventy-five percent," Paris recalls sadly.[15] His training seminars and posing exhibitions had been among the most popular in the sport; suddenly no one would sponsor them. Judges began whispering audibly at meets that "they'd never let a queer win a contest."[16] In spite of his superb physical condition, he found that he could not even place in competition. Joe Weider, the leading impresario of bodybuilding contests around the country and publisher of the sport's leading periodicals, expressed himself in no uncertain terms. "I don't have any use for you anymore," he told Paris.[17] As far as the IFBB was concerned, Paris's career as a celebrity athlete had ended. They wanted him to disappear.

The career of Dennis Rodman makes an interesting counterpoint to that of Bob Paris. No country boy, Rodman grew up in the urban ghettos of South Dallas, a product of the housing projects and of abject poverty. Even as a very young child, he witnessed scenes of excruciating violence during race riots and gang wars. His father abandoned the family when Dennis was only three, and his mother threw her adolescent son out of the house because he had become unmanageable. At twenty, he was mopping floors and cleaning out restrooms on the graveyard shift at the Dallas–Fort Worth Airport. He lost that job when he was arrested and jailed for shoplifting.

Rodman freely admits that he considers himself an ugly man; he says he can barely stand to look at his own reflection in a mirror. In fact, he does not have conventional good looks, although he does have a personal magnetism which—now that he has become a celebrity—attracts a generous female following. In contrast, Rodman is almost certainly telling the truth when he says that during his days as a janitor and a drifter, he attracted few black women and no white women at all. Rodman likes to expatiate with journalists about his obsessive masturbation during those years: "I've had my share of lonely nights with Judy (my right hand) and Monique (my left hand)."[18]

He was, Rodman says, the original invisible man: "Life was a f—ing confusion plus a bunch of goddamn agony. You just hoped for some part-time happiness once in a while." Did the black church comfort Rodman in his despair or help him to find a sense of direction? "I have no purpose in life at all," he says. "I mean, we can always pray to the holy spirit to whisk us away and make everything better, but who knows if that prayer ever gets there? It's only a mirage."[19]

Throughout those empty years, Rodman found his only source of pure pleasure—and his only source of personal pride—on the basketball court. Years later, *Sports Illustrated* would say that he might be the best rebounder of all time. Quite accidentally, an assistant coach for Southeastern Oklahoma State University happened to see Rodman play in 1981 and decided that he had enormous potential. In 1986, Detroit Pistons coach Chuck Daly risked the twenty-seventh pick of the NBA draft on the unknown who became, at twenty-five, the oldest rookie in the league. During the next two seasons, Daly promoted Rodman into the starting lineup of the well-known Bad Boy Pistons. In the 1988–89 season, Rodman averaged 9.4 rebounds per game, and Detroit swept the Lakers and took their NBA title. "I knew I would have been just another nigger if I didn't play basketball," Rodman says of his feelings in the midst of these triumphs.[20]

Although Rodman owes his rescue from poverty and obscurity to professional basketball, he is quite cynical about the sport that has made him a superstar. To him, professional basketball is only "a cold-hearted business. . . . There is no loyalty, no commitment, no anything."[21] Most athletes are only in it for the money. "Paying players $90 million is ridiculous," Rodman laughs. "Even $30 million—think of the lifetimes people work to get that much money." Should athletes strive to perform as role models for the younger generation? "No," Rodman answers. "People think athletes and entertainers are role models for kids, but they're wrong. Kids today have more options than we ever had. . . . These kids are 15 years old, partying their asses off. Every day is Woodstock."[22]

Oddly enough, Rodman has made himself astonishingly popular with the fans by his displays of poor sportsmanship on the court, like shoving Scottie Pippen into the stands, leaving him with a vicious gash on his face and Rodman with a five-thousand-dollar fine. But the fans do not seem to mind this conduct or even his graphic boasting about his sexual exploits. They apparently even admire his ambition to top Wilt Chamberlain's record of having had sex with twenty thousand women. And they are not seriously disturbed by his wife's allegations that he beat her. Interestingly, fans evidently also enjoy Rodman's accounts of his adventures as a transvestite. He has appeared in public more than once wearing make-up and women's clothes, and he admits to dressing up as woman in private for sex thrills. "We all have a little homosexual in us," Rodman theorizes. "We pat each other on the ass. We kiss. I kiss transsexuals. If I think a guy is attractive, I can tell him, 'You are a beautiful motherf—er.' I'll hug him and kiss him." Does Rodman enjoy assuming the passive role in sex? "Giving it or getting it, taking or giving, don't matter," he answers. "It's all about getting what sensations you want."[23]

Why does white America find Dennis Rodman so fascinating and Bob Paris so unacceptable? Rodman thinks he knows why: "I give them a little thrill, all the people who forgot that life is fun.

It's like 'Phantom of the Opera.' It might scare them, but they like it."[24] On this point, Rodman almost certainly understands the psychology of the average fan better than all of the theologians, psychologists, and moralists who have pretended to explain the phenomenon of homosexuality. He knows that most men find the idea of homosexual adventures titillating, but they also need to classify them as evil. They covertly enjoy the fantasy of forbidden sexual experiences, but they dread appearing feminine, soft, or emotionally vulnerable.

Rodman skillfully manipulates these contradictory emotions to enhance his bad-boy image and keep himself firmly in the limelight: "It's all about self-confidence. . . . I can go out to a salon and have my nails painted pink, and then go out and play in the NBA on national television." He can be frank about his rationale for such pranks: "It gives me a psychological edge; now they're looking at me like they don't know what I'm going to do next."[25] In this context, even cross-dressing can become an act of aggression.

Rodman self-consciously intimidates people by acting out their own most secret fantasies: "Most people are afraid to let themselves go. They're afraid to take the chance because they might find out something about themselves they don't want to know. . . . I'm the kind of person who can do anything." Rodman boasts that his well-oiled publicity machine has turned his private life into a species of pornography for his fans: "That's what pornography is all about. . . . Why do you have sex magazines? So you can go out and buy it and beat off, and hope someday it happens to you. . . . Some people are just bolder about asking for it."[26]

As pornography, as aggression, as lawlessness, even as anarchy, homosexuality has become acceptable to most American men—acceptable and even enviable, perhaps. It's evil but it's fun. But when a clean-cut gentleman from the American heartland like Bob Paris asks us to believe that love between men is something holy—something entirely admirable and necessary to the building up of our human community—most men get angry. This is not what they wanted to hear. And what do our churches tell us about this? Do they help people to sort out these conflicted feelings? Do they try to make moral sense out of moral chaos?

John Boswell argued twenty years ago that homosexual promiscuity was different from heterosexual—qualitatively as well as quantitatively. Marital infidelity, frequent divorce, spousal abuse, and teenage pregnancy all represent lapses from heterosexuals' moral codes that have been well-documented and receive ample publicity. At least straights know what the moral standards are that they have violated. Homosexuals can hardly say the same. "I am extremely sensitive to the heterosexual majority on this point," Boswell writes. "I think their attitude comes rather from the following. They think they know what heterosexual ethics they fall short of. They don't understand what homosexual ethics might be or what ethical standards gay people fall short of. Do gay people plan to be regulated by the same moral norms that regulate straight people? Do they expect special privileges?"[27]

In fact, our churches have failed consistently to think creatively about the ethics of love between men. Instead, they have wasted their time in rehashing ancient theological arguments based on premises that few educated people today can accept. The Episcopal church, for example, has even put itself through the ridiculous spectacle of a heresy trial involving a much-loved elderly bishop and the young gay man whom he ordained. Often when the churches have agreed to work together, they have found common ground in their fears and hatreds. For example, Louis Farrakhan and the Southern Baptist Convention (who seldom agree about anything) both have denounced the Disney corporation as the enemy of family values because it provides benefits for the spouses of gay and lesbian employees. How can we get beyond such jeremiads, which only deepen confusion and perpetuate painful conflicts?

CRUSADERS AGAINST LOVE

The most ironic thing about homosexuality—a subject riddled with ironies—is the motivation of those who most militantly oppose it. If one had to make a list of America's most adamant homophobes in our time, then surely men like Francis Cardinal Spellman, Senator Joe McCarthy, Red-baiter Roy Cohn, and "G-man" J. Edgar Hoover would certainly head that list. In public, no one denounced the threat of the "lavender menace" more vehemently than they did; somehow they convinced the average citizen that "perverts" lurked under every bed and behind every bush.

Yet even in their lifetimes, rumors circulated that each of these men practiced homosexuality in private. After their deaths, the revelations began to pour out—revelations so outrageous that they might have been incredible if they were not so well evidenced. Thus, intimate associates confess that they saw bulldog Hoover dressed as a woman at drag parties, where he performed homosexual acts publicly and had himself photographed doing so. Joe McCarthy was entrapped into propositioning a young man in a Washington men's room. Roy Cohn died of AIDS. Many young men who once served Cardinal Spellman as altar boys now denounce him for trying to intimidate or bribe them into granting sexual favors.[28]

On the surface, such behavior can seem like little more than just old-fashioned hypocrisy. Something more complex may be at work here, however. If studied in the light of well-documented cases such as Jean Genet, then the psychology of a Hoover or a Cohn can look more complex. Thus, one biographer of Spellman calls him a rabid moralist: "He ranted against movies, plays, and films that treated sex even lightly, let alone those that exploited sexuality as a major theme." Spellman may genuinely have hated anything that even remotely savored of sexuality; he almost certainly despised homosexuality, especially his own. Men strongly committed to patriarchal values and motivated largely by the desire for power inevitably fear and deny their own human vulnerability, especially when it takes a form that they think of as unmanly or even feminine. Because they cannot repress that vulnerability, they hate it all the more. When Hoover ruined men's careers because they "walked funny" or wore flamboyant neckties, he may well have acted with a completely sincere conviction of his own righteousness. For without acknowledgment of compassion between men, such "friendly" competition is the incomplete and ruthless language for relationships.[29]

The Accidental Homosexual

Equally ingenious are the arguments such men can use to justify their own attitudes. They feel sure that the Bible is on their side, along with the laws of nature, reason, and common sense. Sartre said of this type of man that he "never thinks of himself when someone is branded in his presence with the name 'homosexual.'" True, his sexual tastes will draw him into secret contacts with such strange characters, but he somehow believes he can have sex with homosexuals without being himself a homosexual: "Elsewhere there is a category of comic, shady people whom he jokes about with 'straights,' namely the queers. He is the one who receives with horror the name homosexual. It is not one quality among others; it is a destiny, a peculiar flaw of his being."[30]

Nor is this kind of madness necessarily a thing of the past. Even today, a shy, introverted, intense young man like Timothy McVeigh—who apparently never really dated or had a girlfriend— feeds his paranoia with literature that blames rising crime rates, falling wages, and hard-core unemployment on "race mixing, homosexuality, political corruption, and other evils in Washington, D.C." McVeigh justified urban terrorism as an attempt to eradicate "the filthy creatures who are overruling America." At the other end of the social hierarchy, Supreme Court Justice Antonin Scalia, in his dissenting opinion to *Romer v. Evans*, frets that "those who engage in homosexual conduct . . . possess political power much greater than their numbers, both locally and statewide." Justice Rehnquist warns of an insidious *Kulturkampf* in which a degenerate elite with "enormous influence in media" plot the, "piecemeal deterioration of the sexual morality favored by a majority." In short, he seeks to stem "creeping perversion."[31]

Luminous Common Sense

By contrast with such theater-of-the-absurd, anyone who reads Carpenter attentively finds that most of his thinking (however outlandish some of his ideas might sound in the abstract or out of context) possesses a luminous common sense which renders it at least persuasive, and at best irresistible. Rather like the little boy in the well-known tale "The Emperor's New Clothes," he says aloud what has been in front of everyone's eyes all along. He is honest enough to recognize and courageous enough to denounce the hypocrisy so manifestly at the foundation of much of what now passes for Christian civilization.

"If our Gospel is veiled, it is veiled to those who are perishing," wrote Saint Paul (2 Cor. 4:3). Certainly Carpenter could echo those words and say with the apostle John, "I am writing you no new commandment but an old commandment that you have had from the beginning. Whoever loves his brother lives in the light, and there is no cause for stumbling" (1 John 2:7a, 10). One may ask where Carpenter draws his inspiration from, who he quotes as authorities to substantiate his positions; the answer is simple. Unlike some psychiatric advocates of tolerance for homosexuals active in the Germany of his time (or the America of our time), Carpenter never appeals to scientific research, cites case histories, or lists statistical tables. The names that come up again and again in his work are no more obscure than those of Socrates and Jesus—the foundational figures of Western culture.

The strange fact is that the homogenic experience—for all the ferocity of its long, drawn-out persecution—has always been at the heart of Western religious and ethical thought. Both Socrates and Jesus, each in his own distinctive way, validated the spiritual importance and meaning of love between men. In dialogues such as the *Symposium*, the *Phaedrus*, and the *Charmides*, Plato specifically demonstrated that love is an end in itself, that love between men can be a deeply spiritual experience, that there is nothing unnatural about this love, and that it can even serve as a kind of moral cement that helps to hold society together. This message, furthermore, is so obvious on the face of his work that it is nearly miraculous that the church allowed the dialogues to survive and that Christian philosophers have been able to read them for centuries while still failing to see the obvious import of Plato's words.

Jesus and the Love of Men

The homogenic message of the Gospels is certainly less apparent, but just as certainly it is there for anyone who does not actively refuse to see it. It is there, for example, in Jesus' sudden impulse of love for the rich young man who wanted to be perfect, in the copious tears he shed for Lazarus, in his special intimacy with John—as the editors of *The Men's Devotional Bible* discovered, rather in spite of themselves. But even more importantly, it is there in what feminists refer to as Jesus' rejection of patriarchy and in what Carpenter terms the "androgyny" of Jesus.

Carpenter is nowhere more shocking (or more obviously correct) than when he points out that the image of Jesus as represented in our churches, portrayed in our art galleries, and pictured in our homes is markedly androgynous. Nor is this a result of nineteenth-century sentimentality or Renaissance cryptopaganism. From the beginning, without knowing it, Christians have been worshiping a homosexual as the "perfect man." Yet Thomas F. Matthews contends, in his *The Clash of the Gods,* that no subject in history is more taboo than the sexuality of Jesus. "Christ in early Christian art often showed a decidedly feminine aspect which we overlook at our own risk. It is not unanswered but unasked questions that undermine discourse and lend an unbalanced slant to the entire field."[32]

For Matthews, the androgynous Christ is a problem for art history. For Carpenter, it was the key to an understanding of the inmost nature of the spiritual life. He felt that the higher self of every person—the self which, according to Plotinus, Eckhart, and Augustine, always remains "hid with Christ in God"—is beyond all distinctions of gender, as it is also beyond distinctions of race, class, occupation, and nationality. As Paul put it, "There is neither Jew nor Greek; there is neither slave nor free; there is neither male nor female; for you are all one in Christ Jesus" (Gal. 3:28). As the perfect man, Christ incarnates that dimension of humanity that transcends the artificial distinctions and hierarchical structures which are so important here below and which cause so much pointless suffering.

For Carpenter, this is not a theological detail that lacks potential for application. The recognition of the androgyny of Christ is, for him, the key to transforming society—and not just for the homogenic minority. What Carpenter wants is moral transformation from within, a return to the spiritual Source. For him, to acknowledge the sexuality of Christ fully means a rediscovery of the sacredness of human sexuality. And that is, in itself, potentially a new way of looking at human relatedness.

Well-known sexologist Marina Raye suggests in a recent interview what the full implications of sacred sexuality are: "We must heal our sexual woundedness and find sexual peace, both individually and as a society. This healing work is a prerequisite to facing the challenges of rebuilding our lives and the planet we have come close to destroying." For Raye, sexual puritanism, with its excessive emphasis on self-control, only reflects patriarchal values and male dominance. If we can free ourselves from our guilt-ridden past, we will be able to direct our sexual energy in creative ways. For Raye, sexual freedom does not mean simple hedonism: "What we need in society are more opportunities to recognize that sexuality is sacred. People want to know how to reinvent sexuality."[33]

THE TRAGIC FACE OF LOVE

The 1994 study *Created Equal: Why Gay Rights Matter in America* purports to be a new manifesto for the gay liberation movement in the twenty-fifth anniversary year of the Stonewall riots. Its authors follow the familiar gay liberation party line and define gay rights as a libertarian movement focusing on the private freedoms of the individual. "The key contribution of the gay and lesbian movement to the history of civil rights and civil liberties is a re-emphasis on the individual," they write. They do not believe that there is or can be a gay community. "There is no reason to believe that the millions of lesbians and gay men in fact share connections. The deepest source for sharing arise from a common oppression."[34]

Edward Carpenter would have found it ironic—as would Marina Raye—that members of a minority defined by its sexuality would share no connection except fear. Apparently sexuality is not a force which connects people or brings them together. Apparently sexuality is an entirely selfish appetite, to be gratified privately (preferably with pornography as a partner?) and without affecting other human beings—whether negatively or positively. And yet Milton described sex as "the source of all the charities," the ultimate source of every form of love, whether between husband and wife, parent and child, or brother and sister. Or is it only sexual contact between men that is so entirely separated from love, which divides men rather than brings them together?[35]

Certainly anyone who accepts this kind of thinking should logically accept the inevitability of homosexual promiscuity, for if love cannot hold people together, what can? The twin curses of promiscuity, however, are loneliness and disease. And to the extent that promiscuity has helped create the AIDS pandemic, you could say that gay men are dying from hate as much as from a virus. According to the law described by Ralph Waldo Emerson in his essay "Compensation," which Carpenter loved, every material hardship in life brings with it an opportunity for spiritual enrichment. The suffering caused by, say, AIDS is difficult to calculate, difficult even to think of seriously, but it does seem to have brought with it its own peculiar forms of spiritual blessing. Sherwin Nuland, in *How We Die: Reflections on Life's Final Chapter*, writes that "it is impossible to observe homosexual AIDS patients without being struck by the way a circle of friends, not necessarily all gay, will almost predictably come together as a man's family and assume responsibility for what a wife or parents might otherwise do." He has called this phenomenon "the caring surround," which he also calls "a communal act of love."[36]

Even for most gay men, it came as something of a surprise that such caring existed in the gay community. When AIDS becomes a fact of life, all talk of individual rights and civil liberties and private freedoms tend to seem irrelevant. Suddenly only the fact of suffering and compassion for those who suffer is present. One of the ironies of gay life is that the specter of death seems necessary in order to end all of the arguments about the nature of gay community or about whether or not such a thing exists or can exist. One gay young man explained this to Nuland: "In many cases, the traditional family has rejected us. So the affinitive family is much more important."[37]

"The affinitive family," "the caregiving surround," "communal love"—such terms dropped from the rhetoric of gay liberation a long time ago. It took an epidemic to bring them back with an unparalleled force. And yet, over a century ago, Edward Carpenter was writing about love between men in precisely such terms.

For all his idealism and optimism, Carpenter could be much the hard-headed realist when it came to facing the tragic aspects of love between men in the modern world. Subject to long episodes of depression, Carpenter knew what it meant to be tormented by the thought of dying alone, the horror of facing the desolate end of a seemingly empty and wasted life. "The dread inexorable past, the nothing left to live for, death coming slow, with pain and foul disease."[38] "It's not a gentle world," John Rechy once wrote of the gay subculture, and especially not so for the sick and dying. "You entered it alone—and you're still alone, and so did I, and so am I, and so did he, and all the others now and forever, alone."

Carpenter understood only too well the disgust with life that makes death seem desirable. He clearly understood that the forces acting to obstruct and destroy the possibility of love between men were formidable indeed, and that for many, only death can liberate one from fear of such love and from the loneliness which this fear creates. Carpenter does not speak metaphorically when he writes that the soul "forsakes this world and seeks a fairer one."

There was nothing fanciful or indefinite about his belief that love between men brings with it the promise of life after death. "Some deep and profound suggestion there is in all this beauty, some hint of a life whose very form and nature is love." This life finds its deliverance and nativity only through the abandonment of the body— "even as our ordinary life, conceived in love, finds its delivery into this world through what we call birth."[39]

THE DRAMA OF LOVE AND DEATH

For those who cannot quite rise above the feeling that death may be the final no to every human hope, Carpenter recalls how "the iris-veil of our ordinary existence [was] truly rent" at the time of our first awakening to sexual experience as a passion of the heart. Especially for men destined to love their fellow men most passionately, we really did die to our old selves through our first experience of desire—but only to be reborn into an entirely unanticipated and, ultimately, much larger and richer life. So it will be again with the actual dissolution of the physical body at its biological death. Love will already have taught us that the visible world, the world we know, is "no longer now a film on the surface of an empty bubble, but a curtain concealing a vast and teeming life, reaching down endless, in layer on layer, into the very heart of the universe."[40]

Carpenter can, in fact, be astonishingly literal in presenting his understanding of human immortality. Like Saint Teresa or Dante, he talks about heaven with the easy confidence of someone who has been there—if only in a vision. What is novel with him is his insistence on a comparison between the experience of dying and that of falling in love—or sexual surrender. Thus, in one of his poems he writes of the feelings of the soul freshly escaped from the prison of a dying body:

> You must look at your own body lying dead there quite calmly,
> (If you have ever loved and quietly surrendered that love
>   you will understand what I mean).
> The dear fingers and feet, the eyes you have looked in
>   so often—they are yours no longer;

You are not bound to them; you are something else
   than you thought.
Now you see that these things are only a similitude;
A new and wonderful life opens out—so wonderful![41]

The same Love that revealed to us the depths of our own inner lives will also draw aside the curtain of death, and the new
revelation will be no less surprising and beautiful than the one
before. "Life is more full and rich on the other side of death than
on this side," Carpenter said with absolute conviction.[42]

In this sense, the love of men for one another truly is a religious issue—and at a deep level. Thomas Traherne, the Anglican
divine, could express Carpenter's point well:

I will utter Things that have been kept Secret
from the foundation of the World,
Things Strange, yet Common;
Incredible, yet Known;
Most High, yet Plain;
infinitely Profitable, but not Esteemed.[43]

Carpenter announces his message in much the same spirit.
He is only reminding us of what in our hearts we have always
known. Carpenter expressed his religious understanding of homosexuality in "The Ocean of Sex," one of his most interesting
and moving poems. This was the faith that sustained him through
the struggles and loneliness of his own life. Frustration, misunderstanding, conflict, jealousy, resentment, competition, and loneliness are all forces that mar the joy of friendship and sexuality in
this world. But the power of eros comes from God, and this power
leads ultimately, through many painful detours, back to the divine. This is the real mystery of life and death, self and other, us
and God.

O wonderful Ocean of Sex,
Mirror of the starry Universe,
Ocean-river flowing ever on through the great trunk and
   branches of Humanity,
From which after all the individual only springs like
   a leaf bud.

Ocean which we so wonderfully contain (if indeed we do
  contain thee),
and yet who containest us.
To hold in continence the great sea,
The great ocean of Sex, within one,
With flux and reflux pressing the bounds of the body,
The beloved genitals, Vibrating, swaying
Emotional to the star-glint of the eyes
Of all human beings,
Reflecting Heaven and all Creatures,
How wonderful
O wonderful Ocean of Sex
Mirror of the very universe
Ocean-river flowing ever on through the great trunk
And branches of Humanity,
From which after all the individual only springs
Like a leaf bud!
Ocean which we so wonderfully contain (if indeed we do
  contain thee),
And who containest us!
Sometimes when I feel and know thee within,
And identify myself with thee,
Do I understand that I also am, of the dateless brood
Of Heaven and Eternity.[44]

NOTES

1. The Line between Friendship and Love

1. Dirk Burrsma and Martha Mankas Foster, *The Men's Devotional Bible* (Grand Rapids, Mich.: Zondervan Publishing, 1984), iv, vi.

2. Ibid., 1147.

3. Ibid., 286.

4. Geoffrey Faber, *The Oxford Apostles: A Character Study of the Oxford Movement* (London: Faber & Faber, 1933), 226).

5. David Kuebrich, *Minor Prophecy: Walt Whitman's New American Religion* (Bloomington: University of Indiana Press, 1989), 152.

6. Lucy Kaylin, "I Love You, Man," *Gentleman's Quarterly* (November 1996): 220–26, 218.

7. Charles Gaines, *Pumping Iron: The Art and Sport of Bodybuilding* (New York: Simon & Schuster, 1981), 73.

8. Ibid., 98.

9. Ibid., 11, 98.

10. Ibid., 97.

11. Michael Segell, "The Second Coming of the Alpha Male," *Esquire* (October 1996): 76.

12. Ibid., 77.

13. Plato, *The Collected Dialogues*, ed. Edith Hamilton and Huntington Cairns (Princeton, N.J.: Princeton University Press, 1941), 537.

14. Ibid., 536, 544.

15. Arno Karlen, *Sexuality and Homosexuality* (New York: W. W. Norton, 1971), 187. Benkert in 1870 believed he had identified a new form of moral insanity, calling it "homosexuality" and defining it as a contrary sexual feeling that required medical therapy. In an argument still used today, many nineteenth-century doctors maintained that society should not blame homosexuals for their "problem"; nature had simply made an outrageous mistake, somehow assigning a female brain to a male body, the anatomical male who thinks and feels like a woman. This would remain the medical approach to homosexuality for more than a century.

16. Edward Carpenter, "Homogenic Love," in *Sexual Heretics*, ed. Brian Reade (New York: Coward-McCann, 1970), 330.

17. Ibid., 325.

18. Ibid., 336.

19. As quoted in Kenneth R. Dutton, *The Perfectible Body: The Western Ideal of Male Physical Development* (New York: Continuum Publishing, 1995), 253.

20. Carpenter, "Homogenic Love," 341; Edward Carpenter, *Iolaus, an Anthology of Friendship* (London: Albert and Charles Boni, 1935), 205.

21. Carpenter, *Iolaus*, 330.

22. Ibid., 340.

23. Edward Carpenter, *Love's Coming of Age* (London: Mitchell Kennerley, 1911), 122.

24. Horace Traubel, *With Walt Whitman in Camden*, ed. Gertrude Traubel (New York: Mitchell Kennerley, 1915), 5:161.

25. Edward Carpenter, *Towards Democracy* (London: George Allen & Unwin, 1931), 321, 382.

26. Thomas Aquinas, *Summa Contra Gentiles: Creation*, trans. James F. Anderson (London and Notre Dame, Ind.: University of Notre Dame Press, 1956), 276.

27. Carpenter, *Iolaus*, 200.

28. Plato, *Collected Dialogues*, 562.

29. Christopher Isherwood, *Christopher and His Kind* (New York: Farrar, Straus & Giroux, 1976), 129.

2. A History of Love between Men

1. Bruce Bawer, *A Place at the Table* (New York: Poseidon Press, 1993), 24.

2. Peter McWilliams, *Ain't Nobody 's Business If I Do: The Absurdity of Consensual Crimes in a Free Society* (New York: Prelude Press, 1993), 603.

3. Urvashi Vaid, *Virtual Equality* (New York: Anchor Books, 1995), 24, 37.

4. Ramsey Colloquium, "The Homosexual Movement: A Response by the Ramsey Colloquium," March 1994, 1; Wainwright Churchill, *Homosexual Behavior among Males: A Cross Cultural and Cross Species Investigation* (New York: Hawthorne Books, 1967), 159.

5. See, for example, Leo Bersani, *Homos* (Cambridge: Harvard University Press, 1995), 161; and Armistead Maupin, quoted in Frank Browning, *The Culture of Desire* (New York: Crown, 1993), 80.

6. Jean Genet, quoted in Edmund White, *Genet: A Biography* (New York: Alfred Knopf, 1993), 384.

7. Plato, *Collected Dialogues*, 561.

8. Vaid, *Virtual Equality*, 180.

9. Churchill, *Homosexual Behavior*, 160.

10. Ibid.

11. Bruce Bawer, *A Place at the Table* (New York: Poseidon Press, 1993), 265.

12. Philo of Alexandria, *On the Contemplative Life*, trans. Andrew Hallerin (Boston: J. Osgood, 1911), 325; Aldous Huxley, *The Devils of Loudun* (New York: Caroll & Graf, 1952), 123; Raymond DeBecker, *The Other Face of Love* (New York: Grove Press, 1969), 107.

13. Maralyn French, *Beyond Power: On Women, Men, and Morals* (New York: Summit Books, 1958), 245.

14. Some of the highlights of this bizarre history are as follows. The famous psychologist R. von Kraft-Ebing, author of the influential *Psychopathia Sexualismus* and an early pioneer of scientific sexual psychology, felt sure that frequent masturbation caused homosexuality by draining a boy's "virile bodily fluids."

In contrast, Wilhelm Stekel in *Fear of Women* (trans. R. Hertz [New York: New World, 1948], 386), a disciple of Freud, felt that exaggerated fears of masturbation were the true culprits. Such fears induced castration anxiety, which, in turn, led to an obsessive fascination with the penis, which led to fellatio, which led to . . . , and so forth.

German Dr. Arthur Weil in *Notebooks* ([New York: Penguin Books, 1975], 23) confirmed in 1923 his long-held suspicion that homosexuals had extremely small penises, supporting the castration-anxiety theory.

Paul Tardieu's research indicated, however, that the homosexual penis tended to be *trop volumineux* (observed in Pierre Hahn, *Nos Ancestres Les Pervers; La Vie des Homosexuels sous le Second Empire* [Paris: Olivier Orban, 1979], 198). Kraft-Ebing confirmed this finding, remarking on "the strong sexual equipment of this class of persons," which explained why homosexuals are obsessed with sex (227).

The Jesuit psychologist Father Glass observed that homosexuals had flabby muscles and shunned sport just like women (in James H. VanderVeldt and Robert Odenwald, *Psychiatry and Catholicism* [New York: McGraw-Hill, 1952], 591). Criminologist Alfred Moll, in *The Treatment of Sexual Perversion* (trans. R. Feldman [New York: Grove Press, 1923], 418),worried about the many homosexuals he found in prisons and the army whose muscular hypertrophy seemed abnormal and suggested a penchant for violent sexual crime.

15. Chandler Burr, "Homosexuality and Biology," *The Atlantic* (March 1993), 52. I can testify from my own experience that as late as 1970, the staff psychologists at Harvard University were discussing—and occasionally recommending—castration or shock treatments as an appropriate treatment for homosexuality. And this exciting quest for the true cause and cure of homosexuality continues, with geneticists now claiming to have found a gay gene and neuroendocrinologists saying they have found a gay gland in the brain.

16. Erich Fromm, *The Art of Loving* (New York: Harper & Row, 1956), 7.

17. Ibid., 34.

18. Edward Carpenter, *My Days and Dreams* (Charles Scribner's Sons: New York, 1916), 223.

19. Carpenter, "Homogenic Love," 324–47.

20. Ibid., 331.

21. Edward Laumann, Robert Michael, and Stuart Michaels, *The Social Organization of Sexuality* (Chicago: University of Chicago Press, 1994), 159.

22. French, *Beyond Power*, 201.

23. Carpenter, "Homogenic Love," 344.

24. Ibid., 326, 341.

25. Ibid., 326.

26. Ibid., 328.

27. For the myth of Ganymede, see Carl G. Jung, *The Undiscovered Self* (New York: Harper & Row, 1956), 256; George Bull, *Michelangelo: A Biography* (New York: St. Martin's Press, 1995), 432.

28. David M. Halpern, *One Hundred Years of Homosexuality* (New York: Rutledge, 1990), 46.

29. Lillian Hellman, *Six Plays* (New York: Modern Library, 1956), 81.

30. DeBecker, *Other Face of Love*, 96; evidently mutual masturbation was his preferred form of sexual activity.

31. C. S. Lewis, *The Four Loves* (New York: Macmillan, 1962), 93, 91.

32. Ibid., 96; Carpenter, *Love's Coming of Age*, 122.

33. French, *Beyond Power*, 323.

34. Carpenter, "Homogenic Love," 341.

35. Lewis, *Four Loves*, 91, 103.

36. Carpenter, "Homogenic Love," 330.

37. Story told in Jean Paul Sartre, *Saint Genet* (New York: Mentor Books, 1963), 113; see also Jean Genet, *The Thief's Journal*, trans. Bernard Frechtman (New York: Grove Press, 1963).

38. Lewis, *Four Loves*, 91; Carpenter, "Homogenic Love," 48.

39. Plato, *Collected Dialogues*, 341.

40. Carpenter, "Homogenic Love," 345.

41. Ibid.

42. Edward Carpenter, *Civilization: Its Cause and Cure* (New York: Charles Scribner's Sons, 1921), viii.

43. Chushichi Tsuzuki, *Edward Carpenter, Prophet of Human Fellowship* (Cambridge: Cambridge University Press, 1980), 80.

44. Carpenter, *Civilization*, viii., 4.

45. Sigmund Freud, *Civilization and Its Discontents*, trans. James Strachey (New York: Norton, 1961), 33.

46. Friedrich Engels, *The Origin of the Family* (New York: Globe Publishing, 1899), 233.

47. Carpenter, *Civilization*, 4, 6; French, *Beyond Power*, 195.

48. Turnbull quoted in French, *Beyond Power*, 489, 490, 66.

49. Engels, *Origin of the Family*, 129.

50. French, *Beyond Power*, 38.

51. Ibid.

52. Carpenter, *Civilization*, 40.

53. Ibid., 29.

54. French, *Beyond Power*, 271.

55. Carpenter, *Civilization*, 56.

56. W. T. Stace, *The Philosophy of Hegel* (New York: Dover, 1955), 491; Engels, *Origin of the Family*, 129.

57. Carpenter, *Civilization*, 41, 57.

58. Anthony Burgess, *The Life and Work of D. H. Lawrence: Flame into Being* (New York: Arbor House, 1985), 197.

59. Carpenter, *Civilization*, vii.

60. Sheila Rowbotham, "In Search of Carpenter," *History Workshop Journal* (spring 1977): 3,118; Fromm, *Art of Loving*, 11.

61. Fromm, *Art of Loving*, 33.

62. Fromm is quoting Diderot, "l'ame n'a pas de sexe," in Fromm, *Art of Loving*, 15 (my translation).

63. Edward Carpenter, *Intermediate Types among Primitive Folk* (London: Allen & Unwin, 1919), 162.

64. Fromm, *Art of Loving*, 33.

65. Carpenter, *Civilization*, 79.

66. John Boswell, *Same-Sex Unions in Premodern Europe* (New York: Villard Books, 1994), 77.

67. Carpenter, *Intermediate Types*, 162.

68. Ibid., 164.

69. Kate Millett, *Sexual Politics* (New York: Doubleday, 1970), 259, 345; Carpenter, *Intermediate Types*, 92.

70. Colin Powell, quoted in Eric Schmitt, "The Top Soldier Is Torn between Two Loyalties," *New York Times*, February 6, 1993, A9.

71. Carpenter, *Intermediate Types*, 96, 100.

72. Ibid., 99, 101.

73. Boswell, *Same-Sex Unions*, 77.

74. Carpenter, *Intermediate Types*, 94, 129.

75. Aristotle quoted in Carpenter, *Intermediate Types*, 127; for a description of brotherhood-unions, see Carpenter, *Civilization*, 124.

76. Carpenter, "Homogenic Love," 146.

77. Carpenter, *Intermediate Types*, 134.

78. Engels, *Origin of the Family*, 144.

79. Carpenter, *Intermediate Types*, 82.

80. Ibid., 56, 33.

81. Ibid., 33, 22.

82. Ibid., 77.

83. John Dollison, *Pope-Pourri* (New York: Simon & Schuster, 1994), 118; Carpenter, *Intermediate Types*, 77.

84. Carpenter, *Intermediate Types*, 78, 78; Carpenter, *Towards Democracy*, 332.

85. Carpenter, *Towards Democracy*, 268; Caroline W. Bynum, *Holy Feast and Holy Fast: The Religious Significance of Food to Medieval Women* (Berkeley: University of California Press, 1987).

86. Carpenter, *Intermediate Types*, 64.

87. Carpenter, *Towards Democracy*, 332, 80.

88. Lewis, *Four Loves*, 91; Anna Kingsford and John Maitland, *The Credo of Christendom* (London: John M. Watkins, 1916), 261.

89. French, *Beyond Power*, 151.

90. Carpenter, *Intermediate Types*, 58.

91. French, *Beyond Power*, 538.

92. Carpenter, *Love's Coming of Age*, 103; Engels, *Origin of the Family*, 145.

93. Fromm, *Art of Loving*, 34; C. S. Lewis, *Four Loves*, 145.

94. Matthew Arnold, *Culture and Anarchy* (Cambridge: Cambridge University Press, 1932), 84, 103.

95. Carpenter, *Love's Coming of Age*, 103, 35, 37.

96. Tsuzuki, *Edward Carpenter*, 123; Carpenter, *Love's Coming of Age*, 84.

97. Carpenter, *Love's Coming of Age*, 88, 91.

98. Ibid., 44.

99. Ibid., 87.

100. Ibid., 55.

101. Ibid., 56.

102. Ibid., 135.

103. Ibid., 57.

104. Ibid., 86.

105. Ibid., 141, 137, 110.

106. Ibid., 150, 163.

107. Ibid., 175, 122.

108. Jerry Falwell, *The New American Family* (Dallas: Word Publishing, 1992), 53, 55, 138.

109. French, *Beyond Power*, 323.

110. Carpenter, *Towards Democracy*, 326.

111. Carpenter, *Love's Coming of Age*, 93.

112. Ibid., 23.

113. Carpenter, *Intermediate Types*, 162.

114. Carpenter, *Love's Coming of Age*, 179.

115. Ibid.

116. Allan Bloom, *Love and Friendship* (New York: Simon & Schuster, 1993), 523; Carpenter, *Towards Democracy*, 390.

117. Carpenter, *Love's Coming of Age*, 173, 162; Marsilio Ficino, *Commentary on Plato's Symposium on Love*, trans. Sears Jayne (Dallas: Spring Publications, 1985), 158.

118. Spencer Klaw, *Without Sin: The Life and Death of the Oneida Community* (New York: Penguin Press, 1993), 157; Carpenter, *Love's Coming of Age*, 27,

119. Carpenter, *Love's Coming of Age*, 20; Edward Carpenter, *The Drama of Love and Death: A Study of Human Evolution and Transfiguration* (London: Mitchell Kennerley, 1912), 153, 124.

120. Carpenter, *Drama of Love and Death*, 124.

121. Ibid., 215.

122. Ibid., 170; Carpenter, *Towards Democracy*, 390.

123. Bloom, *Love and Friendship*, 550.

124. Carpenter, *Love's Coming of Age*, 179; Elizabeth Barrett Browning, *Aurora Leigh* (New York: C. S. Francis, 1857), 203.

125. Carpenter, *Love's Coming of Age*, 179.

126. Ibid.

127. Edward Young, *The Complaint, or Night Thoughts* (London: William Pickering, 1852), 67.

128. Carpenter, *Towards Democracy*, 390.

129. Plotinus, *The Enneads*, trans. Stephen MacKenna (New York: Penguin Books,

1991), 433; Josiah Royce, *The Conception of God* (London: Macmillan, 1897), 157; Aquinas, *Summa Contra Gentiles*, 180.

130. Aquinas, *Summa Contra Gentiles*, 180; Young, *The Complaint*, 277. To expand these points: As a finite human individual, each person is, in God's eyes, everything one thinks he or she is at this moment in time. But each is also infinitely more. Who ever imagined that he or she had exhausted all personal potential, that he or she had exhausted the capacity of experience? Who ever imagined that the realization of his or her true self could ever be completed outside eternity?

131. Meister Eckhart, *Sermons and Treatises* (Rockport, Mass.: Element, 1979), 275.

132. Traubel, *With Walt Whitman*, 1:161.

133. Ibid.

134. Edward Carpenter, *Days with Walt Whitman* (London: Allen & Unwin, 1915), 6.

135. Carpenter, *Towards Democracy*, 121; Tsuzuki, *Edward Carpenter*, 121.

136. Carpenter, *Towards Democracy*, 228, 186; Jung, *Undiscovered Self*, 146.

137. J. N. Findlay, *Ascent to the Absolute* (New York: Allen & Unwin, 1970), 198; Carpenter, *Love's Coming of Age*, 200; Elizabeth Barrett Browning, "Sonnet 15," *Sonnets from the Portuguese* (Oxford: Henry Frowoe Ltd., 1908), 326; Carpenter, *Towards Democracy*, 188.

138. Carpenter, *Drama of Love and Death*, 153, 3; Ficino, *Commentary*, 144.

139. Ficino, *Commentary*, 144.

140. Carpenter, *Drama of Love and Death*, 153.

141. Carpenter, *Love's Coming of Age*, 152.

142. Ibid., 119.

143. Ibid.

3. The Culture of Greed and the Culture of Brotherhood

1. Vaid, *Virtual Equality*, 206, 180.

2. Carpenter, "Homogenic Love," 345.

3. See Edward Carpenter, "A Mightier than Mammon," *Towards Democracy* (London: George Allen & Unwin, 1931), 320.

4. See Kenneth Clark, *The Nude* (Princeton, N.J.: Princeton University Press, 1971), 23; and Will Durant, *The Life of Greece* (New York: Simon & Schuster, 1939), 301.

5. Margaret Mead, *Cultural Patterns and Technical Change* (New York: Mentor Books, 1955), 11, 12.

6. Vaid, *Virtual Equality*, 180.

7. Edward Carpenter, "Transitions to Freedom," in *Forecasts of the Coming Century*, ed. Horace Traubel (Manchester: Labour Press, 1897), 137, 190; Carpenter, *Civilization*, 192.

8. Edward Carpenter, *The Healing of Nations* (London: George Allen & Unwin, 1920), 216.

9. Zbigniew Brzezinski, *Out of Control: Global Turmoil on the Eve of the Twenty*

First Century (New York: Charles Scribner's Sons, 1993), 7.

10. Dominic Lieven, *Nicholas II: Twilight of Empire* (New York: St. Martin's, 1993), 248.

11. Carpenter, *My Days and Dreams*, 220.

12. Brzezinski, *Out of Control*, 32.

13. Allen Mays, "Future Schlock," *Buzz* (May 1994), 14; Malcolm Muggeridge, *Chronicles of Wasted Time* (New York: William Morrow, 1973), I, 44; Brzezinski, *Out of Control*, 32.

14. Dominic Lieven, *Nicholas II: Twilight of Empire* (New York: St. Martin's Press, 1993), 251;

15. Jean-Paul Sartre, *Existentialism and Humanism*, trans. Philip Mairet (London: Methuen, 1966), 643; Lester Thurow, *Head to Head: The Coming Economic Battle among Japan, Europe and America* (New York: William Murrow, 1992), 245; Malachi Martin, *The Keys of This Blood* (New York: Simon & Schuster, 1990), 172; Brzezinski, *Out of Control*, 32.

16. Edward Carpenter, *The Healing of Nations* (London: Allen & Unwin, 1920), 216.

17. Carpenter, *Towards Democracy*, 410.

18. Adolf Hitler, quoted in Brzezinski, *Out of Control*, 39.

19. Francis Fukuyama, *The End of History and The Last Man* (New York: Macmillan, 1992), 197.

20. Clinton Rossiter, *Conservatism in America* (New York: Alfred A. Knopf, 1956), 23.

21. Martin, *Keys of This Blood*, 172.

22. William Graham Sumner, quoted in Mortimer J. Adler, *Haves without Have Nots: Essays for the 21st Century on Democracy and Socialism* (New York: Macmillan, 1991), 17.

23. Richard Nixon, *Beyond Peace* (New York: Random House, 1994), 21.

24. Carpenter, *Towards Democracy*, 87.

25. Ibid., 87.

26. Ibid., 89.

27. Ibid., 18; Nixon, *Beyond Peace*, 5; Fukuyama, *End of History*, 320, 171.

28. Carpenter, *Towards Democracy*, 89.

29. Nixon, *Beyond Peace*, 236, 239; Fukuyama, *End of History*, 336.

30. Carpenter, *Towards Democracy*, 81, 51.

31. Richard J. Barnet and John Cavanagh, *Global Dreams: Imperial Corporations and the New World Order* (New York: Simon & Schuster, 1994), 139.

32. Edward Carpenter, *Angel's Wings: Essays on Art and Its Relation to Life* (London: Allen & Unwin, 1898), 240.

33. Edward Carpenter, *England's Ideal* (London: Swan Sonnenschein, 1912), 7; Gandhi, quoted in Tsuzuki, *Edward Carpenter*, 4.

34. Carpenter, *Towards Democracy*, 26.

35. Sartre, *Existentialism and Humanism*, 634.

36. Carpenter, *England's Ideal*, 70.

37. Carpenter, *Towards Democracy*, 61.

38. Ibid., 31, 102.

39. Ibid., 31.

40. Ibid., 32.

41. Carpenter, *Civilization*, 132.

42. Regarding urban gangs and violence, see Leon Bing, *Do or Die* (New York: HarperCollins, 1991), 271 ff.; Carpenter, *Civilization*, 151.

43. Carpenter, *Towards Democracy*, 76, 127.

44. Peter Gay, *The Cultivation of Hatred: The Bourgeois Experience, Victoria to Freud* (New York: Alfred A. Knopf, 1931), 15; Henry Kissinger, *Diplomacy* (New York: Simon & Schuster, 1994), 161.

45. Carpenter, *Towards Democracy*, 129.

46. Edmund Morris, *The Rise of Theodore Roosevelt* (New York: Ballantine Books, 1979), 12; Kissinger, *Diplomacy*, 161.

47. Kissinger, *Diplomacy*, 54.

48. Carpenter, *Intermediate Types*, 58.

49. Ibid., 68.

50. Carpenter, *Healing of Nations*, 58, 54.

51. Ibid., 24.

52. Ibid., 147, 14.

53. Ibid., 30; for an analysis of trade rivalries in the two cases noted, see Robert K. Massie, *Dreadnought: Britain, Germany, and the Coming of the Great War* (New York: Random House, 1991), 218, 597.

54. Carpenter, *Healing of Nations*, 35.

55. Ibid., 164, 31.

56. Ibid., 89.

57. Ibid., 31. For a more recent analysis of how these two forms of violence conspired in Flint, Michigan, at the closing of GM plants, see Warren Farrell, *The Myth of Male Power* (New York: Simon & Schuster, 1993), 215 ff.; for how they conspired in the Gulf War, see Noam Chomsky, *What Uncle Sam Really Wants* (Berkeley, Calif.: Ondonian Press, 1992), 201 ff.

58. Carpenter, *Healing of Nations*, 139.

59. Ibid., 156.

60. Carpenter, *Healing of Nations*, 144.

61. Winston Churchill, quoted in Nixon, *Beyond Peace*, 13; Carpenter, *Healing of Nations*, 156; consider, as an illustration of this point, Hitler's hatred and rage against the German people in the last year of World War II.

62. Carpenter, *Healing of Nations*, 134, 217.

63. Carpenter, *Civilization*, 233, 224.

64. Carpenter, *Healing of Nations*, 218.

65. Ibid.

66. Ibid., 217.

67. Farrell, *Myth of Male Power*, 167, 166.

68. Carpenter, *Civilization*, 229.

69. Carpenter, *Towards Democracy*, 67; Carpenter, *Healing of Nations*, 184, 195.

70. Carpenter, *Healing of Nations*, 199.

71. Ibid., 200, 202.

72. Ibid., 206, 109.

73. Ibid., 326.

74. Carpenter, *Towards Democracy*, 229, 276.

75. Ibid., 226.

76. Bawer, *Place at the Table*, 224; Carpenter, *Towards Democracy*, 230.

77. Pope Leo XIII, "De Rerum Novarum," *Ridpath Library of Current Literature*, ed. John Clark Ridpath (New York: Ridpath, 1899), 543; Carpenter, *Towards Democracy*, 274.

78. Carpenter, *Towards Democracy*, 274.

79. Ibid., 287; in his poem "A Sprig of the Aristocracy," Carpenter describes one such young man, whose simple and unpretentious ways seemed to him England's best hope.

80. Robert Conquest, *V. I. Lenin* (New York: Viking Press, 1972), 342, 344, 346.

81. Ibid., 348.

82. Carpenter, *Towards Democracy*, 401.

83. Paul Kennedy, *Preparing for the Twentieth Century* (New York: Random House, 1993), 235.

84. Brzezinski, *Out of Control*, 113; E. J. Dionne, *Why Americans Hate Politics* (New York: Simon & Schuster, 1991), 331.

85. Peter Kropotkin, *The Essential Kropotkin*, ed. Emile Capouya and Keith Tomkins (New York: Liveright, 1975), 54; Plato, *Collected Dialogues*, 535.

86. E. M. Forster, "Some Memories of Edward Carpenter," in *Edward Carpenter: In Appreciation*, ed. Gilbert Beith (New York: Haskell House, 1973), 78.

87. Carpenter, *Towards Democracy*, 47.

88. Kropotkin, *Essential Kropotkin*, 68.

89. Carpenter, *Towards Democracy*, 164, 96.

90. Thomas Aquinas, *Summa Theologica* (Westminster, Md.: Christian Classics, 1981), Pt. II–II, Q. 66, Art. 2; John Locke, quoted in Adler, *Haves without Have Nots*, 10.

91. Carpenter, *Towards Democracy*, 56; Frank J. Tipler, *The Physics of Immortality* (New York: Doubleday, 1994), 41, 47.

92. Aquinas, *Summa Theologica*, Pt. II–II, Q. 118, Art. I; Carpenter, *Towards Democracy*, 148.

93. Carpenter, *Healing of Nations*, 110.

94. Carpenter, *Towards Democracy*, 52, 54, 53.

95. Ibid., 53.

96. Thurow, *Head to Head*, 138.

97. Ibid., 139, 140, 170.

98. Ibid., 124; Carpenter, *Healing of Nations*, 226; Carpenter, *Towards Democracy*, 326.

4. The Rediscovery of Sacred Sexuality

1. For one treatment of Jesus' sexuality, see Phipps, *The Sexuality of Jesus* (Cleveland: Pilgrim Press, 1996), esp. 69–72; Carpenter, "Homogenic Love," 343.

2. Carpenter, *Towards Democracy*, 228.

3. Georg W. F. Hegel, *The Philosophy of History*, trans. J. Sibree (New York:

Prometheus Books, 1990), 381; Augustine, *The City of God: Basic Writings*, trans. Whitney J. Oates (New York: Random House), 503.

4. Vaid, *Virtual Equality*, 223.

5. Edward Carpenter, *My Days and Dreams* (New York: Charles Scribner's Sons, 1916).

6. Traubel, *With Walt Whitman*, 5:104; Whitman, quoted in Kuebrich, *Minor Prophecy*, 73.

7. These exchanges are quoted in Traubel, *With Walt Whitman*, 253.

8. Plato, *Collected Dialogues*, 485.

9. Arnold, *Culture and Anarchy*, 1211; Thomas Huxley is described in Dollison, *Pope-Pourri*, 111.

10. Fromm, *Art of Loving*, 34.

11. Fyodor Dostoyevsky, *Notes from the Underground* (New York: Dell, 1960), 52.

12. Stephen Hawking, *Black Holes and Baby Universes* (New York: Bantam Books, 1994), 14.

13. Carpenter, *Civilization*, 63.

14. Thomas Kuhn, "The Structure of Scientific Revolutions," *International Encyclopedia of Unified Science*, 2d ed., vol. 2, no. 2 (Chicago: University of Chicago Press, 1970); Carpenter, quoted in Del Ratzsch, *Philosophy of Science* (Downer's Grove, Ill: Inter-Varsity Press, 1986), 44, 55; Carpenter, *Civilization*, 104.

15. Paul Monette, *Becoming a Man* (New York: HarperCollins, 1992), xi.

16. Carpenter, *Civilization*, 120.

17. Carpenter, *Drama of Love and Death*, 112.

18. Carpenter, *Civilization*, 121.

19. Ibid.

20. For a fuller description of Madam Blavatsky's life, see also Gertrude Marvin Williams, *The Passionate Pilgrim: A Life of Annie Besant* (New York: Alfred A. Knopf, 1946), and Gertrude Marvin Williams, *Priestess of the Occult* (New York: Alfred A. Knopf, 1953); Howard Murphet, *Yankee Beacon of Buddhist Light: Life of Col. Henry S. Olcott* (Wheaton, Ill.: Theosophical Publishing House, 1987), 38.

21. Carpenter, *My Days and Dreams*, 244.

22. Ibid.

23. For Besant's ease with gay men, see Gregory Tillett, *The Elder Brother: A Biography of Charles Webster Leadbeater* (London: Routledge & Kegan Paul, 1982), 83; for Besant's assessment of Carpenter, see Tsuzuki, *Edward Carpenter*, 90.

24. Edward Carpenter, *Pagan and Christian Creeds: Their Origin and Meaning* (New York: Harcourt, Brace, 1921), 203, 292.

25. Carpenter, *Drama of Love and Death*, 156; Carpenter, *My Days and Dreams*, 242; Theresa of Jesus, *The Interior Castle*, trans. E. Allison Peers (New York: Sheed & Ward, 1957), 24.

26. Edward Carpenter, *The Art of Creation: Essays on the Self and Its Powers* (London: Allen & Unwin, 1904); Edmund Husserl, *Cartesian Meditations* (Boston: Marinus Nijhoff, 1973); Jean-Paul Sartre, *The Transcendence of the Ego: An Existentialist Theory of Consciousness*, trans. Forrest Williams and Robert Kirkpatrick (New York: Farrar, Straus, & Giroux, 1957).

27. Carpenter, *Pagan and Christian Creeds*, 43.

28. Carpenter, *Love's Coming of Age*, 78.

29. Carpenter, *Pagan and Christian Creeds*, 57–58.

30. Edward Carpenter, *Towards Industrial Freedom* (London: Allen & Unwin, 1917), 284, 282, 394.

31. Sartre, *Transcendence of the Ego*, 33; Carpenter, *Art of Creation*, 79, 231.

32. Carpenter, *Art of Creation*, 55, 181; Carpenter, *Drama of Love and Death*, 55.

33. Carpenter, *Drama of Love and Death*, 78.

34. Ibid., 79.

35. Ibid., 76.

36. Sartre, *Transcendence of the Ego*, 33.

37. Ibid., 78; Carpenter, *Pagan and Christian Creeds*, 298; Plotinus, *Enneads*, 165.

38. Carpenter, *Pagan and Christian Creeds*, 298; Carpenter, *Art of Creation*, 30.

39. William James, *The Varieties of Religious Experience* (Garden City, N.Y.: Dolphin Books, 1962), 384; Robert Flint, *Theism* (New York: Charles Scribner's Sons, 1907), 126; Carpenter, *Art of Creation*, 30.

40. Carpenter, *Art of Creation*, 47.

41. Ibid., 47.

42. Simone Weil, quoted in Iris Murdoch, *Metaphysics as a Guide to Morals* (New York: Penguin Books, 1992), 504; Thomas Traherne, *Poems, Centuries, and Three Thanksgivings*, ed. Anne Ridler (London: Oxford University Press, 1966), 253; Carpenter, *Art of Creation*, 275.

43. Carpenter, *Towards Industrial Freedom*, 304, 306.

44. John Henry Newman, *Parochial and Plain Sermons* (London: Longmans, Green, 1914), 125; Carpenter, *Drama of Love and Death*, 261.

45. Carpenter, *Civilization*, 116.

46. Ibid., 219; Carpenter, *Towards Democracy*, 306; Carpenter, *Drama of Love and Death*, 49; Carpenter, *Art of Creation*, 234.

47. Carpenter, *Drama of Love and Death*, 49.

48. Carpenter, *Art of Creation*, 62.

49. Carpenter, *Towards Democracy*, 322.

50. Bawer, *Place at the Table*, 38.

51. Carpenter, *Drama of Love and Death*, 125.

52. Ibid., 80, 257.

53. Ibid., 149; Carpenter had read Sigmund Freud, *On the Interpretation of Dreams*, and found in it the confirmation of much he had already surmised; Carpenter, *Pagan and Christian Creeds*, 100.

54. Carpenter, *Art of Creation*, 11.

55. Ibid., 14.

56. John F. Finamore, *Iamblichus and the Theory of the Vehicle of the Soul* (Chico, Calif.: Scholar Press, 1985),160,102; Proclus, *The Elements of Theology*, trans. E. R. Dodds (Oxford: Clarendon Press, 1933), 101.

57. Dionysus the Areopagite, *The Divine Names: Complete Works*, trans. Colm Luibheid (New York: Paulist Press, 1987), 63; William Temple, *Nature, Man and God* (London: Macmillan, 1964), 80; Gottfried Wilhelm Leibniz, *Monadology* (La Salle, Ill.: Open Court Publishing, 1985).

58. Temple, *Nature, Man and God*, 148; Paul Weiss, *Modes of Being* (Carbondale: Southern Illinois University Press, 1958), 302; Tipler, *Physics of Immortality*, 12.

59. Carpenter, *Art of Creation*, 128, 123.

60. Ibid., 136.

61. Ibid., 139.

62. Ibid.

63. Carpenter, *Pagan and Christian Creeds*, 205.

64. Anna Kingsford and John Maitland, *The Perfect Way* (London: John M. Watkins, 1995), 253.

65. Ibid., xii.

66. Thomas Aquinas is quoted in Francesco Nagni, *Divine Intimacy* (New York: Desclee, 1963), 77; J. N. Findlay, *The Transcendence of the Cave* (New York: Humanities Press, 1967), 182; Charles E. Hartshorne, *The Logic of Perfection* (La Salle, Ill.: Open Court, 1962), 24.

67. Carpenter, *Drama of Love and Death*, 80.

68. Ibid., 273.

69. Carpenter, *Drama of Love and Death*, 152.

70. Aquinas, *Summa Theologica*, I, 42, 1; Carpenter, *Drama of Love and Death*, 43.

71. Carpenter, *Drama of Love and Death*, 212.

72. Ibid., 259, 59.

73. Ibid., 171, 80.

74. Ibid., 168.

75. Ibid.

76. Carpenter, *Pagan and Christian Creeds*, 120.

77. Ibid., 65.

78. Ibid., 236.

79. Sigmund Freud, *Moses and Monotheism* (New York: Harper & Row, 1913), 79; Carpenter, *Pagan and Christian Creeds*, 210.

80. Arnold, *Culture and Anarchy*, 109; Carpenter, *Pagan and Christian Creeds*, 210.

81. Carpenter, *Pagan and Christian Creeds*, 210.

82. Meister Eckhart, *Sermons and Treatises*, 183; Robert Barclay, *An Apology for the True Christian Divinity: Being an Explanation and Vindication of the People Called Quakers* (Philadelphia: Joseph James Printers, 1789), 144; Kingsford and Maitland, *Perfect Way*, 324.

83. Carpenter, *Pagan and Christian Creeds*, 169.

84. Ibid., 208.

85. Carpenter, *Art of Creation*, 165.

86. George Feuerstein, *Sacred Sexuality* (New York: Putnam, 1992), 91.

87. Ibid., 129.

88. Carpenter, *Pagan and Christian Creeds*, 183.

89. Ibid., 249; for one investigation into rituals of sacred sexuality, see Boswell, *Same-Sex Unions*.

90. Carpenter, *Pagan and Christian Creeds*, 220.

91. Ibid., 191, 126.

92. Ibid., 192, 267.

93. Baron Friedrich von Hugel, "Loisy, Alfred Firmin," *Encyclopaedia Britannica* (1911), 927; Carpenter, *Pagan and Christian Creeds*, 266.

94. Carpenter, *Pagan and Christian Creeds*, 191.

95. Tillett, *Elder Brother*, 169.

96. Albert Camus, *Resistance, Rebellion, and Death*, trans. Justin O'Brien (New York: Alfred A. Knopf, 1961), 308.

5. Gay Suffering and the Promise of Immortality

1. Carpenter, *Towards Democracy*, 37.

2. Carpenter, *Love's Coming of Age*, 12; Traherne, *Poems, Centuries, and Three Thanksgivings*, 174.

3. Although Carpenter did not have access to more-recent scholarship (see, for example, Phipps, *Sexuality of Jesus*, esp. 69–72), his assumption has plausibility; Traherne, *Poems, Centuries, and Three Thanksgivings*, 183.

4. Schmitt, "The Top Soldier Is Torn between Two Loyalties," 1A.

5. Howard Menas, *Colin Powell: A Biography* (New York: Ballantine Books, 1992), 173.

6. Philip Shennon, "Despite New Policy, Military Asks about Homosexuality," *New York Times*, February 27, 1996, A18.

7. David W. Dunlap, "Recognizing a Ruling, and Battles to Come," *New York Times*, May 21, 1996, A20.

8. Linda Greenhouse, "Colorado Constitution Violates Guarantee of Equal Protection," *New York Times*, May 21, 1996, A20.

9. Ibid.

10. Bob Paris and Rod Jackson, *Straight from the Heart: A Love Story* (New York: Warner Books, 1994), 128.

11. Bob Paris, *Gorilla Suit: My Adventures in Bodybuilding* (New York: St. Martin's Press, 1997), 117–18.

12. Paris, *Straight from the Heart*, 122.

13. Ibid., 188.

14. Ibid., 197.

15. Paris, *Gorilla Suit*, 262.

16. Ibid., 270.

17. Paris, *Straight from the Heart*, 254.

18. Dennis Rodman with Tim Keown, *Bad As I Wanna Be* (New York: Dell Publishing, 1996), 195.

19. Kevin Cook and Bill Marovitz, "Dennis Rodman: A Candid Interview with the NBA's Boa-clad Bad Boy," *Playboy*, June 1997, 68.

20. Rodman, *Bad As I Wanna Be*, 32.

21. Ibid., 65.

22. Cook and Marovitz, "Dennis Rodman," 64.

23. Ibid., 171.

24. Ibid., 60.

25. Rodman, *Bad As I Wanna Be*, 209.

26. Ibid., 195.

27. John Boswell, *Rediscovering Gay History* (London: The Gay Christian Movement, 1985), 13.

28. Anthony Summers, *Official and Confidential; The Secret Life of J. Edgar Hoover* (New York: Pocket Books, 1994), 296; John Cooney, *The American Pope: A Biography of Francis Cardinal Spellman* (New York: Times Books, 1984), 332.

29. Cooney, *The American Pope*, 51.

30. Sartre, *Saint Genet*, 97.

31. Brandon M. Strickney, *All-American Monster: The Unauthorized Biography of Timothy McVeigh* (Amherst, N.Y.: Prometheus, 1996), 246; Linda Greenhouse, "Victory for Gay Rights," *New York Times*, May 21, 1996, A1.

32. Thomas F. Matthews, *The Clash of the Gods: A Reinterpretation of Christian Art* (Princeton, N.J.: Princeton University Press, 1993), 122.

33. Marina Raye, "Sacred Sexuality," *Magical Blend* (July 1994): 63–68, 66.

34. Michael Nava and Robert Dawidoff, *Created Equal: Why Gay Rights Matter in America* (New York: St. Martin's, 1994), 21.

35. John Milton, *Paradise Lost*, bk. 4, l. 755.

36. Sherwin Nuland, *How We Die: Reflections on Life's Final Chapter* (New York: Alfred A. Knopf, 1994), 88.

37. Nuland, *How We Die*, 206.

38. Carpenter, *Towards Democracy*, 290.

39. Ibid., 300.

40. Carpenter, *Drama of Love and Death*, 118.

41. Carpenter, *Towards Democracy*, 289.

42. Carpenter, *Drama of Love and Death*, 118.

43. Traherne, *Poems, Centuries, and Three Thanksgivings*, 169.

44. Carpenter, *Towards Democracy*, 312.

0